Trauma, Taboo, and Truth-Telling

Critical Human Rights

Steve J. Stern and Scott Straus

Series Editors

Books in the series Critical Human Rights emphasize research that opens new ways to think about and understand human rights. The series values in particular empirically grounded and intellectually open research that eschews simplified accounts of human rights events and processes.

How do silence and taboo shape the expressive culture and politics of human rights, even among activists pushing to dismantle lies and establish the truth of state atrocity? *Trauma, Taboo, and Truth-Telling* shatters the comfortable temptation to reduce human rights culture to a struggle between voice and silence. The focus is the acutely poignant case of postdictatorship Argentina, whose military junta of 1976–83 not only "disappeared" perhaps thirty thousand citizens but also organized the trafficking of babies born to pregnant prisoners. Years later, the dual family identity of the adopted babies became a fraught issue—one example, among several analyzed in this book, of the weave of talk and taboo that together tell a human rights story. This bold yet sensitive study shows that even activists who push hard against forgetting can generate troubling new silences. The result is striking insight into the human consequences of atrocity, and into the power of silence to communicate difficult truths.

Trauma, Taboo, and Truth-Telling

Listening to Silences in Postdictatorship Argentina

Nancy J. Gates-Madsen

The University of Wisconsin Press

The University of Wisconsin Press
1930 Monroe Street, 3rd Floor
Madison, Wisconsin 53711-2059
uwpress.wisc.edu

3 Henrietta Street, Covent Garden
London WC2E 8LU, United Kingdom
eurospanbookstore.com

Printed in the United States of America

This book may be available in a digital edition.

Library of Congress Cataloging-in-Publication Data

Names: Gates-Madsen, Nancy J., author.
Title: Trauma, taboo, and truth-telling : listening to silences in
    postdictatorship Argentina / Nancy J. Gates-Madsen.
Other titles: Critical human rights.
Description: Madison, Wisconsin : The University of Wisconsin Press, [2016] |
    ©2016 | Series: Critical human rights
Identifiers: LCCN 2015036813 | ISBN 9780299307608 (cloth : alk. paper)
Subjects: LCSH: Dictatorship—Argentina—History—20th century. | Collective
    memory—Argentina. | Collective memory and literature—Argentina. |
    Victims of state-sponsored terrorism—Argentina—History—20th century. |
    Disappeared persons—Argentina—History—20th century. | Human
    rights—Argentina—History—20th century. | Argentina—History—Dirty War,
    1976–1983.
Classification: LCC F2849.2 .M323 2016 | DDC 323.0982—dc23 LC record available at
http://lccn.loc.gov/2015036813

ISBN 9780299307646 (pbk.: alk. paper)

For Greg,
Anja, and Evan

Contents

Illustrations

Acknowledgments

Those who know me well recognize the irony of a person like me writing a book about silence. I am not known for my reticence, and only on rare occasions have I found myself in trouble for something I *didn't* say. Yet although this book advocates listening to what is left unspoken, I am delighted to proclaim my sincere thanks to the many individuals who supported me throughout the research and writing process. Without their unwavering belief in the project, I never could have found my voice.

I owe a profound debt of gratitude to Ksenija Bilbija for encouragement and assistance at many stages of the process. Not only did she help me explore the language of silence in ways I had only imagined, but her conversations and advice also proved invaluable to the work's completion. She encouraged me to write about the Parque de la Memoria in Buenos Aires, which culminated in my contribution to the volume she coedited with Leigh Payne, *Accounting for Violence*, and ultimately led to my research on the ex-ESMA. Her work proved foundational to my own, and I could not ask for a better mentor and friend. Discussions with Leigh also informed my thinking about the topic of silence and memory, as did her work on postauthoritarian societies. I have been privileged to collaborate with Leigh at conferences and workshops, and I deeply value her continued friendship and support.

Other friends and colleagues aided the evolution of my thinking and served as sounding boards during the early stages of the project. Coauthoring a piece on art and transitional justice with Becky Atencio helped illuminate the important interplay between cultural production and societal reckoning with a difficult national past. Her work on the cycles of cultural memory in Brazil served as inspiration for my research, and I could not have completed this book were it not for her wisdom and friendship.

Several individuals in Argentina facilitated the research and writing of this book. I am grateful to Jonathan Perel for helping me access his documentary films, and I thank the Grandmothers of the Plaza de Mayo for granting permission to use an image related to one of their identity campaigns. I also appreciate the thoughtful responses of the tour guides at the ex-ESMA to questions regarding the history of the site and its current place in the landscape of memory.

Many colleagues at Luther offered support throughout the process, and I am happy to recognize them here. The fabulous members of the G-10, Victoria Christman and Elizabeth Steding, helped keep me on track and provided necessary feedback on early drafts of chapters, and I appreciate their willingness to delve into issues that are related only marginally (if at all) to their respective research. I thank my departmental colleagues for supporting my work and offer special recognition to Alfredo Alonso for his insights regarding the language of cinema. Particular thanks go to Thomas C. Johnson for providing me with sources related to documentary film and for reading an early version of chapter 6, and I remain indebted to my former student Kirsten de Jarlais for supplying invaluable research assistance at an opportune moment.

I am delighted to recognize the individuals at the University of Wisconsin Press who were instrumental in bringing this project to completion, in particular the coeditors of the Critical Human Rights series, Steve J. Stern and Scott Straus. This book could not have found a better home. Steve's work on Chile—especially his insights regarding memory politics and the recognition of the understudied nature of silence—informed my work in the Argentine context, as did the notion of the "human rights paradox." Special thanks are due to editorial director Gwen Walker, who provided valuable guidance along the way, and also to her assistant Matthew Cosby. I also wish to thank the anonymous reviewers of the manuscript for comments that shaped the evolution of the argument and structure of the book.

To Kathy Buzza and the folks at the Luther College Interlibrary Loan department, I extend a special thank-you. Without their unfailing ability to locate sources, I could not have carried out the research for this book. I also appreciate the sabbatical leave support from Luther College that allowed me to complete a research trip to Argentina and gave me uninterrupted time for writing. I am deeply grateful to grammar maven Linda Winston for assistance in editing portions of the final manuscript, and I especially appreciate her taking the time to work on the document under less than optimal conditions. Heartfelt thanks go to Nan Hibbs, who was able to transform a photo I had taken at the Parque de la Memoria in Buenos Aires into the striking image that appears on the cover of the book. The photo depicts an art installation by

Claudia Fontes, titled *Reconstrucción del retrato de Pablo Míguez* (Reconstruction of the portrait of Pablo Míguez), which pays tribute to one of the youngest victims of the dictatorship. Thanks also go to Germano Streese for sharing his vast knowledge of Zotero (in multiple languages) and to Samuel Haefner for preparing the images that appear in chapters 4 and 6. I gratefully acknowledge the assistance provided by many other people too numerous to mention individually who helped in large and small ways to bring the book to completion; at the same time, I take full responsibility for any errors.

Finally, I want to thank my family, who have supported me throughout this long process. This includes my father, a fine academic whose advice was almost always welcome, and my mother, who would have loved to have read this book. I especially want to acknowledge my husband, Greg, who has lived with this project for many years, provided much needed encouragement, and kept me grounded. Words cannot express how much I value his generosity and support. My husband and children are the inspiration for all I do, and I dedicate this book to them.

An earlier version of chapter 1 appeared as an article in *Latin American Theatre Review* (vol. 42, no. 1). An abridged version of chapter 4 can be found in the volume *Pushing the Boundaries of Latin American Testimony: Metamorphoses and Migrations*, edited by Louise Detwiler and Janis Breckenridge (New York: Palgrave Macmillan, 2012), under the title "Bearing False Witness? The Politics of Identity in Elsa Osorio's *My Name Is Light* (*A veinte años, Luz*)." An earlier version of chapter 5 was published in *Letras Femeninas* (vol. 31, no. 2). I am grateful to the editors for permission to reprint these works.

Trauma, Taboo, and
Truth-Telling

Introduction

Listening to Silences

A striking moment occurs near the end of Luis Puenzo's 1985 film *The Official Story*. After wrestling with her conscience, the protagonist Alicia has come to accept that her "adoptive" daughter Gaby is most likely a child of a woman who was disappeared during the so-called Dirty War in Argentina (1976–83).[1] She seeks out Gaby's possible biological grandmother, Sara, at a march at the Plaza de Mayo. As they ride together on the subway afterward, Alicia turns to Sara with an agonizing question, "If Gaby is your granddaughter, what do we do?," to which neither woman has a reply. A long moment of silence follows, while the camera (and the viewer) watch the two women struggle with the complicated and emotional situation in which they find themselves. The camera first registers Sara's look of compassion, resignation, and pain, as she meets Alicia's gaze squarely, then slowly looks away; the viewer then sees Alicia's troubled expression as she ponders an uncertain future. A long shot shows the women sitting side by side, staring straight ahead, saying nothing, surrounded by the other passengers, the only sound the rushing of the subway car over the track. This poignant silence captures well the dilemma of those caught in the tangle of emotion and politics in postdictatorship Argentina, for it calls attention to the powerful silence of an unanswered question.

Asking a question with no answer is like dropping a pebble down a well with no bottom: one remains suspended in the moment of waiting for the faint sound that never comes. There exists a strong tendency to focus on the answers, on the sound the pebble will surely make when it falls in the water, yet unanswered questions resist any neat closure. Rather than the resolution of the fall, there is only the endless, silent drop, yet the silence itself merits attention. Since the return to democracy in Argentina, human rights groups, victims, and academics have most often advocated breaking the silences left in the wake of the military dictatorship, finding the answers at the bottom of the well. Argentina's position as an innovative global leader in its responses to human rights abuses rests to a great extent on its protagonism in the realm of truth commissions and trials, mechanisms designed to voice crimes of the past in a public manner.[2] Testimonial narratives and human rights groups highlight the importance of exposing the crimes of the military and giving voice to the voiceless. Meanwhile, calls for memory often associate speech with remembering and silence with oblivion or societal amnesia. After years of addressing the military's refusal to respond to agonizingly simple questions such as *¿Dónde están?* (Where are they?), a search for answers is understandable.

Nevertheless, the cultural landscape of postauthoritarian Argentina has long been marked by silence and silencing: by unasked, unanswered, or unanswerable questions, by censorship, disappearance, or taboo topics. The pressing issues of the postdictatorship period include subjects that defy expression such as torture, complicity, or the legacy of large-scale disappearance. Even human rights discourse and testimonial narratives addressing the past violence contain silences that point to taboos within the human rights community, such as when unpalatable or difficult stories may be suppressed in favor of those that uphold more triumphalist interpretations of the recent past. Victims whose stories do not conform to expected narratives—a recovered grandchild who feels ambivalence regarding identity restitution, for example—remain marginalized by the preservation of taboos that distort or suppress their complicated experiences. Identifying and unpacking these lingering taboos acknowledges in a more inclusive or democratic way the experiences of a wider group of victims and can help articulate the depth and breadth of the painful legacies of the dictatorship's systematic violation of human rights.

Attention to the silences that populate representations of trauma not only exposes the limits that govern truth-telling about past violence, even among the very groups and individuals who demand accountability, but also reveals the expressive nature of silence itself. Just as an abundance of words does not always lead to greater understanding, an absence of speech does not necessarily indicate an absence of meaning, and often what an author or character does *not* say carries more interpretive weight than what they do. When telling the tale of state terror, silence does not simply equal lack of meaning or oblivion but rather represents a way of making meaning out of the past. Artistic and societal silences invite the critic to read between the lines and notice how the dictatorship's legacy is comprised of both what is articulated openly as well as what is suggested through silence. In visual terms, a more comprehensive picture of past violence emerges by observing both the positive and the negative space of the image.

At first glance Argentina may seem like an unlikely candidate for a study of the unspoken or taboo, since the country is hailed for the pioneering steps it has taken to break silences.[3] In fact, examining the silences and taboos that still persist after a truth commission and trials leads to a deeper, more comprehensive understanding of the debates that shape the memory of the dictatorship as well as how they evolve over time. Argentina's leadership role makes it an ideal case study of silence and taboo, for the gaps and lacunae reveal what remains beyond the reach of even the boldest initiatives to voice the crimes of the past. Moreover, the insights an exploration of taboos and silences in the Argentine context provides may be applied to other nations following similar paths.

This book examines the interplay between societal and artistic silences seen in dramatic, literary, and cultural texts that emerged around the time of the memory "boom" in Argentina, when many artists and authors sought to bear witness to the horrors of the dictatorship. Ignited in 1995 when former repressor Adolfo Scilingo confessed on television to throwing drugged prisoners into the River Plate as part of the "death flights" employed by the regime, the memory "boom" represents a critical juncture in the shift from a politics of amnesia to a politics of memory.[4] With renewed possibilities of judicial action, new actors in the human rights scene (such as the H.I.J.O.S. group, comprised of children of the disappeared and their allies), and a proliferation of acts of memory and memorialization regarding the dictatorship, the boom served to break repressive silences surrounding the years of military rule.

It is easy to view the memory boom as a hinge point, when oppressive silence is replaced with liberating memory discourse. However, an exploration of the interplay between textual and contextual silences reveals a more nuanced portrait of pre- and postboom engagement with the legacy of authoritarianism.[5] The silences seen within artistic representations of the postdictatorship period respond to societal silences outside the works themselves and can help call attention to taboo topics or the way in which silence informs an understanding of trauma. As this work aims to demonstrate, the boom did not simply break repressive silences but fractured or multiplied them; shattering one oppressive silence often reveals a concomitant (and entrenched) taboo. Put simply, the breaking of silence is also the making of silence. Furthermore, the silences before the memory boom are not unequivocally negative, denoting an absence of meaning, but can serve to articulate the vestiges of violence and terror. Through a close examination of cultural production that responds to and engages with societal silences—works that expose taboos by breaking silences and those that employ silence as an expressive language in itself—this book illuminates not only the importance of listening to the silences that emerge in the wake of dictatorship but also how unpacking these silences facilitates an understanding of memory politics and the character of memory itself.

By its very nature, silence opens itself up to many interpretative possibilities. Any treatment of the subject must therefore consider what is encompassed by this broad and ambiguous term. Nevertheless, exact definitions can prove elusive, precisely because silence operates on many levels: in artistic expression and in society, and in both the *form* and *content* of cultural representations.[6] In literary works, silence manifests itself at the formal level of language, seen in the spaces between words, or pauses marked by punctuation (dashes, parentheses, and the suggestive use of ellipses, for example). Unclear, absurd, or hermetic language also constitutes a type of silence by introducing obstacles to understanding. Silence can express itself through mute characters, unfinished statements or thoughts, a beginning in media res or an open ending, the silencing of certain actions (such as the crime in detective fiction), or the omission of information. In a similar fashion, the visual language of film can also employ silences, such as an absence of dialogue or (in a documentary) a lack of voice-over. Finally, visual art, monuments, and memorials also utilize a silent language of shape and space to communicate with a viewer. Yet silence also figures as the content of artistic representations of the dictatorship, for example when censorship, disappearance, or inexpressibility features prominently in a particular work. The prevalence of such themes challenges the traditional assumption that silence denotes an absence of content or meaning.

Given the many levels of interpretation associated with silence, a few words regarding how I approach the subject are warranted; in particular, what this study aims to accomplish and what it does not. First, this work does not attempt an exhaustive taxonomy of silence. The choice to eschew a comprehensive, universally applicable taxonomy is deliberate, for such a structure is both unwieldy and insufficient to address the complexities involved in the analysis of silence. Silence manifests itself on so many levels in text and context that attempts to exhaustively categorize the phenomenon are insufficient at best and reductionist or simplistic at worst. Second, for similar reasons this study deliberately avoids a structure by genre. While types of silences may vary from narrative to film, a theoretical approach that privileges genre considerations also risks molding the fundamental ambiguities that are central to understanding silence into an easily digestible (yet possibly artificial) theoretical structure. This is not to say that differences between genres do not matter, or that this work has no organizational framework. Rather, because silence cuts across genre lines and by nature resists categorization, I have chosen to avoid structures that could lead to a formulaic treatment of the subject. I therefore organize the text along chronological lines, employing the memory boom as a central point of departure around which to analyze taboos and silences that manifest themselves in text and context during different periods of the postdictatorship.

Within this chronological framework, this study explores the interplay between textual and contextual silences in representations of fundamental human rights issues of the postdictatorship period: the legacies of torture and disappearance, the crime of appropriation, the nature of remembering a traumatic past, and the interpretation of sites of memory. The chapters that follow explore how cultural production not only engages with preboom institutional silencing but also complicates the view of the postboom climate as one of openness and memory initiatives. The silences in literary and cultural expression call attention to taboo topics outside the works themselves, stemming both from the regime itself (such as the military's refusal to offer information regarding missing persons) and from within the human rights community (a reluctance to acknowledge uncomfortable truths regarding the legacies of torture or the appropriation of babies). Preboom silences embodied in the military's "pact of silence" or a societal culture of amnesia cede to postboom taboos regarding which stories can or should be told and which elements figure in the telling. More recently, the fusion of official discourse with human rights discourse during the Kirchner years—the terms of Presidents Néstor (2003–7) and Cristina Kirchner (2007–15)—offers new challenges to truthtelling. Each chapter demonstrates how the silences seen within cultural representations of the postdictatorship period respond to broader societal issues regarding truth and justice and how the meaning of these silences relates to the evolution of memory discourse before and after the memory boom.

In broad terms, this work explores two simultaneous ways in which silence makes meaning in the postdictatorship period. Silent expression first refers to what remains unsaid: the unanswered or unanswerable questions as well as ideas or thoughts that remain unarticulated. These silences encompass both the impossibility of language to represent trauma (silences rooted in inexpressibility) as well as the reluctance to articulate difficult truths (taboos related to a particular historical moment or linked with certain social actors).[7] But silent expression also refers to how silences can communicate: how a lack of words or information actually speaks. Attempts to express indescribable horror can illustrate its fundamental incomprehensibility, while taboo topics call attention to tensions regarding which tales of trauma can (or should) be told. An attention to the relationship between cultural and societal silences in and around the memory boom acknowledges the way in which an apparent absence of words can effectively communicate trauma, while also recognizing the impenetrable opacity of certain "unspeakable" acts.

This book makes three central claims regarding cultural production that addresses institutional and societal silences in and around the memory boom. The first is the most basic, although easy to overlook: silence is a legitimate mode of expression rather than a symbol of oblivion or an absence of meaning. Especially in a context of trauma, silence may even "speak" more than words, for the full story of violence is informed not only by speech but also by absence, inexpressibility, and muteness. Although one can conceive of the boom as an explosion of memory discourse that blows apart a repressive silence, the silences in and around the boom are not unequivocally negative states that must be "broken."

Second, attention to the silences in cultural works illustrates the shifting nature of taboos in the postauthoritarian period. The limits governing which aspects of the dictatorship's practices of terror find expression and which remain silenced change depending on the political climate—what is taboo directly after the return to democracy may become more accepted with the passage of time. Furthermore, censorship and taboos are not the exclusive domain of the military regime and its apologists; the needs of human rights groups also determine which tales of trauma can be told. These lingering taboos represent what I term the fallout of the memory boom: pockets of silence left in the wake of the explosion of memory discourse that signal uncomfortable or unpalatable legacies of the dictatorship, such as complicity, betrayal, or the use of memory for political gain.

Finally, looking at cultural production with an eye (or ear) to silence underscores the importance of ambiguity in the expression of trauma. Silence proves especially suited for expressing the postdictatorship period because of its capacity to move beyond the many dichotomies traditionally associated with memory discourse. The possibility to articulate trauma is often viewed as a struggle between opposing poles, speech *versus* silence, memory *versus* forgetting, resistance *versus* complicity, or power *versus* powerlessness. Nevertheless, when it comes to representing the nature of extreme violence, the ambiguity inherent in silent expression may prove more successful in capturing the authentic nature of trauma than any attempt to represent violence through precise language, which often relies on the aforementioned oppositions. The power of silent expression comes not from its ability to align with one extreme or the other but its position in the ill-defined ambiguous middle ground. Although the inability to fix any univocal meaning to silence can be vexing, it is this very ambiguity that gives silence its power, for it calls attention to the tension between the poles and the way in which trauma resists any definitive "meaning."

Cultural production in the postdictatorship period engages with complicated issues regarding the legacies of torture and disappearance, topics that resist straightforward efforts of truth-telling. Attention to the interplay between cultural and societal silences illuminates the conflicts over the meaning of memory—which stories are being told and, more importantly, which are being silenced—as well as the evolving nature of the debates themselves. To come to a deeper, more comprehensive understanding of the postauthoritarian period in Argentina—one that acknowledges the fundamental complexity of trauma and memory and allows room for the messiness of victim experiences—one must examine not only the voices that seek to articulate the past but also the silences themselves.

Silence and Memory in Argentina

"Si no hay justicia, hay escrache" (If there is no justice, there is *escrache*). Starting in the mid-nineties, the *escrache*, or public outing of former perpetrators of state terror, served as a public shaming of those implicated in the repressive mechanism of the dictatorship. Given the absence of legal justice, the loud, almost carnivalesque protests in front of the homes of ex-repressors provided an antidote to societal amnesia, as they obliged passersby to recognize and witness publicly unacknowledged violence.[8] Organized by H.I.J.O.S., the highly vocal and visible demonstrations were a direct response to the climate of impunity that reigned at the time and a clear signal that, for those in the human rights community, silencing the crimes of the dictatorship through pardons and amnesty laws was tantamount to forgetting. The link between silence and oblivion even manifests itself in the name of the H.I.J.O.S. group, Hijos por la Identidad y la Justicia contra el Olvido y el Silencio (Sons and Daughters for Identity and Justice against Forgetting and Silence): silence and forgetting represent two faces of a common enemy.

The emergence of H.I.J.O.S. in 1995, at the beginning of the memory boom, and their expressed mantra to work "against silence" supports the long struggles of human rights groups to voice the crimes of the dictatorship. Although organizations such as the Mothers and Grandmothers of the Plaza de Mayo worked ceaselessly to bring the military's atrocities into the public eye and clamored for accountability, the years of state terrorism from 1976 until 1983 and their aftermath remain marked by societal silence and state secrecy.[9] During the dictatorship years, knowledge became dangerous, and the climate of fear that settled across the country discouraged open communication. In fact, the military strategy to eliminate "subversives" from society was predicated on what Michael Taussig terms "public secrets," events or practices that are generally known to the populace but cannot be articulated openly.[10] Policies such as invading homes and businesses or kidnapping people off the street and spiriting them away to clandestine detention centers to an unspecified yet sinister fate were designed to be at once highly visible but ultimately unwitnessed actions. Diana Taylor labels the military's methods of making the visible invisible "percepticide," an attack on the population's ability to see and witness.[11] Broad policies of censorship complemented the silences represented by missing persons and governmental stonewalling. Argentina had a history of censorship during previous military regimes and simply extended many policies designed to restrict artistic expression. Yet even the official policies were so wide sweeping and deliberately vague that anything could be interpreted as censurable material, and many artists and writers consequently employed a form of self-censorship during the years of military rule.[12]

The struggle against institutional silencing continued after the return to democracy in Argentina. Despite hopes that Raúl Alfonsín's government (1983–89) would be able to hold the military accountable for their actions and provide answers regarding the missing victims, a full reckoning with the past proved impossible. In 1984 the CONADEP (National Commission on the Disappearance of Persons) published its *Nunca Más* report (*Never Again*), an investigation into the fate of disappeared victims, which compiled thousands of testimonies attesting to the brutal state terrorism.[13] Meanwhile, the well-publicized Trial of the Juntas in 1985 sought to bring those responsible for unleashing the violence to justice. Nevertheless, under pressure from the military, the government implemented the Full Stop (1986) and Due Obedience (1987) Laws, which effectively placed an end to most prosecutions of suspected perpetrators.[14]

The subsequent administration of Carlos Saúl Menem (1989–99) continued to erode away the possibility of attaining legal justice. With the support of a large portion of society, Menem advocated a policy of protective amnesia. Claiming that dwelling upon the painful past was unproductive for a society that should be looking forward, Menem pardoned many individuals implicated in the violence, including those officials who had been prosecuted and were serving sentences as a result of the Trial of the Juntas (1989, 1990). Those who testified against the military saw their efforts to combat institutional silencing initially crumble under the weight of eventual pardons, amnesties, and laws restricting future legal action. Menem's politics of amnesia suppressed public discourse of the dictatorship, and for several years the military's practices of brutality were publicly "forgotten" by all but the continually vocal human rights groups, until Scilingo ignited the memory boom with his televised confession in 1995.[15]

The boom brought discussion of the dictatorship years back into the public eye. The continued work of the Mothers and Grandmothers was complemented by that of the next generation of H.I.J.O.S., who established innovative modes of protest such as the *escraches* to ensure suspected perpetrators could not hide behind a veil of silence. The proliferation of memory initiatives—such as the rebroadcast of images from the Trial of the Juntas, the establishment of sites of memory, and the guerrilla artistic interventions of the Grupo de Arte Callejero (Street Art Group), whose modified traffic signs called attention to past violence—served to characterize the boom phenomenon of the mid to late nineties. Furthermore, the struggle to bear witness to the dictatorship years in the legal realm extended to the new millennium, despite Menem's earlier institutional attempts to curtail any type of reckoning with the past.

With the election of President Néstor Kirchner in 2003, Argentina ushered in an era of increased attention to the memory of the dictatorship, and a spirit of collaboration between governmental and human rights organizations emerged, seen for example in Kirchner's push to overturn the amnesty laws. The Supreme Court's 2005 decision to strike down the laws as unconstitutional, coupled with continued prosecutions of crimes that lay outside the purview of the laws (such as the appropriation of minors), has meant a resurgence of court cases against perpetrators. As of August 2014, 121 trials had been conducted to investigate suspected human rights abuses including killings, disappearances, and torture; 503 defendants had been convicted and sentenced for their crimes, and another 1,611 suspects were under investigation.[16] The wave of cases that arose from the nullification of the amnesty laws implies that protective amnesia is ineffective; like a vacuum, the official silence regarding the fate of victims has proved intolerable. At the same time, renewed action in the legal sphere has also led to one case of further silencing, when Jorge Julio López, a key witness in the trial against former repressor Miguel Etchecolatz, disappeared from his home after providing damning testimony that helped secure a guilty verdict.[17]

Given the military's pressure in the late 1980s to curtail legal action against suspected perpetrators, followed by the Menem administration's policies designed to suppress public discussion of the dictatorship years, the H.I.J.O.S. group's proclamation to operate "against silence" is understandable. Silence is easily equated with repression, stonewalling, and a lack of meaningful justice or answers regarding the fate of the disappeared. In a similar fashion, attempts to voice the crimes of the past or tell the tale of trauma are often interpreted as unquestioningly positive, for they lead to an open reckoning with the past—

the boom symbolizes a proliferation of memory discourse that reveals hidden truths. Yet the relationship between speech and silence proves more complicated than a simple struggle of speech "against" silence. An examination of how cultural production responds to silences before and after the boom demonstrates both the limits restricting truth-telling efforts—and their troubling repercussions—as well as the expressive nature of the silences surrounding torture and disappearance.

Attention to the silences in cultural works exposes how the needs of human rights groups can inform the rendering of trauma. Alongside the layers of silence and silencing represented by miscarried or severely delayed justice, societal amnesia, and absent victims, one finds a profound reluctance to engage the more uncomfortable or unpalatable issues related to profound violence. One can easily understand why governments sympathetic to the military might attempt to discourage meaningful investigation into the crimes of the dictatorship, yet a deeper exploration of the silences present in postdictatorship Argentina uncovers taboo topics within the human rights community as well. Practices of torture, disappearance, and appropriation of children create situations that challenge the definition and limits of ethical behavior, and the aftermath can be difficult to process, leading to representations marked by silence or absence. An examination of cultural production therefore reveals which taboos can be broken and which remain entrenched. Furthermore, looking at how cultural texts attempt to engage with these issues of complicity, monumental memory, or the politics of identity reveals how the human rights community generates and perpetuates silences of its own, through prescribing interpretations of the past in a top-down fashion. By calling attention to this tendency, my intention is not to critique the work of the human rights organizations themselves, with which I sympathize, but rather to acknowledge another difficult and underacknowledged byproduct of the dictatorship's violence, one that is also taboo. An exploration of these taboos reveals the troubling and lasting legacy of dictatorship, signaling the limits that still govern truth-telling in Argentina. Understanding the wide-reaching effects of the dictatorship's violence, how it has generated and continues to generate taboos even among groups that aim to shed light on human rights violations, facilitates a broader comprehension of the challenges to redressing crimes against humanity.

The complex nature of taboos within and without the human rights community reflects what Steve J. Stern and Scott Straus refer to as the "human rights paradox": how the perennial tension between universal rights and local realities shapes the understanding of human rights.[18] As Stern and Straus note, while human rights are universal, local conditions determine how rights are interpreted or addressed—ranging from "what constitutes an abuse," or which universal values "can gain traction," to the particular outcome of violations—and this paradox informs both the practice and scholarship of human rights.[19] In the case of Argentina, the tension between global and local plays out on many levels, from the particular (which perpetrators are brought to trial) to the more broad (how universal concepts of "truth," "memory," and "justice" are understood and interpreted).[20] Viewing taboos in the human rights community through the lens of the human rights paradox reveals how locality also shapes which stories find traction and which remain more marginalized. Furthermore, it exposes the tension between universal claims to "remember" and local conditions that shape the nature of what is remembered, and how.

Stern and Straus's work emphasizes the importance of considering both the global and the local when analyzing issues of human rights. An analysis of silence in the postdictatorship period responds to this call for a "deeply contextualized multilevel analysis," for it engages the paradoxical connections between the universal and the particular in two fundamental ways.[21] First, by its very nature, silent expression denotes a universal inexpressibility of trauma, while at the same time it signals taboos rooted in a particular historical moment, and this tension (not unlike the human rights paradox) informs an understanding of silence itself. Second, a close analysis of the textual and contextual silences related to the expression of trauma in Argentine cultural production reveals how local conditions in the human rights community engender or reinforce taboos, even when invoking universal calls for "truth" and "memory." Through its exploration of the many layers and interpretations of silence, this work provides a nuanced understanding of complicated issues of the postdictatorship period, such as the legacies of torture, the nature of disappearance, the appropriation of children, and the preservation and use of sites of memory.

The Nature of Silence

Unpacking the relationship between cultural and societal silences proves critical to understanding the process of memory making in postdictatorship Argentina, yet little scholarship to date has focused explicitly on what such silences mean (or how they make meaning).[22] In the Chilean context, Michael Lazzara notes the importance of exploring "the silences and lacunae implicit in every testimonial act," and his work underscores the fundamental role silence plays in representations of the postdictatorship and lays an important foundation for studies of artistic expressions of trauma.[23] Yet despite its importance in cultural representations of past violence, silence proves a problematic concept to interpret because of its fundamentally ambiguous nature.[24] With no words to hint at a meaning, how does one determine the difference between voluntary and imposed muteness? Between a silence of resistance and one of compliance, indifference, or desperation? Compared with its counterpart, silence requires a much greater interpretive effort to reveal its meaning, which makes it much more difficult to assign it an unequivocal interpretation. This inability to fix meaning makes silence very complicated to understand or interpret, especially in contexts of trauma, which may help explain the traditional call to break repressive silences rather than examine their deeper meanings.

In a maddening paradox, while silence's ambiguity hinders easy interpretation, at the same time silence depends on such interpretation to express any meaning at all. Put simply, the language of silence does not speak for itself. With few linguistic clues as to its meaning, the reader or audience consequently plays an extremely active role in determining the meaning and worth of textual gaps and absence of speech. The poignant silence in *The Official Story* compels the viewer to ponder the possible solutions to Alicia and Sara's dilemma. As the only mother Gaby has ever known, Alicia shares a loving bond with her little girl; at the same time, Gaby represents Sara's only connection to her missing daughter and son-in-law. Can both women "win" or does one have to "lose" in this emotionally wrenching situation? This dependence on external interpretation calls attention to the shared production of meaning between artists and their audience. By using silence in their work, writers and artists entrust the reader or audience with more of the responsibility for determining its meaning.[25]

But by conferring such responsibility onto the audience, these artistic works oblige the reader or viewer to become involved in difficult and often polemical issues surrounding the postdictatorship period. A story with an open ending invites the reader to fill in the missing pieces, while a lack of voice-over in a documentary film compels the viewer to form interpretations and draw conclusions based solely on the images shown. For example, *The Official Story* ends with a scene of Gaby sitting in a rocking chair, singing a song about the land of "I Don't Remember," but the viewer does not know what the future holds for this particular victim of the dictatorship's violence.[26] Will Sara enter into Gaby's life in a meaningful way, or will Alicia attempt to preserve some aspects of the comforting status quo? Both interpretations are possible, yet they also appear mutually exclusive, and it is the film's silence regarding Gaby's fate that allows for these multiple, contradictory interpretations.[27] In short, silence obliges the audience to stake a claim to an interpretation and define his or her position vis-à-vis the violence, which leads to a second paradox regarding the language of silence. Silence appears to be a "neutral" form of expression—by nature it does not provide a clear meaning and resembles an empty vessel. Nevertheless, this very "neutrality" actually obliges the audience to become a more active participant in the creation of meaning. In other words, silence is an empty vessel that asks to be filled: its very neutrality of form makes any type of impartial interpretation impossible.[28]

The ambiguous nature of silent expression is not the only challenge to interpreting the silences left in the aftermath of dictatorship. Limits also arise when identifying the various silences related to the postauthoritarian period. For example, the silences that prick an outsider's eyes or ears may often be the most explicit ones, while local eyes and ears are privy to other, more hidden taboos. Overt silences imposed by the state may resound with deafening force; at the same time, those related to other social actors or human rights groups may be more covert. Moreover, one group's taboo may be another's truth, indicating a need to recognize the differences between state-driven silences and those that arise within the human rights or even academic communities. Given the challenges that face any outside scholar's attempts to identify and explore postauthoritarian silences, this study focuses specifically on silences in literary and artistic endeavors and on how taboo topics manifest themselves (or not) in the public sphere of cultural production. Although the silences in such works may offer an incomplete view of the landscape of truth-telling in Argentina, an analysis of cultural texts that engage with the more blatant silences of the postdictatorship period often reveals lingering taboos that have been buried or veiled.

Cultural representations of trauma that respond to the silences encompassed in taboos or disappearance can promote understanding of the complicated legacies of authoritarianism, for like the postdictatorship period itself, silence is shot through with contradiction, paradox, and ambiguity.[29] Given the importance of understanding cultural and societal silences, coupled with the inherent challenge in interpreting them, literary and cultural representations that address the Argentine dictatorship are especially suited to helping describe, define, and understand the silences that populate the postauthoritarian landscape as well as exploring how such silences make meaning. When it comes to unpacking the complex issues of truth and justice in postauthoritarian societies, forms of expression that embrace contradiction, complexity, and ambiguity—such as novels, plays, films, and other cultural production—can facilitate an understanding of the limits of truth-telling and the tensions surrounding the representation of dictatorship.[30]

Expressing Past Violence through
Speech and Silence

Cultural and scholarly production that emerges from periods of repression tends to privilege the voice, as can be seen in the truth-telling efforts of testimonial narrative and the scholarship of memory studies. Literary and legal testimonial narratives emphasize the importance of breaking silences and exposing the crimes of the past. Indeed, the central role of testimony—to break an oppressive silence—has remained constant despite debates regarding almost every other aspect of the genre. Although critics have disagreed regarding the exact definition of testimonio, argued over issues of truth-value and agency (e.g., the Rigoberta Menchú controversy ignited by David Stoll), and questioned its ability to provoke action, the central purpose of testimonial narrative remains constant: to bear witness to a silenced story of trauma, to give voice to the voiceless.[31]

For the purposes of this study, I include fictional works as part of the testimonial project. At first glance, it may seem surprising to consider fictional dramatizations of torture or disappearance as testimonial narratives that bear witness to past horror. Although a precise definition of testimonio still provokes debate, many leading theorists—including John Beverley, René Jara, Marc Zimmerman, and Elzbieta Sklodowska, to name a few—define the genre as a first-person, mediated text, in which a member of a subaltern class shares a story with an interlocutor in order to provide a testimony of an event or significant life experience that might otherwise be silenced or forgotten. Whether they emphasize the importance of testimonio's truth value (Beverley), its urgency (Jara), its claim to witness (Beverley and Zimmerman), or its collaborative nature (Sklodowska), these theorists do not consider fiction to be part of the testimonial genre. After all, testimonio, like autobiography, invokes a "pact of truth" so the reader will assume the events are true, while fiction requires a "suspension of disbelief" so the reader will unquestioningly accept unbelievable events in the narration.[32]

Yet the division between testimony and fiction is rarely straightforward, especially in contexts of trauma. Jacques Derrida argues in *Demeure: Fiction and Testimony* that testimony cannot help but be "fictional"—the boundaries between the two are fluid and ever changing. As he states, "If the testimonial is by law irreducible to the fictional, there is no testimony that does not structurally imply in itself the possibility of fiction, simulacra, dissimulation, lie, and perjury."[33] In other words, because testimony depends on the faith that the eyewitness is telling the truth—there is no other way of empirically verifying its validity—it must always remain "haunted" by the possibility of fiction.[34]

For Derrida, there is no such thing as a pure, nonfictional testimonial account of an event, for testimony always is implicated by fiction.

In a similar vein, while some might claim that fictional accounts by definition betray the truth of an experience, many authors and critics recognize that a representation need not be "realistic" to portray an event "realistically." Writing about literary production after the Holocaust, Berel Lang asserts, "The claim is entailed in imaginative representation that the facts *do not* speak for themselves," and that the author's figurative manipulations actually represent the historical subject "more compellingly or effectively—in the end, more truly—than would be the case without them."[35] In contexts of extreme violence that defy easy understanding, the facts do not always point to the truth, revealing the importance of fictional truth-telling.[36]

Regarding trauma narrative in particular, Shoshana Felman and Dori Laub have emphasized the difficulty of fully articulating horrific events, for such moments simultaneously demand and resist witnessing. These representative challenges mean that oftentimes literary or artistic witnessing becomes a necessary element of the trauma narrative.[37] Cathy Caruth similarly argues that traumatic events must be "spoken in a language that is always somehow literary: a language that defies, even as it claims, our understanding."[38] Trauma defies expression; therefore its articulation by necessity incorporates fictional modes of telling.

Given the imprecise distinction between fiction and testimony, especially in the context of historical trauma, it can be useful to turn to Kimberly Nance's broad definition of testimonio, based primarily on the goal of such writing rather than the mode. In *Can Literature Promote Justice? Trauma Narrative and Social Action in Latin American Testimonio*, Nance defines testimonio as "the body of works in which speaking subjects who present themselves as somehow 'ordinary' represent a personal experience of injustice, whether directly to the reader or through the offices of a collaborating writer, with the goal of inducing readers to participate in a project of social justice."[39] Although Nance's definition indicates the nonfiction quality of testimonio, the emphasis on the texts' *purpose* (a representation of trauma that aims to promote action) rather than *mode of expression* (a first-person, mediated narrative) allows for a much broader inclusion of works under the umbrella of testimonial representation.

A definition based on purpose avoids the issue of truth-value that has plagued much of testimonial theory over the past decade. For despite the differences of opinion regarding the definition of testimonial narrative, its goal remains invariable: testimonio speaks truth to power; it seeks to break a repressive silence regarding a traumatic event in the spirit of Never Again. Furthermore, putting Nance's definition in conjunction with Derrida's theory implies that texts do not have to be first-person eyewitness accounts to fall into the realm of testimony—*any* fictional tale that engages the legacies of "real" victims of trauma must automatically be considered part of a testimonial project.[40] While Derrida, Lang, Felman and Laub, and Caruth approach the blurry boundary between fiction and testimony from the side of testimony, it can be equally useful to approach the boundary from the fictional side when examining works that engage with the historical reality of the Argentine dictatorship. In short, just as testimony is always "haunted" by fiction, fictional representations of historical trauma are, in turn, always "haunted" by testimony, and works that address real world issues such as torture and disappearance construct a dialogue with the surrounding society concerning the difficult issues associated with the legacy of dictatorship. The fictional works under consideration in this book therefore situate themselves squarely in the realm of testimonio.

In considering cultural production as part of the testimonial project, this study aligns with recent scholarship that addresses the intersections between art and testimonio in the Latin American context. Lazzara's work regarding post-Pinochet Chile reveals how literary and artistic responses to trauma can offer a particular kind of "truth" regarding the past.[41] In the context of post–Shining Path Peru, Cynthia Milton upholds the power of "art as a means to bear witness" to atrocity, owing in part to its ability to make the "'unimaginable' imaginable."[42] Finally, Rebecca Atencio outlines the important connections between cultural production and institutional mechanisms of transitional justice in Brazil, further testament to the power of literary and artistic works to speak truth to power in the spirit of testimonial writing.[43]

Testimonial narratives—whether legal or literary—emphasize the importance of the voice, the ability to speak out against a repressive regime. In Argentina, this was perhaps best seen in the *Nunca Más* report compiled by the CONADEP after the return to democracy, which sought to bring to light the silenced stories of the victims of the dictatorship.[44] Many witnesses of the horrors of the dictatorship were encouraged to add their testimonies to the report, confirming the power of the voice to condemn repression. The legal testimonies compiled in the CONADEP report were also complemented by more literary or cultural testimonies, such as Jacobo Timerman's *Prisoner without a Name, Cell without a Number* or Alicia Partnoy's *The Little School*, which also helped reveal the crimes of the military regime.[45] By underscoring the importance of telling the tale of unacknowledged violence, testimonio responds to the need to break the silences left in the wake of dictatorship.

But the traditional emphasis on the power of the voice in testimonial narrative ignores the crucial role silence plays in testimonial expression. On the most basic level, the creation of any testimonial narrative involves a double process of revealing and concealing. To tell any story always implies selecting which details to include and which to leave out. As Doris Sommer notes, silences can take the form of a testimonial subject's secrets—information deliberately withheld from the interlocutor.[46] This process of selection is also impacted by what Nance refers to as the "socially sayable," forms of expression used by testimonial speakers that constitute "the socially acceptable channels for the narration of trauma."[47] In the case of Argentina, the taboo topics under the military regime (talk of the fate of the disappeared) have been replaced by other, equally strong taboos after the return to democracy (the suggestion that the disappeared may have participated in violence rather than been innocent victims, or that the restitution of an appropriated child's identity may not always be unequivocally positive).[48] Rather than a hierarchical relationship in which an oppressive silence is broken by a liberating testimonio, testimonial narrative comprises a complicated interplay between speech and silence, in which both occupy positions of importance and merit equal attention.

Given the importance of silence and silencing in testimonio, it must be considered more than simply a negative space to be filled. Since testimonial narratives aim to tell the hidden stories of trauma, looking at what these texts *do not* say proves just as important as analyzing what they do. For example, when breaking one societal silence, some testimonies may actually contribute to another, as will be seen in chapters 1 and 4, which address the legacies of torture and the appropriation of children. In other cases, attempting to fill silences with words falls short when calling attention to past crimes, and a strategy of describing and defining a silence may prove more effective, as will be seen in chapters 2 and 3, which are about the representation of disappearance. Silence can also serve as a necessary element of telling the story of trauma, as demonstrated in chapters 5 and 6, which explore the interplay between memory and forgetting. In short, to arrive at a fuller understanding of the postauthoritarian period in Argentina, one must move beyond scholarship that privileges the voice (what testimonial narratives *are* saying) in order to listen to silences (what they *are not* saying).

The tendency in testimonial narrative to privilege the voice has traditionally found its echo in the calls to memory following the return to democracy. Indeed, the established paradigm in memory studies equates speech with memory and silence with forgetting—one must speak of the victims and their experience in order to preserve their memory—and there exists a fear that failing to articulate a victim's experience will condemn it to oblivion.[49] Much of the scholarship of the memory of traumatic events such as the Holocaust or the Argentine dictatorship alludes to the dangers of silence and forgetting.

Slogans such as "Nunca más" (Never again) or "Ni olvido ni perdón" (Neither forgetting nor forgiveness) speak to the impulse to remember the crimes of the dictatorship so they may not be repeated, and human rights groups have struggled against the junta's legacy of silencing and secrecy.

In the Latin American context, memory scholars Elizabeth Jelin and Steve Stern both acknowledge the compelling tendency to conceptualize memory as a battle against forgetting. In *State Repression and the Labors of Memory*, Jelin observes that "the space of memory is thus an arena of political struggle that is frequently conceived in terms of a struggle 'against oblivion': *remember so as not to repeat*."[50] Similarly, in his trilogy exploring how Chileans remember the 1973 coup and the Pinochet legacy, Stern notes that starting in the late 1970s the rhetoric of memory versus *olvido* took precedence when describing Chilean reality.[51] In both broad and specific historical contexts, then, traditional conceptual frameworks of memory view the silence of oblivion as a negative space that stands in opposition to the positive memory work of recovering a difficult past.

However, the binary conceptualization of memory against forgetting obscures the complicated reality of how memory operates. Jelin explains that memory does not exist in opposition to oblivion or silence, but rather "what is at stake is an opposition of 'memory against memory,'" seen in multiple (and contradictory) versions of past events.[52] Reducing complicated struggles over the interpretation of the past to a simple opposition between memory and forgetting ignores the important fact that one individual or group's silence is another's memory. Stern similarly describes the process of creating memories in Chile in terms of competing interpretations of the past that are constantly negotiating for public acknowledgment.[53] Stern and Jelin's work supplants a binary model of memory versus forgetting with a pluralistic one that acknowledges not only the many, competing memories but also their corresponding silences.

Silence itself plays a fundamental role in the creation of memory. Jelin emphasizes that "all narratives of the past involve silences,"[54] and her work provides a brief taxonomy of several types of silences associated with the making of memory.[55] Her exploration of different silences negates the assumption that silence is a monolith with one particular form, motive, or meaning, and this recognition of a more nuanced model of silence is useful for the purposes of this study. For his part, Stern addresses the importance of noting what gets left out in any theoretical and analytical framework of memory. In his words, "The same process that brings certain meanings, remembrances, and voices to the fore also buries others."[56] The work of making memory, like that of creating testimonial narratives, involves both revealing and concealing—yet the working of silence and silencing is rarely noted. Although one of the central conclusions of Stern's work is that "the making of memory is also the making of silence," he notes that the importance and meaning of silence in making memory remains understudied.[57]

Despite an acknowledgment of the importance of silence in making memory, theoretical approaches to memory work tend to conceive of the battle between memories as waged in the terrain of words, wherein competing voices regarding a particular past event vie for a listener's attention. For example, although Jelin provides an initial foray into possible meanings of silence, her work tends to focus more on the importance of language when making memory. Basing her argument on Maurice Halbwachs's affirmation that memories must always correspond with words, she concludes that in the case of traumatic events that defy linguistic expression, "there are no words, and therefore there cannot be memories."[58] Memory remains that which can be articulated through language—without such articulation, the silences themselves have no meaning. Meanwhile, while Stern's work recognizes the fundamental importance of paying attention to the silences created in the process of making memory, his trilogy focuses more on the battles for memory in the public sphere, competing voices and their interpretations of the past, and the struggle *against* silencing and olvido (even while recognizing that any particular interpretation by nature silences other options).[59] In general, even when silence is recognized as an agent in the process of making memory, memory is thought of as being shaped by words.

Building on Jelin and Stern's definition of memory as the meaning we give to experience, and the idea that all memory is by nature selective, this book affirms that the meaning assigned to the dictatorship is shaped at least as much by silence as by words. Silence is not simply a lack of memory, and an absence of words does not automatically indicate an absence of meaning. The traditional emphasis on voicing the crimes of the past must be complemented with attention to the silent expression of trauma as well, for an understanding of cultural and societal silences helps illuminate the complicated process of memory making in the postdictatorship period.

Conceptualizing Silence in Text and Context

As can be seen from the discussion above, an exploration of pre- and postboom silences can help provide a richer understanding of post-authoritarian Argentina. Yet although silence proves an essential element of cultural representations of the postdictatorship, it remains an ambiguous and slippery concept to examine. Rather than catalog the many types of silences found in the postdictatorship period, I have chosen to structure the discussion of the relationship between cultural and societal silences around two broad yet fundamental oppositions. The first concerns the underlying motive or explanation for a particular silence: either voluntary or involuntary. The second relates to its manifestation in text and context: either overt or covert.[60] The particular silences examined fall along different points along each axis—a voluntary or involuntary silence may be covert *or* overt, for example, and vice versa. One advantage of such an organization is that it encompasses silences seen in both text and context, rather than creating a distinction between the two, for silences manifest themselves on the textual level (characters who remain silent) as well as the contextual (taboo topics or societal silences). Furthermore, these silences are intimately related. One of the central aims of this work is to demonstrate the essential interplay between literary and societal silences, in particular the way textual silences inform and are informed by societal ones; therefore a broader theoretical framework is critical. This framework also provides a necessary flexibility of scope: conceiving of silence as an interplay between two sets of oppositions allows for a consideration of individual differences depending on the particular silence under scrutiny and also facilitates an understanding of why essentialist interpretations of silence often fall short.

In terms of the motives for silence, the works studied reveal a fundamental distinction between voluntary and involuntary silences—or, as the psychologist Robyn Fivush puts it, "being silent" and "being silenced." This distinction is critical, because it explores the reasons underpinning cultural silence, while recognizing its intimate connection to existing power structures. Fivush explores how dominant societal narratives either silence or empower individuals. For example, an individual who deviates from a culturally accepted "life script" (e.g., not getting married, not having children) often feels the need to justify her choices, whereas those who align with the normative and prescriptive scripts are able to "be silent." As she explains, "When power gives voice, silence is oppressive, but when power gives silence, voice is justification."[61] Silence therefore aligns with or resists an existing power structure. For the purposes of this study, I broaden the definition of "being silent" to include those who make a deliberate choice to remain silent (such as victims of torture who refuse to offer information to their captors). I employ the term "being silenced" as a silence imposed from without, representing a lack of power, and "being silent" as both a silence that aligns with the existing power structure and an individual choice to resist that power—again, the ambiguity is critical. This focus on the motives underlying silence helps emphasize that, when expressing trauma, being *silent* does not always equal being *silenced*.

The second critical opposition concerns the manifestation of silence, whether it expresses itself openly or remains somewhat hidden or concealed. Not all silences take the form of an absence of words, as Vered Vinitzky-Seroussi and Chana Teeger have shown in their examination of collective memory. These scholars draw a distinction between overt silences, "a literal absence of speech and narrative," and covert ones, which are "covered and veiled" by speech that lacks meaningful content; both types of silence facilitate an understanding of silent expression.[62] This distinction between overt and covert silences becomes especially important because the two manifest themselves both in text and context and are often interrelated. The exploration of overt and covert silences exposes the complicated relationship between power and silence in the postdictatorship period, how the breaking of one taboo can unwittingly create another, and how the silences viewed as needing to be broken can shift with the changing political landscape. These two frameworks (voluntary/involuntary, overt/covert) inform an understanding of how silence can indicate both the universally "unspeakable" nature of trauma as well as the reluctance to engage certain taboo topics.

Chapter Overview

Looking at postauthoritarian cultural production from the perspective of what has been silenced or taboo reveals the profound challenges that face a society grappling with issues of truth and justice in a shifting political landscape. The works examined engage difficult subjects such as torture, disappearance, and the appropriation of children, along with the attendant questions related to complicity or split allegiances. Attention to the silences related to these issues demonstrates not only the difficulty of bearing witness to the dictatorship's crimes but also the way in which human rights discourse at times seeks to prescribe meaning or determine what is "socially sayable." Furthermore, the interplay between cultural and societal silences before and after the memory boom attests to the evolving memory discourse regarding the dictatorship years, in particular which issues come to the fore and which remain taboo. Works were selected for their ability to reveal taboos and silences related to dominant human rights issues of the postdictatorship period: the legacy of torture, the nature of disappearance, the appropriation of children, the memory of violence, and the meaning of sites of atrocity. They also represent a variety of approaches to the tale of trauma, as they include traditional literary works, testimonial narrative, documentary film, and sites of memory. The first three chapters examine works that engage with institutional silencing before the memory boom (1989–95), while the final three analyze cultural production in the postboom era in order to illuminate the shifting nature of taboos pre- and postboom as well as to reveal how silence informs cultural production in both a climate of openness and one of amnesia. As a whole, the exploration of silence and silencing in pre- and postboom works demonstrates the fundamental complexity of representing the postauthoritarian period. Although the boom marks a move from a politics of amnesia to a politics of memory, not all preboom silences are negative, just as not all postboom speech is enlightening. Renderings of trauma that respond to and highlight silence's fundamental ambiguity—its lack of answers, its frustrating incompleteness— serve best to represent the dictatorship's horrors and its complicated legacy.

Chapter 1 looks at the representation of torture during the preboom climate of impunity, as seen in Eduardo Pavlovsky's controversial 1990 play *Paso de dos* (*Pas de deux*). The female protagonist categorically refuses to speak even when subjected to brutal torment, and her choice to "be silent" is portrayed as powerful, for it denies her torturer what he most wants: information. Furthermore, the play creates a situation in which the victim's silence becomes her only source of power; by refusing to label her torturer/lover as a hero, the protagonist attempts to condemn his actions. Yet this powerful silence created within the space of the play (an overt silence) reveals reluctance on the part of the playwright to fully engage with the brutal nature of torture (a covert silence). By presenting a reductionist interpretation of silence as power, *Paso de dos* effectively masks torture's vicious reality. Rather than explore the unpalatable aspects of trauma, the play ultimately reveals two uncomfortable (and opposing) societal taboos surrounding the torture experience and demonstrates how attempts to represent the violent practice lead to an unresolvable tension between the two.

Chapters 2 and 3 address the fundamental question of how to write of disappearance during a period when Argentine society avoided directly addressing the dictatorship's brutal legacy. Framing the discussion in terms of the famous Silhouette Campaign or *Siluetazo*, comprised of outlines of human figures pasted to walls and trees around the Plaza de Mayo, the chapters examine a central tension in human rights discourse: the consideration of victims as individuals (a focus on the interior of the silhouette) or part of a collective whole (a focus on the outline). Chapter 2 looks at Eric Stener Carlson's attempt to rescue one victim from anonymity, seen in his testimonial narrative *I Remember Julia: Voices of the Disappeared* (1996).[63] A former volunteer with the Argentine Forensic Anthropology Team (EAAF), Carlson seeks to re-create the life story of "Julia," whose remains he helped exhume from a mass grave outside of Buenos Aires. He compiles interviews with family members, friends, and colleagues of the missing woman in order to tell the most complete story possible of her life and death. Nevertheless, his attempt to fill silences with words in order to rescue one victim from anonymity unwittingly reveals the paradoxes and challenges of simply combating silence with speech, or filling in the outline of disappearance with information and data. Although Carlson aims to focus on Julia's life, a consideration of her violent death inevitably informs the entire project. Furthermore, every answer he discovers leads to more questions and greater ambiguity, and the packaging of Julia's story into a recognizable framework of testimonial narrative serves more to cover than uncover the tale of trauma. While Carlson's narrative highlights the importance of breaking the silences and voicing the tale of trauma, this chapter demonstrates that an excess of words does not always lead to a greater understanding of disappearance.

Chapter 3 analyzes Juan José Saer's 1994 detective novel *La pesquisa* (*The Investigation*), which highlights the blank silhouette itself as a powerful symbol of disappearance. While Carlson's text combats the silence of the disappeared with the speech of survivors, Saer's work refers to disappearance only peripherally. Nevertheless, although the historical catastrophe of disappearance is barely mentioned, with only fleeting references interspersed throughout the narrative, it remains the central (if unspoken) mystery. By developing an interplay of presence and absence, speech and silence, rather than tell the untold story of disappearance, Saer's text illuminates *how* the untold story is not told. *La pesquisa* emphasizes the importance of the silencing of the untold story, calling attention to the poignant power of the empty silhouette. Taken together, chapters 2 and 3 exemplify the twin impulses in the human rights community—a desire to honor the disappeared as unique individuals (through breaking silences) and a need to emphasize the collective scale of the violence (through calling attention to silences)—seen in Carlson and Saer's differing strategies for responding to the absence embodied in massive disappearance.

While the first three chapters unpack the perception that preboom silence represents powerlessness or a lack of answers, the second three address the fallout of the memory boom: the craters of silence left in the wake of memory discourse. Chapter 4 explores the entrenched taboos related to the stories of children born in captivity and given to military families to raise, represented in Elsa Osorio's 1998 novel *A veinte años, Luz* (*My Name Is Light*) and Telefe's 2006 *telenovela Montecristo*. Both the novel and telenovela feature characters who were appropriated as babies and search for their biological identities; both also portray the search as a suspenseful yet relatively uncomplicated process of discovery, thereby embodying one catchphrase of the Grandmothers of the Plaza de Mayo, "Identity cannot be imposed" (*La identidad no se impone*). Yet by romanticizing the experience of the youngest victims of the dictatorship, these cultural representations effectively silence some of the extraordinarily complex issues surrounding the politics of identity. While on the one hand *A veinte años, Luz* and *Montecristo* align with the testimonial impulse to tell the story of children born in captivity and break the military's pact of silence regarding its systematic practice of appropriating children, on the other hand they suppress some critical (if uncomfortable) aspects of the tale of trauma. In this case, breaking the military's overt silence produces a concomitant covert silence regarding the more difficult or unpalatable aspects of the story of the children of the disappeared. By simplifying the complex politics of identity, both representations silence uncomfortable truths about identity restitution and obscure the tragic scope of the original crime of appropriation.

Chapter 5 demonstrates how postboom silence can be an effective tool of expression and affirms that when it comes to remembering past violence, silent expression can be as eloquent as speech. The chapter examines Luisa Valenzuela's *La travesía* (The crossing, 2001), in which secrets and repressed memories prove to be an effective means to process past trauma. While forgetting and oblivion may appear to be akin to silence and silencing, *La travesía* demonstrates that silence can actually be expressive in all its muteness: the silence of forgetting is never a true absence of expression but rather provokes speech. Furthermore, Valenzuela's use of ellipses, incomplete phrases, and blank spaces on the page all suggest not only that language proves inherently unreliable but also that its absence can be eloquent in itself. By highlighting the importance of secrets and silences, the novel emphasizes the paradoxical and ambiguous nature of silence, as well as its central significance when remembering the postdictatorship years. The chapter argues that this ambiguity is fundamental—the issues left in the wake of state terror do not resolve neatly into traditional paradigms that equate memory with speech and silence with forgetting—and Valenzuela's use of silence as both a theme and mode of expression ultimately demonstrate a rich representation of past trauma.

Finally, chapter 6 examines the use of overt silence as a response to an oversaturation of memory discourse in the Kirchner era. It analyzes Jonathan Perel's 2010 documentary of the former Navy Mechanics School (Escuela Mecánica de la Armada, or ESMA) titled *El predio* (The site). A notorious detention center during the dictatorship, the ESMA returned to the center of debate in 2004, when the decision was made to convert the buildings and grounds into the Space for Memory and the Defense and Promotion of Human Rights. Noting the parallel between the historical blindness of state-sponsored percepticide and the current difficulty of perceiving the space because of an excess of memory discourse, the chapter argues that despite the desire that the grounds of the ex-ESMA "speak for themselves," Perel's documentary demonstrates the inability to express a univocal interpretation of the site through verbal or visual means. Employing various techniques of defamiliarization, most strikingly the lack of voice-over or music, *El predio* suggests that one can only approach, but never truly arrive at, a definitive meaning of the space. Furthermore, by eliminating any authoritative voice from his documentary, Perel forces the viewer to participate in the process of telling the story (or more precisely, *a* story) of the site. By calling attention to the fallout of the memory boom, his documentary underscores both the importance of silence as well as the challenge of memory sites to "speak for themselves," and the chapter argues that it is precisely the fundamental ambiguity of silent expression seen in *El predio* that serves to transmit memory of the dictatorship.

Examining the way these cultural representations of the postdictatorship period engage with issues of silence and silencing helps illustrate the complexities of pre- and postboom memory discourse. During the preboom era, victims and human rights groups were "being silenced" by the military's refusal to offer information regarding missing persons as well as the Menem government's attempts to curtail public discussion of the dictatorship. Yet the cultural responses to the preboom repression of memory discourse indicate that, even during a period of imposed silencing, the choice to "be silent" can prove powerful (see chapters 1 and 3), and combating silences with words may not be enough to sufficiently address the aching silence of forced disappearance (see chapter 2). Furthermore, postboom memory discourse does not relegate silence to the shadows. "Being silent" can be an eloquent expression of the aftermath of trauma (see chapter 5) as well as a response to an oversaturation of memory discourse (see chapter 6). Meanwhile, the externally imposed silencing of particular tales of trauma does not always come from the military but may emerge from human rights groups themselves (see chapter 4). The link between silence and power seen in the opposition between being silent and being silenced demonstrates the evolution of memory discourse across the pre- and postboom periods.

Observing the relationship between overt and covert silences in these works also enhances an understanding of the complicated expression of difficult truths. When exploring the taboo topics that remain after the return to democracy in Argentina, for example, a close examination of an overt textual silence can reveal a covert contextual one (see chapters 1 and 4). Attention to overt and covert silences also reveals an unfolding discourse regarding which silences are viewed as negative (in need of breaking) and which may be linked with human rights discourse. For example, the overt silences in the years of "societal amnesia" are often linked with the military: the refusal to offer information regarding the fate of the disappeared or the "pact of silence" regarding the appropriation of children. Nevertheless, overt silence in the Kirchner era can be seen as a response to an excess of memory discourse or a reaction against the use of memory initiatives for political expediency (see chapter 6). A detailed investigation of how overt and covert silences both facilitate and disrupt the expression of past trauma exposes both the promise and the limitations of the boom when reckoning with the past.

The dialogue between textual and contextual silences in the cultural representations under scrutiny underscores the essential role silent expression plays when articulating the tale of the postdictatorship before and after the memory boom. Artists and writers who address past trauma in their work necessarily engage issues of silence and silencing, for to do otherwise would ignore a crucial aspect of postauthoritarian Argentina. Yet the way in which silence is represented in these works demands close attention, for these artistic representations inevitably engage with the broader context to alternately conceal or reveal critical issues regarding trauma and representation, such as taboos surrounding torture or the hidden pitfalls of testimony. The dictatorship and postdictatorship years are marked with ambiguity: the ambiguous loss represented by disappearance, the ambiguous subjectivity of survivors (are they heroes or traitors?), and the struggle over multiple and competing meanings regarding sites of memory. To approach a more complete understanding of the complicated legacy of state terrorism, one must plumb the depths of the bottomless well, attending not just to the explosion of memory but also to the hidden fallout of the memory "boom."

Tortured Silence and Silenced Torture in Eduardo Pavlovsky's *Paso de dos*

> Truthful words are not beautiful, beautiful words are not truthful.
>
> Tao Te Ching

On June 13, 2013, Gloria Di Rienzo gave her testimony in the "Megatrial" in Córdoba of over forty individuals accused of crimes committed in the clandestine detention center La Perla. After first asking the judge for the defendants to be removed from the chamber while she spoke, she related the horrific tortures to which she had been subjected. For one and a half hours, she recounted her experience, recalling names, faces, and abuses in grim detail. Yet toward the end of her testimony she made a startling declaration: "Look, Your Honor, there are details that I will never, ever tell! I will not describe them because they have humiliated my dignity completely! My husband and children are in this courtroom, and I will not share them for anything in this world!" As one journalist wrote in a description of the day's testimony, a question remained in the hearts and minds of all those who heard the witness's emotional declaration: "What else? What other trauma? What other unbearable humiliations had Gloria suffered, if what she had already related demonstrated such intolerable depths?"[1]

Di Rienzo's testimony reveals the complicated role silence plays when relating past abuses, in particular the taboos surrounding the torture experience.

While her testimony initially appeared painfully complete, her final statement revealed that for all the details she shared during her declaration, many others remained suppressed. Rather than simply leave out the unspeakable aspects of her experience, Di Rienzo chose to call attention to the overt silences in her own testimony, leading to several important questions regarding the relationship between silence and torture. When relating such a life-shattering experience, can—or should—one tell the "whole" story? How? Does leaving certain aspects unsaid help or hinder the communication of violence? In short, what elements of torture and its aftermath find expression, what remains taboo, and why?

The questions raised by Di Rienzo's testimony are reflected in fictional representations of torture, which weave painful history—the real-world experience of torture victims—into meaningful story and seek through the telling to express truths about state terror. Yet in a context such as the torture chamber, the path from history to story is marked with representational pitfalls. Given the challenge of finding words to fully express extreme violence, any rendering of trauma necessarily highlights certain aspects of the experience at the expense of others, and the ultimate meaning of a work reveals itself not only through what is expressed but also what remains unsaid. Representing the effects of torture therefore becomes a very complex project of determining which aspects are portrayed and which are effectively silenced, as seen in Eduardo Pavlovsky's controversial play *Paso de dos* (*Pas de deux*).

First performed in 1990, *Paso de dos* emerged at a time of increased suppression regarding public human rights discourse: shortly after Menem's first presidential pardons (1989), and in the wake of the Full Stop (1986) and Due Obedience (1987) Laws, measures designed to apply a soothing balm of amnesia to the societal wounds of the dictatorship years.[2] By detailing the continuing relationship between a torturer—referred to only as Él, or He—and his former victim—Ella, or She—after the return to democracy, Pavlovsky's play worked against institutional silencing regarding the dictatorship. Its dramatization of a "romance" between a torturer and victim, its central themes of complicity and torture, and its overtly sexual and violent staging attracted controversy and debate. In many ways the play aims to unsettle common perceptions regarding repressors and victims, the average person's capacity for evil, and the nature of "collaboration" in a context of extreme violence.[3] By bringing uncomfortable issues to the fore, *Paso de dos* seeks to engage taboos surrounding the torture experience and resist societal silencing regarding the subject. One striking aspect of the production concerns its use of silence as a powerful denunciatory tool, even in a climate of societal amnesia.[4] In particular, *Paso de dos* illuminates the complex relationship between overt silences (information deliberately left unsaid) and covert ones (silences that are hidden or veiled), for the overt silences in the play itself point to uncomfortable covert ones in the broader society regarding the legacies of torture. An examination of these silences reveals which aspects of torture are unsettled by Pavlovsky's work, and what remains taboo.

Staged as a conversation between the torturer and his victim/lover, *Paso de dos* depicts the violent and intimate relationship between He and She as they seek to understand and negotiate the terms of their changing relationship. Throughout the performance, He speaks of his growing obsession with She, and his need to possess her, while She questions him regarding their shared past and strives to understand the relationship that developed between them. Varying between tenderness, violence, resistance, and complicity, they share their tangled feelings, yet as the performance progresses He subjects She's body to physical and sexual torments that ultimately culminate in her death. Meanwhile, the voice of She, played by a different actress sitting in the audience, affirms that She's silence represents not complete annihilation but rather a powerful condemnation of the military's actions.[5]

The overt silence of She, both during torture sessions and after the return to democracy, represents her only weapon, yet an examination of Pavlovsky's attempt to create such powerful overt silences reveals a more disturbing covert silence regarding justice (or its lack) and the relationship between torture, complicity, and betrayal. In their well-known analyses of the play, Diana Taylor and Marguerite Feitlowitz explore how the female character's silence exposes a troubling relationship between gender and power, yet the drama has not received as much attention for its portrayal of the torture experience itself.[6] The play seeks to tell a difficult truth regarding the possibilities of a romantic relationship emerging from the violence of the torture chamber and the consequences of impunity for repressors. Nevertheless, it silences the most uncomfortable or unpalatable aspects of the torture experience and also signals entrenched societal taboos regarding torture victims' militancy or their capacity for "collaboration." Although *Paso de dos* purports to condemn the brutal practices of the dictatorship and honor the victims of violence, it fails to fulfill the testimonial project of bearing witness to the manifold horrors of torture.

Overt Silences in Eduardo Pavlovsky's *Paso de dos*

Paso de dos aims to call attention to the atrocities committed by the military, and this engagement with the reality of state terrorism implicates it in a larger ethical dilemma regarding fictional representations based on historical events.[7] Elizabeth Swanson Goldberg outlines the problem in *Beyond Terror: Gender, Narrative, Human Rights*: "How not to do further violence to these humans, their loved ones, or their descendants by spectacularizing, eroticizing, or otherwise *getting wrong* the representation of pain inflicted in a grave violation of human rights."[8] Through an analysis of several contemporary literary and cinematic representations of human rights abuses in places ranging from Latin America to Iraq, Goldberg outlines a possible ethic for fictional witnessing of atrocity that involves avoiding facile or generic narrative codes. By eschewing simplistic treatments of complex issues, one begins to approach an ethical representation of historical horror.

Such an ethic of representation proves especially appropriate in the case of a torture play, given the difficult subject matter. Any drama that engages the complex legacy of torture and disappearance must be sensitive to the lived experience of the victims themselves.[9] *Paso de dos* features a victim who refuses to reveal information despite suffering horrendous torments, thereby serving as a heroic example of dignity in the face of abject humiliation. In refusing to speak, the victim thwarts the purported object of torture by exercising free will in the face of ostensibly complete domination, thus preserving her humanity in an inhuman situation. Nevertheless, choosing to portray fictional characters who suffer torture in heroic terms risks betraying the memory of those who suffered the dehumanizing torments of torture in the real world and undermining the testimonial function of a work designed to criticize the military dictatorship and its authoritarian legacy.

Paso de dos creates two powerful overt silences within the play. First, the female prisoner categorically refuses to offer information under torture, infuriating her interrogator and denying him the satisfaction of fulfilling the purported goal of the sessions. Overt silence, *Paso de dos* implies, is the victim's only weapon within the torture chamber. Yet the drama also portrays She's overt silence after the return to democracy as an equally powerful weapon against impunity: toward the end of the performance, She refuses to name her torturer/lover's deeds or label him a hero, thereby denying him the "fame" of proclaiming his exploits to others. By emphasizing the force of She's silences, *Paso de dos* inverts the traditional interpretation of silence as absence or lack of power, for She's silence, rather than symbolizing defeat or oblivion, serves to challenge the authority of the repressors. Moving from one extreme to the other, silence is denied as oblivion and recast as power; however, attempts to infuse these overt fictional silences with unequivocal power fail to recognize the inherent (and uncomfortable) real-world ambiguities regarding the legacies of torture. Put simply, an emphasis on powerful overt silences—an essentialist interpretation of silence as power—leads to a simplistic understanding of the postdictatorship period, one that does not address the full spectrum of torture's brutal reality and reveals societal taboos concerning the representation of victim and victimizer.

Overt Silence after the Return to Democracy: Oblivion Recast as Power

Throughout the play, She wields her overt silence as a weapon, as she first keeps silent under torture and later refuses to name her torturer/lover or grant him an identity. He draws a parallel between her two silences, declaring: "You didn't speak before and you won't name me now," followed by "who am I then?"[10] Unable to find his own words, he asks her to explain his relationship—"what we shared was . . . ?"—and articulate his identity— "I was . . ."[11] Seemingly incapable of defining himself or their shared experience, He pleads with her to name or denounce him, implying that he needs her to validate his identity; without her declaration, he will remain anonymous. He further implores her, "I'm asking you to tell the truth / to tell what I did to you / I need it for me."[12] He needs her to acknowledge their relationship, to make public his actions, so that everybody will know he was able to possess her completely. In the final, climactic scene, He is standing at attention in the muddy pit where he has "disappeared" his victim/lover, but her bodiless voice proclaims: "I will remain silent. My silence is your prison. . . . I'll never make you a Hero / you will remain imprisoned in my silence / I won't name you . . ."[13] Employing overt silence as her weapon, this decision to deny him the label of "hero" turns her silence into a cry of condemnation.

Both Pavlovsky and director Laura Yusem insist that *Paso de dos* portrays a positive, empowering vision of the legacy of the dictatorship. Nevertheless, faced with Feitlowitz's suggestion that "the death seems real; her 'triumph' seems a literary conceit,"[14] Yusem emphasizes the importance of She's voice living on as a testimony to her unbroken spirit. Paradoxically, then, this overt silence can be interpreted at one and the same time as a powerful affirmation of the individual's free will or as proof of her complete disappearance. On the one hand, She's decision to remain silent and not grant He an identity through her words can be viewed as a ringing condemnation of the public's perverse fascination with violence (her refusal to label him either a torturer or a hero prevents him from capitalizing on his past); yet on the other, this silence means her experience, like that of many other desaparecidos, will be condemned to oblivion. Furthermore, such silence also implies impunity for the torturers.

As Taylor remarks concerning the female protagonist's silence, "This is hardly *power*. Women have been refused *voz y voto* (voice and vote) throughout much of history."[15] The contradictory character of silence seen in *Paso de dos* testifies to the fundamental ambiguity of silent expression. Is She's silence a *silencio a gritos*, a criticism of the system of oppression? Is it a tacit acceptance of that system? And how can one determine the difference?

In the case of *Paso de dos*, the answer hinges on the disjunction between the textual and contextual interpretation of She's dramatic silence. The conflict between the interpretation offered by the director and playwright and that of critics viewing the play points to the central problem of interpreting a victim's silence in a work situated in the postauthoritarian context: the fact that such an interpretation is constructed within the text itself (Yusem and Pavlovsky's interpretation) but is also informed by its relation to the broader social context of the work (Feitlowitz and Taylor's reading). One can very easily emphasize the power of a victim's overt silence, but at the same time that textual silence can be seen as a mere reflection of extratextual repression. In other words, those who "read" subversion into an overt silence may be trying to limit the interpretation of a character's silence to the insular space of the play or performance itself, without recognizing the extremely important effects of the sociohistorical context in which the play is produced. *Paso de dos* offers an interpretation of postauthoritarian Argentina that did not completely align with the societal reality at the time it was staged, when perpetrators enjoyed the full protection of the controversial immunity laws. Although She attempts to use her silence as a weapon, the strength of her refusal to grant He an identity through her words stems from *his* desperate response rather than a societal affirmation of the power of torture victims' silences. While it remains clear in the performance that He needs She to give him his identity, that She's overt silence (her negation) has a tremendous power over him, the strength of this voluntary muteness does not extend beyond the restricted space of the performance.[16]

Despite the playwright's claims to the contrary, *Paso de dos* is unable to infuse accusatory power into She's overt silence after her torture experience. At the end of the performance, Pavlovsky presents the spectator with a final tableau of a seemingly unrepentant officer standing at attention in the mud that hides She's body.[17] That She's refusal to name him a "hero" seems to hold such a power over He, even after He has "disappeared" She into the mud at his feet, rings hollow in the culture of impunity at the time of the play's performance. Despite his protestations on an individual level, in a society where torturers enjoy complete immunity, He does not need She to label him a "hero," or to denounce him, or to define him—his role and identity as a torturer have already been tacitly acknowledged and accepted by society. Pavlovsky's drama converts She's silence into empty power, because her death, like her silence, remains shatteringly realistic in a postauthoritarian context of miscarried justice.[18] In this case, overt silence only becomes powerful if one ignores the external context, and *Paso de dos*'s essentialist interpretation of silence as power attempts to deny the fundamental ambiguity of silence, in particular its resistance to any univocal interpretation. Furthermore, it reveals a reluctance to tackle the difficult issues of impunity—the uncomfortable covert silences regarding the amnesty laws and their implications. Recasting silence as unequivocal power fails to recognize the important nuances and tensions of postdictatorship Argentina and its legacy of torture and disappearance.

Overt Silence in the Torture Chamber: When Victims Become Heroes

Paso de dos's production during a period of state-sponsored impunity demonstrates the difficulties with infusing power into She's silence after the return to democracy; despite Pavlovsky's efforts to create a strong overt silence, a torture victim's silence too often represents powerlessness, whether because of a lack of words to express the experience, a lack of a forum in which to speak, or a lack of a sympathetic public willing to listen. Nevertheless, *Paso de dos* succeeds in bestowing a positive and even powerful value upon She's overt silence in the torture chamber. The work emphasizes the resistance inherent in She's silence, and Pavlovsky shows the power a victim acquires when she chooses to "be silent."

The female victim's implacable silence under torture proves a powerful tool of resistance. While initially He fears that she will give in too quickly, thereby terminating "the intensity" of their experience,[19] her relentless silence eventually infuriates her torturer. He recalls, "Why always evasions *winning in your silence* / I wanted you to shout out all the truth."[20] At one point he attempts to communicate with her through gestures, offering her a cigarette as he asks her a question. Yet she rejects the cigarette and refuses to answer, repudiating her torturer on both verbal and nonverbal levels of communication.[21] Finally, her stubborn silence takes a different form in the interrogation scene included in the play; in this case She deigns to speak, but the words have no meaning:

HE: Who?
SHE: She

HE: She who?
SHE: She who
HE: Who she who?
SHE: She who who[22]

Despite He's repeated insistence that "I don't believe you" and "I'm being serious," She fails to provide any actionable information during the torture session.[23] She clearly holds a power over He through her refusal to provide answers, as can be seen when He despairingly states, "I finally asked you to invent names I only needed a made-up name so you would say something . . . it became important that you pretended to give in."[24] Her unyielding character serves to subvert the torture experience, in which He supposedly has complete power over She.

She's unwavering silence aligns with the heroic portrayal of victims who refuse to betray any information under torture. The victim's silence may lose potency after a return to democracy, but during the moments of maximum repression—the torture sessions themselves—overt silence does indeed translate into power. And herein lies one paradox of silence within authoritarian and postauthoritarian contexts: it is most powerful during the moments of greatest repression. At the same time that a regime employs tactics of repression and censorship to actively "silence" its victims, it is this very repression that grants silence its power. In other words, while on one hand the repressive power gains control of the official discourse because it manages to silence its victims (She dies as a result of her torment), on the other, the victims are able to resist such complete domination because their silence is converted into power. Yet the force of overt silence is very tenuous in a postdictatorial setting, because it depends so much on a specific future interpretation of past events. For the silence of victims such as She to be viewed as powerful, not only must their memory be preserved—spoken of a posteriori—but society must also believe in the amorality of the military's actions. Given that silence depends on external context for its interpretation, if a strong undercurrent of thought remains that the victims of military repression in some sense "deserved" their fate—the infamous "por algo será"—She's silence is voided of all its power.[25]

Despite the challenges of interpreting silences in a context of impunity, overt silence remains a powerful tool of resistance in the torture chamber. By refusing to speak, the victim undermines the purported object of the practice of torture through exercising free will in the face of ostensibly complete domination, thus preserving her humanity in an inhuman situation. Yet She's implacable overt silence within the space of the play reveals a covert societal silence regarding the relationship between torture and "betrayal" and the limits of representing torture, best seen through a close analysis of how *Paso de dos* cultivates ambiguity, unsettling facile interpretations of torture, and where it falls short. In brief, the play presents a nuanced characterization of the torturer, and to a certain extent the torture victim as well, which serves to bear witness to the complexity of the torture experience. Nevertheless, the representation falters in one crucial area: the victim's steadfast silence under torture precludes a nuanced treatment of the practice, revealing a reluctance to address some of the more uncomfortable legacies of this particular tool of repression.

Pavlovsky emphasizes that his work engages difficult questions regarding torture and its aftermath. He insists that his intention was to explore the ambiguity of torture, stating in an interview with Feitlowitz that "the theme must be dealt with in its *complexity*."[26] Granted, the decision to portray a "love affair" between a torturer and his former victim explores an aspect of the legacy of torture that is generally considered unthinkable. As Estela Patricia Scipioni emphasizes in her analysis of the play, "*Paso de dos*, whether or not it has treated the theme [of "romantic" relationships between victims and victimizers] from the correct perspective, has the merit of having forced us to consider and debate the issue."[27] By depicting a continuing relationship between a former victim and her captor, the play raises thorny questions regarding the relationship between power, violence, and passion, thus directly confronting a taboo topic related to the torture experience.[28]

The fictional relationship between She and He raises uncomfortable issues of complicity between victims and torturers. As Ana Longoni observes, female prisoners who developed relationships with repressors are often stigmatized in fictional and testimonial portrayals; even when the women maintain silence under torture, they are labeled "traitors" nonetheless.[29] Longoni muses, "If a traitor is somebody who betrays others, and these women did not do that, what converts them into traitors? Their betrayals, then, are of a different order: sexual, or even loving."[30] Rather than giving up names, addresses, or other compromising information, these women "gave up" their bodies, an act that often translates into unforgivable disloyalty in the fictional and testimonial realms.

Although Pavlovsky's play explores the territory of complicity, She is not characterized as a "traitor" for developing a connection with her torturer, thereby unsettling this common perception. Considering any relationship between victimizer and victim a "betrayal" on the part of the female prisoner maintains an easy distinction between "good" and "evil." Victims who resist any type of collaboration with repressors remain firmly situated on the moral high ground, while those who develop a bond with a torturer cross over to the side of the enemy and deserve condemnation. Nevertheless, representations and interpretations that draw a clear line between repressor and victim—the former unquestionably evil and the latter an innocent victim—ignore the way in which torture challenges simplistic categories of good and evil. By depicting a torturer-victim relationship that does *not* condemn the female prisoner as a traitor, Pavlovsky attempts to avoid a simplistic condemnation of complicity on the part of the female victim.[31]

Other works of Pavlovsky delve into the mind of the repressor in order to denounce the traces of authoritarianism even in the postdictatorship. As Brenda Werth explains in *Theatre, Performance, and Memory Politics in Argentina*, "Pavlovsky explores the role of the repressor to demystify the myth of the torturer as an inhuman monster and expose the banality of evil."[32] Keenly interested in the psychology of repressors, Pavlovsky aims to offer emotionally rich characters in his dramas. The emphasis on creating well-rounded, human characters rather than flat caricatures points to one of the key ways in which Pavlovsky seeks to engage the complexities of torture, and *Paso de dos* deliberately avoids creating a Manichaean relationship between a victimizer who embodies evil and a victim who embodies goodness. In particular, the drama rejects any one-dimensional characterization of the torturer as a psychopathic monster, depicting him rather as a normal, if corrupted, individual.

Pavlovsky's play offers readers and spectators a complicated vision of the torturer. The two participants in the torture sessions "fall in love" in spite of (or perhaps as a result of) the violent experience they share, and their relationship continues after the prisoner's release.[33] Although he commits some savage acts throughout the play, He is not the incarnation of an inhuman torturer. He does not describe his indoctrination in the practice of torture, but he relates an incident of childhood humiliation that helps explain his formation in a world of violence.[34] She even goes so far as to claim "distance is what makes us recognize each other / what mystery passes between us / making us forget so much of the past *who knows if we are that different* / what grew so strongly between us?,"[35] indicating the potential similarities, however disturbing, between the two. While the play explores to some extent the unique discomfort that arises from their emotionally charged relationship, the fact that the two are able to develop a certain form of intimate bond, and the allusion to his difficult childhood, imply that He is not an aberration of the human race.

It is worth noting that the portrayal of the repressor as a normal person corrupted by circumstance reflects the real-world evolution of torturers. As Edward Peters explains in his classic study of the practice of torture, "Torturers are deliberately trained in such a way as to alter their personalities, make them accept a fabricated political reality in which their victims have been set outside the pale of humanity, and sustain this illusion by both coercion and reward."[36]

Pilar Calveiro, a survivor of several clandestine camps in Argentina, similarly believes that the structure of the system allowed normal men to perform barbaric acts, explaining that they were "part of a mechanism, constructed by themselves, which led to a dynamic of bureaucratization, routinization, and naturalization of death, which appeared as simply a line item on an official form."[37] The characterization of the torturer in *Paso de dos* therefore aligns with the testimonial impulse to voice the truth about the practice of torture.

The portrayal of torturers as human beings rather than inhuman monsters to a certain extent prevents the audience from dismissing victimizers as marginal members of society. Faced with brutal torments carried out by seemingly ordinary people, audience members must consider their own capacity for evil. The human characterization of the victimizer may also avoid the danger of the torturer-as-most-fascinating-character, for rather than creating a voyeuristic spectacle of a psychopathic fiend, *Paso de dos* exposes the manner in which torture becomes normalized or routine. By portraying a human torturer, *Paso de dos* therefore prevents the comfortable distancing that could occur if the victimizer were completely barbaric, or only marginally human, thereby preserving the interpretive complexity needed to avoid "getting wrong" the portrayal of torture.

Considering the extent to which the play dismantles the perception of victimizers as inhuman, one would expect this complex character development to extend to the victim as well, to better approach a fuller account of the brutal experience. Indeed, the victim's response to torture and interactions with her torturer demonstrate a depth of character that to a certain extent balances the multifaceted depictions of the torturer. Nevertheless, the capacity of the victim to express a broad range of human emotions and behaviors remains limited because of the emphasis on the victim's refusal to speak, revealing restrictions that govern which aspects of the torture experience can be told and which are effectively silenced.

In *Paso de dos*, She does not remain a passive victim but interrogates He about their past shared experience. Throughout the entire play she is continually questioning him, demanding explanations, descriptions, answers. At the very beginning she presses him to articulate the type of conviction he had when touching her for the first time, as well as his eventual obsession with her. When he suggests that his actions had no deeper motivation than simple "inclination" (*ganas*), she probes further: "Nothing more than that, absolutely nothing more?"[38] Her questions about his family lead to He performing a soliloquy about the childhood incident in which his father humiliated him—in an ironic twist, the "confession" in this case comes from the torturer rather than the victim.[39] She's side of the dialogue even begins to resemble that of a torturer, with a series of questions that recall the torture chamber: "Shall we stop or continue? / You are tired / Shall we resume or stop here?" Beginning to suffer under her barrage of questioning and her charge that they try to "remember every detail of the events with the same original intensity," he gasps, "I need air," in an attempt to stem the tide of her questions. But she simply twists his plea into further questions, demanding, "How much do you need, one liter, two?," continuing to mock him: "You've always been precise before, why not now?"[40] She turns the tables on her former captor and takes on the role of interrogator, thus demonstrating a broad emotional range.

The complexity of the female protagonist extends to her psychological development as well, for throughout the play She appears deeply conflicted regarding her relationship with He. Her dialogue often alternates between a rejection of their shared violent past and an attempt to maintain the connection between them. For example, when He is gasping for breath as a result of her questions, she reflects upon their relationship:

> Now is the moment
> Maybe we can reconstruct
> words help us forget, many times we tried to talk in order to forget
> Do you remember those long conversations we had in order to forget what
>   had happened? . . .
> We tried to forget what had grown between us
> that's what it's about
> about reconstructing everything
> the mystery of each event in exact detail
> Is it even possible to talk about all this? . . .
> Finally we two are together, how many others with their heads in the mud?
> without being able to breathe
> naked, mutilated bodies, finally we two are together
> finally, finally
> We can remember together, shall we?[41]

The progression from attempting to forget what had happened, to attempting to forget what had grown between them, to meditating upon other nameless, faceless victims, to ultimately hoping to remember, reflects the protagonist's discomfort with her connection to He. In particular, the juxtaposition of their continuing relationship ("finally we two are together") with those whose lives ended in the torture chamber ("how many others with their heads in the mud?") highlights the violence and tension at the root of their relationship. While at some moments she appears to reject him completely, remembering the violence and the horror, at others she offers reflections such as "what a strange space we have invented / that sometimes I can't stop talking to you despite myself."[42] The conflicting emotions experienced by She as she alternately participates in and struggles against this sexual relationship with the man who, through exercising complete control over her in the torture chamber, became obsessed with possessing her, do indeed entail a complex characterization of the female protagonist as an individual struggling with issues of attraction and complicity.[43]

Paso de dos thus demonstrates a multifaceted nature for the tortured as well as the torturer. By highlighting the slippage between victim and victimizer and focusing on the mental struggles of the victim as she confronts their ambiguous situation, the work questions the seemingly clear-cut positions of power and complicity and therefore responds to the complexities of torture and its aftermath. Nevertheless, despite the efforts to present a more complicated vision of the torturer and his victim, the drama falls short on one critical level. Although the torturer in this work is not a monster, and the victim is portrayed in all her humanity to the extent that she may face profound internal struggles or take on aspects of her antagonist's behavior, one facet of the victim's conduct is never questioned: her overt silence under torture.

Given the ambiguities explored in *Paso de dos* and the range of emotions exhibited by the victim, it seems especially surprising that her behavior under torture is presented as unambiguously laudable. The play explores the taboo surrounding relationships between victims and victimizers, challenging the stigmatization of the female victim as a "traitor"; meanwhile, She works through the extraordinarily complex ramifications of this continued relationship with her torturer. Yet She categorically refuses to give up information. Ambiguities regarding complicity or an individual's capacity for evil abound, but such uncertainties do not extend to She's behavior under torture, as she unequivocally remains an "ideal" victim who did not reveal any information. By exhibiting a strong overt silence during torture, She subverts the expected role of torture victim, becoming a heroic agent instead of a passive prisoner and suggesting a limit to the amount of nuance this fictional representation can cultivate: ambiguity regarding the torturer's character or the victim's complicity (through a sexual/emotional relationship) is acceptable; ambiguity regarding the victim's capacity for "betrayal" (of others) remains taboo.[44]

The theatrical representation of the silent torture victim is quite common, as Severino Albuquerque observes in *Violent Acts: A Study of Contemporary Latin American Theatre*. His consideration of torture plays reveals how the prisoner's refusal to confess becomes a source of power over the torturer. While his analysis centers on the way in which the "unrepresentable" act of torture is made visible on stage through the interplay of verbal and nonverbal languages of violence, the numerous plays that he cites, written under military rule in

Brazil and Argentina, all conform to a greater or lesser extent to the mythology of the stubbornly silent torture victim in Latin American theater.[45] The prevalence of such characterizations of the victims reinforces the wide scope of this discourse of the torture victim as silent hero.[46] Silence is perceived as the only weapon available to the torture victim, for if they speak, their capitulation signifies they have lost everything, including the choice to remain silent. Small wonder that those who attempt to tackle the difficult task of dramatizing an experience as shattering as torture employ the victim's overt silence as a cornerstone of their representations, for it allows for a conscious choice—the decision not to speak—to emerge as a heroic symbol of humanity amid brutal attempts to break down the individual through torture.

But the victim's overt silence under torture does more than make her a heroic symbol of resistance. This refusal to speak also signals an implied militancy on the part of the victim, thereby revealing a tension between representing torture as a human rights crime (against a presumably innocent victim) or as a practice implemented against a group of people of a particular political persuasion (often with a militant aim).[47] When *Paso de dos* emerged in the cultural scene, human rights advocates tended to understate victims' participation in militant organizations in order to accentuate the military's violation of human rights. Attention to victims' militancy fed into the theory of the "Dos demonios" or "Two demons," which claimed that the military's violence was simply a response to armed guerrilla groups, thereby implying a struggle between two equal foes, rather than an asymmetrical encounter in which the military annihilated an undermatched enemy with excessively brutal force. Returning to Stern and Straus's identification of the tension between the universal and the local, local conditions clearly shaped the framing of this human rights crime.[48] Andreas Huyssen notes that in the years following the return to democracy, the urban guerrilla groups were publicly "forgotten" in order to speak of "innocent" victims of the brutal dictatorship, yet he emphasizes that although these silences are "politically desirable"—because they allow an unequivocal condemnation of the military's actions—they still "distort and erode memory" by suppressing key aspects of the dictatorship period.[49]

In *Paso de dos*, although He's interrogation of She involves names and addresses, the script makes no direct mention of She's political leanings or relationship to any guerrilla organizations. Politics and militancy remain notably absent from their conversation, and the staging and dialogue presents torture primarily in individual terms (their personal experience) as well as those of greater human rights (She's references to other victims of torture).[50] But, as Eugenio Di Stefano argues regarding *Pedro and the Captain*, a well-known Uruguayan play by Mario Benedetti that depicts the interrogation of a militant, a focus on the infliction of pain and victimhood discounts the specifically polit-ical context of torture: the discourse of human rights supplants any ideological commitment on the part of the victim.[51] In the case of *Paso de dos*, by effacing direct mention of militancy, torture appears as a crime against humanity rather than a crime against a particular group of politically dedicated individuals.

Nevertheless, She's overt silence complicates the interpretation of torture purely in terms of human rights, for the portrayal of a torture victim who withstands the torments of the torture chamber without "betraying" informa-tion appears to imply a level of commitment to a cause that one would not expect from an "innocent" victim. At one point near the end of the play, He remarks that "they said I wouldn't be able to get a single name out of you,"[52] indicating that She upholds what Longoni labels the "moral mandate to resist torture" common in militant groups.[53] While a lack of political discourse and emphasis on the violence of the torture experience serves to suppress the pos-sible militancy of the victims (and maintain the covert silence that considers victims as primarily "innocent"), underscoring the victim's silence under tor-ture implicates them as part of a militant political cause. *Paso de dos*'s focus on the overt silence of the victim thereby reveals a tension between framing torture within the discourse of human rights (thereby effacing its political implications) or within a struggle informed by political ideals.

Furthermore, by suggesting that a torture victim's humanity and dignity rest on maintaining silence under torture, *Paso de dos* forges a connection between humanity and militancy, leaving no fictional space for either innocent victims or those who provided information. The play creates a chain of causa-tion in which the victim's dignity (and the preservation of her humanity) is predicated on her silence, which in turn implies militancy. Ergo, dignity comes from militancy. The uncomfortable ramifications of such a premise illustrate the complications that arise when the victim's only agency comes from overt silence under torture.

The victim's steadfast refusal to provide information causes the drama to resemble what Herbert Lindenberger terms "martyr plays" in his study *His-torical Drama: The Relation of Literature and Reality*. Although She displays a breadth of character regarding love and complicity, her steadfast refusal to provide information aligns with the ethics of martyrdom Longoni analyzes in militant groups.[54] As Lindenberger observes, by their nature "martyr plays tend to cultivate as little ambiguity as their audiences—or the writers' artistic consciences—will let them get away with."[55] Pavlovsky takes pains to avoid the simple dichotomy between "monster/tyrant" and "saint/martyr," recognizing Lindenberger's assertion that such terms "are much too absolute . . . for a work which cultivates the subtle shading of its characters,"[56] yet *Paso de dos* only appears to fully question or develop one half of the dichotomy. The drama goes to great lengths to break down the tyrant's side of the dualism in order to prove that torturers are not inhuman monsters, but the victim retains a heroic aura. While the complexities demonstrated in some aspects of She's behavior partially mitigate this "aura," her categorical refusal to speak under torture ultimately precludes the "subtle shading" of her character.

The reluctance to portray the ambiguity of the victim's behavior under torture risks converting her into a one-dimensional symbol of resistance rather than a well-rounded human character. As Lindenberger explains, "although they may begin by showing common human weaknesses, martyrs by their very nature are heroes whom the audience must come to recognize as superhuman,"[57] an especially ironic situation given the extent to which the torturer is shown as a complex individual, characterized as all too human. After all, it is just as dangerous to portray victims as heroes as it is to portray torturers as monsters. Given that one of the reasons for portraying the torturer as human rather than monstrous is to avoid creating a play in which the torturer is the most interesting character, the contrast between a well-rounded victimizer and a somewhat flat victim serves to undermine this important goal, as the torturer may inadvertently end up being the most fascinating character simply by virtue of appearing more human. In other words, to avoid a dichotomy between a human torture victim and an inhuman (monstrous) torturer, *Paso de dos* errs on the side of contrasting a human torturer and an inhuman (heroic) victim. Neither of these dogmatic portrayals does justice to the memory of those who suffered torture, for they fail to fully acknowledge the complexities of the brutal practice.

From Overt to Covert: The Unspoken Legacy of Torture

The idealized portrayal of the silent torture victim in *Paso de dos* points to two "convenient truths" about torture, to use Darius Rejali's term for uncomplicated interpretations of the practice that do not cause discomfort.[58] The first views torture as merely an information-gathering device, while the second characterizes the torture victim's speech as a betrayal. But these convenient truths serve as "cover stories," covert silences that mask uncomfortable realities—or inconvenient truths—regarding the practice of torture.

Regarding the first "convenient truth," the fundamental structure of torture the play presents—with violence inflicted as a simple means to gather information—differs greatly from the reality of the practice. As Elaine Scarry reminds us in *The Body in Pain: The Making and Unmaking of the World*, the description of torture as a method for "information-gathering" is a calculated fiction designed to legitimize the infliction of pain in the extraction of information.[59] While the military justified the use of torture by claiming that inflicting a limited quantity of pain would prevent greater injury (the rationale behind the oft-cited example of a captured terrorist who knows the location of a bomb that is about to kill many innocent people), the reality of the situation rarely, if ever, matched such hypothetical urgency.[60]

The absurdity of justifying torture as a method of gathering information is painfully illustrated by the significant number of survivors who testify to torture sessions absent of any interrogation, or questions concerning activities about which they had no knowledge. Many accounts in the Argentine *Nunca Más* report detail brutal torture sessions that are seemingly unrelated to information gathering of any kind, either because the victim has no knowledge that would allow him or her to answer the questions posed, or because he or she is subjected to torture without any type of interrogation at all. Such testimonials belie the classification of torture as a pure "information-gathering" device and seem to support Scarry's assertion that torture is in fact a practice designed to transform the prisoner's pain into the torturer's power. Scarry explains the mechanism of this procedure by describing how torture values form over content: "While the content of the prisoner's answer is only sometimes important to the regime, the form of the answer, the fact of his answering, is always crucial,"[61] as seen in He's desperate attempts to extract a confession from She. The utterances emitted during torture may bear little if any resemblance to usable information, but they serve rather to demonstrate how torture destroys both language and the self. When the prisoner's world is reduced to his or her immediate pain, his or her voice has been completely co-opted by the repressive regime. In her study *Torture and Truth*, Page duBois similarly argues that the object of torture is not to have the victim reveal a hidden truth but to eradicate the subversive truth they possess (communism, nationalism, or any other political belief that threatens the regime). She states, "This truth, located in the body of the revolutionary, the student, the dissident, must be rooted out, extracted and dominated, in the process of torture."[62] Nevertheless, the common perception of torture remains that it serves as a tool to gather information.

The second "convenient truth" concerns the tricky relationship between torture, "confession," and "betrayal." As Scarry observes: "There is not only among torturers but among people appalled by acts of torture and sympathetic to those hurt, a covert disdain for confession."[63] Yet the very confession extracted during torture is, in Scarry's estimation, mistakenly considered a "betrayal." Her intricate analysis of torture makes it clear that such intense physical pain destroys an individual's relation to the world, explaining that this destruction is "experienced spatially as either the contraction of the universe down to the immediate vicinity of the body or as a body swelling to fill the entire universe."[64] When the victims' world becomes pain, or, conversely, when their pain becomes their world, any true "confession" is impossible, because "one cannot betray or be false to something that has ceased to exist."[65] While these words still do have some type of "meaning" in the larger political context, in the intimately brutal space of the torture chamber, they are released from their referent and cannot be viewed as a simple act of betrayal. According to Scarry, the fact that those who inflict, experience, or witness torture (through testimony) are still able to place the burden of responsibility on the victim is proof of torture's ability not only to completely destroy a victim and his or her world but also to cover its tracks and create a reading of the event that allows those who practice torture to elide the moral responsibility for their actions and blame the victim for the consequences. In the case of *Paso de dos*, this "covering"—or covert silence—presents the torture experience in terms of heroism and betrayal rather than revealing its full brutality.

Testimonial evidence about the myriad responses to torture, coupled with critical analysis of its structure and meaning, stand as a testament to the issue's complexity. Faced with such a difficult subject, one must consider the elements of torture that Pavlovsky chooses to voice and those he leaves unvoiced. The portrayal of a victim who is able to exercise a clear choice between remaining "loyal" to an exterior world that is arguably rendered absent through torture and "betraying" that world and its inhabitants converts the experience of torture into a very manageable world of clear choices between "good" and "bad" and subsequently forces the victim to choose between being a "hero" or a "traitor." This is especially notable given Pavlovsky's refusal to stigmatize the female prisoner as a "traitor" merely because she developed a relationship with her captor. While the drama avoids easy demarcations between "good" and "evil" regarding her sexual collaboration, such ambiguities do not extend to her capacity to "betray" others.

This subsequent packaging of torture into an easily understandable system with clearly demarcated rules upholds "convenient truths" regarding the practice. Yet these interpretations cover the real truth. Too often the "choices" offered those subjected to torture are not nearly so straightforward. One survivor of one of Argentina's clandestine detention centers tells the tale of a man who broke under torture and offered information to his captors. But when they asked for more, he refused, even when they threatened to kill both him and his mother. His torturers eventually killed them both, causing the survivor who told the tale to challenge: "So here's the question. . . . Under torture he cracked, but given a free choice he gave up his life. Is he a hero? A traitor?"[66] This example, far from illustrating a clear demarcation between heroes and traitors, highlights the desperate ambiguities involved in such systematic violence.

By choosing to preserve the covert silences regarding torture and betrayal, the play confines this crucial aspect of the practice of torture to the fictional realm. Taylor warns of the possible consequences of such dogmatic representations of human brutality in *Theatre of Crisis: Drama and Politics in Latin America*: "Along with the (false) element of choice enter notions of responsibility: if the victim *chooses* to suffer rather than answer or 'confess,' we (as spectators) are relieved of the moral responsibility of interfering with that choice. Good audiences stay in their seats and let the actors fight it out."[67] Put another way, the less ambiguity cultivated in a representation of torture, the less discomfort the audience experiences, and consequently the less they understand about the brutal reality of the practice.

This is not to say that spectators of *Paso de dos* did not experience discomfort.[68] As Feitlowitz and others have noted, the play generated a high level of controversy and prompted a boycott from the Mothers of the Plaza de Mayo.[69] Yet the discussion in the public sphere was not rooted in the representation of torture as an information-gathering device or the victim's capacity for "betrayal" but rather the portrayal of a violent sexual relationship between victim and victimizer and the voyeuristic nature of the performance. An audience reaction that focuses on the sexualized violence between He and She rather than the other equally disturbing aspects of the torture experience serves to silence the "inconvenient truths" regarding the practice, despite the play's capacity to provoke discomfort.

Paso de dos invites, encourages, or even forces contemplation of some very difficult issues regarding torture and complicity in the postauthoritarian period: the average person's capacity for evil, and the nature of relationships developed in the torture chamber. However, when it comes to perhaps the most difficult aspect of torture—its potential to completely devastate a human being and his or her world—the play retreats to the safety of uncomplicated silent torture victims. The victim's overt fictional silence reveals a more disturbing covert silence on the part of the playwright regarding pain and "betrayal"— the torture victim may be given leave to resemble a torturer but never a traitor. Additionally, although the definition of traitor proves somewhat flexible (in *Paso de dos*, a prisoner who "collaborates" with a repressor through a sexual or emotional relationship is not automatically considered a traitor), providing information that "betrays" others remains strictly taboo.

The divergence between the testimonial reality of torture and the fictional characterization of its victims—between the stated goals of the playwright to explore the complexities of torture and the actual impact of his work—suggests that writers may unconsciously share a "covert disdain" for confession. Indeed, there exists in Argentina a stigma surrounding survivors of clandestine detention centers—just as the phrase "por algo será" (there must have been a reason) was used to justify the military violence (e.g., "If Fulano was taken away, there must have been a reason"), some human rights activists similarly condemn those who came out alive as traitors or collaborators (e.g., "If Fulano *survived*, there must have been a reason"). As Longoni explains, "While the disappeared are considered martyrs and heroes, survivors are stigmatized as traitors."[70] Through examining several testimonial novels that emerged out of the military dictatorship, Longoni reveals how writers persist in portraying survivors as traitors, and she wonders to what extent such representations may contribute to the perpetuation of this negative labeling. In the case of the play under consideration in this chapter, while it may expose certain taboos surrounding the torture experience, it unwittingly reveals a profoundly disturbing reluctance to engage the uncomfortable reality of how torture can destroy body and mind as well as an unwillingness to question the misconceived relationship between torture and betrayal.

Conclusion

Meditating on their tortured relationship, She declares, "We use our words to forget,"[71] an allusion to the fundamental silences that reside at the heart of their relationship. He and She use words to "cover" the truth of their intense experience, and *Paso de dos* directly exposes this particular covert silence. Yet other important silences regarding the legacies of torture remain unvoiced. The emphasis on the power of She's overt silence demonstrates the limits that govern which stories of torture find representation and which remain suppressed. Regarding issues of complicity and collaboration between victims and victimizers, while the female character can be portrayed as developing an emotional bond with the torturer, she may not provide information that "betrays" others, demonstrating the strength of the taboo regarding torture victims and "betrayal." Meanwhile, the focus on the victim's silence under torture further signals a tension between two mutually exclusive representational taboos regarding the torture experience: first, the direct mention of militancy; and second, providing information under torture. By eliminating overt references to armed struggle, *Paso de dos* appears to support the suppression of public discourse regarding the victims' militancy; nevertheless, the parallel focus on She's implacable silence under torture implicates the prisoner in the revolutionary cause. While the taboo regarding "betraying" others proves stronger (her stubborn silence inevitably suggests militancy), the struggle between two visions of a victim that are impossible to maintain concurrently leads to representational ambivalence regarding the female prisoner's connection to militant groups, a testament to the strength of both taboos.[72]

Portraying torture appears to involve an inescapable paradox. On the one hand, attempts to create a strong fictional torture victim accept information gathering as the central premise for torture and implicate victims in a philosophy of revolutionary martyrdom, thereby justifying the practice and disregarding the suffering of real victims. Furthermore, it requires creating an unequivocally powerful overt silence, turning victims into heroes and linking humanity with militancy. On the other hand, an attempt to do otherwise and engage the incredibly difficult issue of "betrayal" denies the "sacrifice" of the victims of torture and prevents any hope from emerging out of the horror. Just as the torturers and those who tacitly condone torture need to believe that such actions are justified ("*por algo será*"), those who attempt to honor the legacy of the victims also need to find meaning out of the horror ("*para algo será*").

Protective narratives that assign heroic meaning to trauma stem from the commonplace human tendency to want to find meaning in desperate situations. However, attempts to form horrific events into coherent and heroic narratives can be as dangerous as they are noble, for they take a real person's inexpressible pain and convert it into a simplistic, easily digestible story.[73] Tales of triumph emerging from trauma offer comforting words that, citing Lawrence Langer's critique of some Holocaust fiction, "make us feel better" but consequently do not "help us *see* better."[74] Yet choosing to see clearly can be too much to bear. Hopeful portrayals of horrific events ultimately mask a fear that were we to look carefully for the "real" meaning of such experiences, we would discover that such meaning proves intangible, nonexistent, or beyond our comprehension, thus rendering us truly powerless in the face of radical evil.

Of course one could easily argue that fictional representations create spaces where historical truths can be suspended or set aside. Playwrights, after all, have the right to portray history not as it *actually* happened but as it *could* or *should* have happened. However, is the purpose of such representations to honor the victims of such a life-shattering experience, to bear honest witness to their trauma, or to portray a more palatable version of torture, one more suited to those who remain outside the experience? The overt silences of fictional torture victims point to uncomfortable covert ones regarding the legacy of torture, and in the end, heroic tales of torture provide an additional burden for victims who lived to tell the tale, compounding the brutal physical victimization with the psychological blow that anything less than martyrdom constitutes a failure or betrayal.

There are no easy answers to the ethical dilemma of representing torture. If Di Rienzo's testimony at the beginning of the chapter reveals the challenges victims face when articulating the experience, Pavlovsky's attempts to fictionalize torture point to equally thorny issues of bearing witness to a victim's pain. In search of a possible path through the representational minefield, one can turn to "The Garden of Forking Paths" by Jorge Luis Borges, a tale that features an incomprehensible novel. In most fiction, characters make one decision at the expense of all others, and yet in this paradoxical text, each time a character encounters a situation in which he is obliged to make a choice (to kill or to be killed, to speak or to keep silent), the character chooses every possibility. The result is a labyrinthine, contradictory novel, impossible to comprehend in all its complexity. But such decisions are not limited to the fictional sphere. Authors make similar choices when deciding what to write. By electing one particular plot twist or characterization, many possible alternatives are effectively silenced. Spectacles of torture that allow easy, satisfying, or comfortable interpretations of heroism and betrayal let the spectator off the hook. They sanitize the experience instead of forcing those faced with the act of witnessing the drama to consider uncomfortable issues or inconvenient truths regarding their own attitudes about justice (or its lack); the relationship between torture, complicity, and betrayal; or the acceptability of the violence portrayed. The experience of torture involves a labyrinth of conflicting motivations and jumbled utterances, all played out through a prism of unspeakable pain. To portray it in all its complexity, one risks creating a confused tale, impossible to comprehend, or a tale that proves too difficult to accept—the horrifying legacy of radical evil. Yet the alternative would seem to be a dangerous silencing of some of the most difficult and crucial aspects of the torture experience, leaving the heart of the violence ultimately unvoiced. In the search for a representation of torture that honors the victims and bears witness to their trauma, we must not forget that the price of coherence is always a silenced story.

Filling in the Space of Disappearance

Eric Stener Carlson's
I Remember Julia:
Voices of the Disappeared

ne September morning in 1983, near the end of the dictatorship, the disappeared returned to the Plaza de Mayo. This was not a literal return but a symbolic one, embodied in life-sized silhouettes of human figures that were pasted to walls, monuments, and trees in and around the Plaza. Known as the *Siluetazo* (or Silhouette Campaign), this artistic and human rights event defied the institutional silence regarding the military's practices of terror, as each faceless figure interrogated passersby with its silent presence, calling attention to the absent victims. Over time the silhouette has come to serve as a stand-in for the disappeared, a visual rendering of the presence of absence, yet the use of an outline of the human form to symbolize the missing victims underscores a central tension in human rights discourse regarding the crime of disappearance. On the one hand, a blank silhouette prompts a desire to fill in the interior, to provide defining characteristics that will allow a consideration of victims as *individuals*, each with a unique story. Personalizing silhouettes with names or other features responds to the need to view the disappeared as distinctive and irreplaceable persons. On the other hand, the empty space of the silhouette situates the victim as part of a *collective group*, underscoring the violence as a crime against humanity in the broadest sense. A seemingly endless line of identical figures highlights both the extent of the violence and the gaping hole left in its wake.[1] These two interpretations of the silhouette pull in opposite directions, raising the question: does one (considering victims as individuals, considering victims as part of a collective whole) inevitably silence the other?[2]

Attempts to write the story of disappearance respond to this tension. When the object of the story has vanished without a trace, when the specific circumstances surrounding that vanishing are unknown yet terrifying, should authors strive to fill in the outline of the silhouette or call attention to its poignant emptiness? Which approach best serves to break the societal silence and make visible the trauma of disappearance? This question was particularly pressing in the early 1990s, when the physical absence of the disappeared was compounded by a political climate that suppressed public discussion regarding the victims of state terror, prompted by President Menem's pardons of military officers and institutional stance against pursuing justice for human rights violations in all but certain cases.[3] This chapter and the next explore two different renderings of disappearance that arose in this climate of impunity and silencing, one an investigative account of the life and death of an actual victim of the dictatorship, the other a fictional detective tale seemingly removed from Argentina's legacy of state terrorism. The first, Eric Stener Carlson's *I Remember Julia: Voices of the Disappeared*, seeks to break the overt silence of disappearance by filling in the outline of one particular victim, while the second, Juan José Saer's *La pesquisa (The Investigation)*, highlights the silence contained in the silhouette itself.[4] A consideration of these two approaches reveals the inherent challenges of telling the story of a vanished subject as well as how such seemingly opposite renderings of disappearance paradoxically complement each other, even when appearing mutually exclusive.

I Remember Julia: Voices of the Disappeared marks the writer Eric Stener Carlson's attempt to re-create the life of "Julia," a victim whose remains he helped exhume from a mass grave on the outskirts of Buenos Aires when working as a volunteer for the Equipo Argentino de Antropología Forense (EAAF) in 1991.[5] Though it was impossible to identify the vast majority of the close to four hundred victims in the Avellaneda cemetery site, the case of one young woman proved exceptional. This particular individual had undergone a rare heart operation that allowed the forensic team to positively identify her remains. Her family held a small memorial service for her at the cemetery, affording them some form of closure denied to so many others. Witnessing these events, Carlson felt compelled to investigate the woman's life more fully in order to bring her experience to light and listen to the voices of those touched by the dictatorship. He remarks in the introduction to his text: "In all of this discourse of guilt-shifting and recrimination—which group was more right or more

Filling in the Space of Disappearance

wrong, the military or the revolutionaries—the people who were murdered in this process are nowhere to be found. They are still disappeared in many ways, even after their exhumations have been performed."[6]

I Remember Julia responds to the silences left in the wake of disappearance in two related—yet at times contradictory—fashions. First, in the name of filling in the silhouette, the text aims to give voice to "Julia" as a unique *individual,* to create as accurate a picture as possible of this particular young woman's life. Second, by framing "Julia's" story within the broader context of the dictatorship's crimes, Carlson also situates this particular victim as part of the *collective group* of the disappeared. With its central emphasis on rescuing one victim from anonymity, the first goal occupies a privileged position, for the work endeavors to provide answers to aching questions surrounding "Julia." To Carlson, talking and filling the silences—attempting to fill in the details of "Julia's" silhouette—is the only response to the poignant emptiness of the outline, yet a close examination of his text reveals the challenges, paradoxes, and limitations of an approach that privileges breaking silences and filling in the lines of the silhouette.

Filling in the Outline: The Challenges of Investigating Disappearance

To piece together a portrait of "Julia," Carlson interviewed family members, friends, and colleagues of the missing woman, and *I Remember Julia* is comprised of these interviews, interspersed with first-person testimonies of other people unrelated to the victim who provide representative glimpses into certain aspects of the dictatorship. Although not a testimonio in the strictest sense of the word, Carlson's project aims to fulfill the testimonial function of speaking truth to power by both providing a forum to speak for those affected by disappearance and exposing the crimes of the military to a broader public. The text also aligns with the broader goals of the EAAF to provide clarity and truth in the face of the military's attempts to hide their actions.[7] In keeping with testimonial narrative's desire to listen to the victims of violence, the invocation of the voice figures prominently in Carlson's discussion, beginning with the subtitle of the book, *Voices of the Disappeared.* He emphasizes that the main purpose of his work was "to listen" to "the voices of the people who lived through those dark times," because he felt that while there was a significant and growing body of literature dedicated to the political and economic effects of the dictatorship, the stories of those most affected by the experience were still being silenced when he conducted his investigations

(1991–93).[8] He describes the "great pains" he took to exclude secondary sources, "focusing instead upon the voices of those persons directly involved,"[9] in a clear attempt to incorporate unmediated accounts of the time period.[10] Carlson's emphasis on the power of the voice, coupled with his desire to break the repressive silences surrounding the disappeared, situate his text within a broader testimonial project.

By privileging the voices of so many witnesses to "Julia's" life and death, *I Remember Julia* attempts to construct an empirical and emotional record of this young woman's story. The chapters tracing the thread of "Julia's" life take their titles from the name or pseudonym of the family member, friend, or colleague interviewed. These stories alternate with other chapters titled simply "Voice 1," "Voice 2," and so on, which relate the testimony of others who lived through the dictatorship, including a religious leader, a psychologist who specializes in the lingering effects of disappearance, a government official, and a representative of the Mothers of the Plaza de Mayo. In keeping with testimonio's strong reliance on the unmediated voice, Carlson avoids providing commentary or judgment about each testimony, streamlining some of it into a coherent third-person narrative but leaving significant portions of direct quotation, a structure that allows the protagonists in the story to speak for themselves.[11] Friends, family members, and colleagues remember their interactions with "Julia," grieve her loss, and offer explanations for her fate. By gathering a wealth of empirical evidence from those who knew "Julia" best, *I Remember Julia* attempts to compile the most complete picture possible of her life and death, thereby fulfilling testimonial narrative's function (and that of the EAAF) to tell the silenced story of trauma.

But this strategy of gathering evidence to "fill in" the outline of the missing victim presents some fundamental challenges. Most important, Carlson's text reveals the tension in human rights discourse between focusing on the body of a disappeared person as evidence of a crime or as an individual with a unique life story. As the historian Thomas Laqueur notes, the rhetoric of the corpus delicti (the body as evidence of a crime) has dominated human rights discourse, yet the body also serves an extrajudicial function, helping survivors to mourn and remember.[12] By investigating "Julia" as an individual, Carlson works against the language of victimhood—her body solely as testament to the crimes committed against her—yet at the same time the exhumation of her body as one of the disappeared victims of the dictatorship prompts the exploration of her life in the first place. The attempt to re-create "Julia's" life and listen to the "voice" of a desaparecida paradoxically ends up reproducing the discourse of the corpus delicti: the focus on her life (the personal details of the silhouette) is constantly informed by her death (the outline itself).

Carlson's efforts to restore "Julia's" identity and explore her life story also reveal the related challenges of constructing a tale grounded in trauma by means of empirical investigation and interviews. His work demonstrates the impossibility of simply combating the overt silence of disappearance with speech, for the answers he discovers lead to more questions and greater ambiguity. By breaking the overt silence of disappearance—re-creating one victim's story—*I Remember Julia* reveals the concomitant covert silences of the testimonial genre itself: its tendency to conceal as much as it reveals. Carlson's narrative foregrounds the importance of breaking the silences and voicing the tale of trauma, yet this view of silence as unambiguously negative fails to recognize that an excess of words does not always lead to a greater understanding of disappearance. Furthermore, the project invokes what Allen Feldman has termed the "prescriptive expectations" of testimony, the idea that testimonies must serve a particular function: legal, moral, cathartic, or therapeutic.[13] The packaging of testimony into recognizable frameworks serves to "cover" the opaque heart of trauma, and breaking an overt silence thereby risks creating a covert one, a "cover story" that masks the unfathomable depths of traumatic experience. The ever-present tension between the victim's life and her death, coupled with the paradoxes and limitations of empirical investigation and testimonial narrative, point to the difficulty of simply breaking the silences surrounding the crime of disappearance, for the interior of the silhouette is not so easily filled.

The Corpus Delicti in Human Rights Discourse: Can Dead Bodies "Speak" of Life?

I Remember Julia responds to two related overt silences regarding the disappeared: specifically, the questions regarding the fate of *one* particular victim—first identified as skeleton 17, later matched with "Julia"—and more broadly, the societal silence regarding the dictatorship, fueled at first by the military's refusal to offer information regarding the fate of missing victims and later by the Menem government's attempts in the early 1990s to close down public discourse in the name of moving forward. Carlson conducted his interviews and research during a two-year period from 1991 to 1993, during which time speaking publicly of the disappeared was still considered taboo among all but the most vocal human rights groups. Carlson alludes repeatedly to the societal silence and concomitant fear, both the silence of those who lived near the cemetery and witnessed the mass burials and also the friends and family members of "Julia" who often spoke only under promises of anonymity.

He marvels at the bravery of those who did come forward to speak to him: "Ex-prisoners and political militants, those who repeated time and time again to me, 'Don't use my real name, because I'm afraid they'll find me,' those who have the most to lose if the military again returns to power, talk. They talk through their fear and through their pain because they cannot stand the silence."[14] This central goal of breaking silences also aligns with Carlson's aim to rescue one victim from anonymity. The gravesite in which the forensic team worked contained remains of approximately four hundred people, yet positive identification of remains occurred in only "a limited number of cases"; "Julia's" case proved the exception rather than the rule and provided some definitive answers to one family.[15] Breaking individual and collective silences surrounding the disappeared is of paramount importance in Carlson's text, in order to fill in the missing details regarding "Julia."

Although the discovery and positive identification of "Julia's" remains serve as the catalyst for Carlson's investigations, he aims to tell the story of this young woman's *life*, rather than simply the story of her death. In keeping with the goal of listening to the "voices" of the disappeared, Carlson seeks to discover who "Julia" was, to fill in the outline of the silhouette with characteristics that define the young woman as an individual, rather than "just another number in an unmarked grave."[16] He notes that human remains are not enough to put a human face to suffering: "because we lack a person, a personality to connect our lives with theirs, we find it extremely hard to imagine that each one, in fact, had been a real person. In this way, ten thousand dead, twenty thousand, thirty thousand come to be mere numbers, arbitrary and lacking in humanity." For this reason, he compiles information from those who knew "Julia" best, to provide "vignettes of who she was, memories of what she meant to them."[17] Rather than focus on her violent death (a tale more easily told from her remains), Carlson aspires to determine "who she was," a goal perhaps best described as putting the "human" back in "human rights." Yet paradoxically, Carlson's attempt to restore "Julia's" identity and individuality rests on the fact that while "Julia" is an individual person with a unique life story, she is also material evidence of a crime. *I Remember Julia* reveals a tension between trying to "hear" the "voice" of a disappeared victim (a forensic project that relies on "Julia's" remains) while at the same time attempting to maintain a focus on her life (rather than her disappearance and death).

Thomas Laqueur observes that contemporary human rights discourse centers around dead bodies. The bodies of victims of human rights violations stand as physical evidence of a crime, "an articulate witness" to the atrocities committed against them, and given the prominence of forensic work at sites of horror, the corpus delicti occupies a privileged space in human rights discourse.[18] Laqueur identifies a tension between two uses of the truth revealed by a forensic examination: judicial truth (the body as evidence of a crime) and "truth in the interests of memory, of narrative closure, of healing, of reconciliation." He questions whether bodies can serve both purposes simultaneously, as evidence of a criminal act and as "the balm of closure," begging the question of whether one function necessarily silences the other.[19] Borrowing Laqueur's framework, can "Julia's" body "speak" of *both* her life and individuality *and* the crime committed against her, or does one particular discourse inevitably silence the other?

As the first place in the world where the techniques of forensic anthropology were used for human rights work, Argentina wrestles with the competing functions of thousands of dead bodies that evidence the crimes of the dictatorship.[20] The anthropologist Ari Gandsman explains that human rights groups such as the Mothers and Grandmothers of the Plaza de Mayo have resisted the corpus delicti as a basis for their work, choosing to focus on the victim's lives and politics rather than their deaths. He elaborates: "For human rights organizations, the disappeared are not defined by their material traces in the present; they are defined by their political activism."[21] To many in the Argentine human rights community, a focus on material remains precludes consideration of the lives and politics of the missing: one cannot fill in the details of the silhouette if the outline itself symbolizes death.

Akin to the human rights groups who strive to reclaim the lives of their missing loved ones, Carlson resists a language of victimhood by trying to rescue "Julia" from the graveyard in which her remains were found. By identifying "skeleton #17" as "Julia Andrea Montesini" and investigating her life, Carlson attempts to portray "Julia" as a woman with a unique personality and set of beliefs that make her an individual. Nevertheless, the project automatically begins with an acknowledgment of her death; it starts from what her body can "tell" the forensic team. Not only does her body determine which victim Carlson investigates (as he states, the vast majority of remains proved impossible to identify), but it also serves as incontrovertible evidence that she was a victim of a crime (the forensic report lists the cause of death as "the passage of a projectile from a firearm through the cranium").[22] The story of *I Remember Julia* begins in the cemetery in a literal sense, yet Carlson also chooses this starting point for the text, as the first chapter details the discovery and identification of the remains as well as the memorial service held for "Julia." Although the work aims to re-create "Julia's" life beyond her situation as a desaparecida, the inevitable grounding of the story in the cemetery, in the language of dead bodies, informs the rest of the tale of "Julia's" life.

Furthermore, the decision to include voices that speak to the dictatorship times more broadly also serves to undermine the focus on "Julia's" life, for such testimonies invariably consider her as a victim of violence rather than an individual. Re-creating "Julia's" life through memories of those who knew her best aims to fill in the details of one individual's silhouette, rescuing her from the anonymity of the mass gravesite, from being considered "just another number" representative of the massive scale of the dictatorship's violence. Including voices of various experts who provide historical context, however, also situates her within the broader collective whole of "the disappeared."[23] This paradox highlights the contradictory nature of the silences Carlson aims to break, which are both individual (what happened to "Julia") and collective (what happened to all the victims, and the societal silence regarding the crimes of the past). By incorporating voices that respond to both types of silences, the text seeks to bridge the gap between the particular and the collective. Nevertheless, the dialogue between the two types of voices—those who talk of "Julia" as a person, those who talk of "Julia" as a victim—creates a tension between a focus on her life (trying to fill in the details of the silhouette) and a focus on her death (acknowledging that she is a victim of violence), akin to the competing interpretations regarding forensic remains.

The use of a pseudonym to identify the victim also contributes to the "collectivization" of "Julia." Carlson explains in the acknowledgments of his book that while the characters and events in the book are "historically accurate," as are the names of the torture centers, the names of certain individuals and other locations and dates were modified to protect those who otherwise would not have contributed to the account.[24] He elaborates:

> It is a testimony to the pain and fear still surrounding the disappearance of the woman whose story appears in the following pages that, almost twenty years after her death, the reader cannot know her real name. The author finds it ironic that he is compelled to take "Julia's" real name away from her in order to promote her memory, for it is the name, first of all, that this disappeared person was robbed of when she was kidnapped. Her name, and thus her identity, her liberty, and her life.[25]

The military took away her identity when they kidnapped her so long ago, so Carlson grants her a substitute identity, "Julia Andrea Montesini," and uses this proper name (unencumbered by quotation marks) throughout the text. A brief allusion to the irony of erasing identity to preserve memory marks Carlson's only reference to "Julia's" true identity.[26]

Yet the inability to name "Julia" is more than simply ironic. As Carlson states, the name was the first thing taken from prisoners; for this reason, the

Filling in the Space of Disappearance

ability to restore her identity in a public fashion would make a powerful statement. Despite the author's compelling reasons for concealing "Julia's" real name, the substitute identity impedes the goal of rescuing this victim from anonymity. The fear that prevents the author from using her real name also speaks to the entrenched taboos at the time of writing. That a book written in English, destined for a North American audience, cannot state the full truth regarding one victim of the Argentine dictatorship stands as a testament to effective military and governmental silencing even years after the return to democracy, demonstrating the limits writers face when attempting to break the silences.[27] Investigating the life of one particular victim is possible; publishing her name is not. In terms of the tension between the particular and the collective, withholding the victim's name compels the reader to consider "Julia" as representative of the collective group of desaparecidos, defined in terms of victimhood and violent death, even as the text aims to present her as a unique and vibrant individual.[28]

The struggle for meaning surrounding "Julia's" body does more than call attention to the constant tension between the judicial truth—"Julia's" body as evidence of a crime—and the truth of "Julia" as a member of a community that needs to mourn and remember. One of the primary reasons human rights groups resist the rhetoric of the corpus delicti is precisely because such language robs the victims of agency. As Gandsman explains, "A politics of dead bodies assumes the passive position of victims. For Argentine human rights groups, an ethics of political action is prioritized over an ethics of dead bodies."[29] For the victims to be remembered as living beings with beliefs, ideals, and agency, the focus must be on their lives rather than their deaths. Furthermore, the emphasis on bodies and forensic evidence situates the victims of the dictatorship within a broad framework of human rights, with its attendant "depoliticizing universalism," to borrow Gandsman's words.[30] The four hundred bodies exhumed from the graveyard in Avellaneda—like bodies exhumed in Bosnia, Guatemala, and South Africa—testify to violent crimes against humanity, yet to view these victims as part of a universal discourse of human rights effaces the individual circumstances of each person whose remains occupy the mass gravesite. This universalization, to a certain extent, works against the text's goal to restore "Julia's" individuality: the outline of the silhouette threatens to overshadow the re-creation of individual details. A human rights paradox in herself, "Julia" is at one and the same time an individual person *and* evidence of a crime against humanity, yet speaking of her death lessens the consideration of her life, while focusing on her life risks downplaying the circumstances of her death.

Concealing and Revealing:
The Limits of Testimony

But the paradox of telling "Julia's" story as an individual person, rather than simply a victim of a crime, is compounded by the challenges of accessing "Julia's" story at all. Carlson's attempt to piece together the life of a missing woman through breaking the overt silences regarding her disappearance reveals the limitations of a testimonial project to fill in the outline of the disappeared victim's silhouette. The methods Carlson employs to uncover "Julia's" life and character—empirical investigation and interviews—exemplify the challenge of hearing the "voice" of a disappeared subject, and *I Remember Julia*'s attempts to provide answers and clarity often lead to more questions and ambiguity.

A central issue when reconstructing the life story of a vanished subject is that of agency, or who has the right to speak. In traditional testimonial narrative, the speaking subject often pertains to a subaltern group, calling attention to the power of the investigator, and many critics argue that the subaltern can only speak through such nonsubaltern (intellectual) interlocutors.[31] Yet while subaltern subjects are "silenced" because of their position on the margins of society, "Julia" *literally* cannot speak for herself but only through those who remember her. The promise encapsulated in the book's subtitle—that the reader will hear the "Voices of the Disappeared"—proves impossibly ambitious, as "Julia's" voice remains inevitably mediated by others. If the struggle to resist the rhetoric of the corpus delicti aspires to reclaim the victim's agency, the necessarily mediated voice of the disappeared subject pulls in the opposite direction. Such a situation begs the question: who possesses the agency of the encounter when the subject has vanished? While in some cases of massive human rights violations the survivor's *testimony* is often all that remains, in "Julia's" case *she* has been destroyed, leaving behind family and friends whose voices combine in a narrative of multiplicity.[32]

The content of the testimonies themselves, while providing insight into the life of this extraordinary young woman, points to many unanswered questions even as they shed light on others. Like many other detainees, "Julia" was pregnant when she was captured, and the fate of her baby remains a mystery. No fetal remains were found in the grave, leading the forensic team to believe that she gave birth, yet the resolution of one issue leads to further questions: "Whether it was aborted naturally or, due to the conditions of the prison cells in which she was held, whether it was born dead or killed afterwards, or whether it was removed and placed in the home of a military family as many other children of the disappeared had been, is impossible to know."[33] "Julia's" mother finds herself scanning the faces of young women on the streets of Buenos Aires, wondering if perhaps the girl she sees could be her granddaughter. Dr. Ester Saavedra, the psychologist interviewed for the book, explains how the possibility of the child's existence keeps the victim's family members in the same type of terrible limbo they experienced when they wondered about the fate of "Julia."[34] The ability to fill in one aspect of the silhouette—determining that "Julia" gave birth—leads to more questions and uncertainty.

The chain of questions and answers is only one obstacle to reconstructing "Julia's" life. Narrative polyphony also undermines any attempts at accessing "who she was"; despite the interviews, many details remain inaccessible. The specifics surrounding her kidnapping prove elusive, for the version of the story Carlson includes in the book is "repeated frequently in testimony by Julia's friends and family" but "cannot, however be confirmed."[35] *I Remember Julia* also contains conflicting reports of the extent of her involvement with the government opposition groups labeled as "subversives." Her older brother Luis Ignacio was heavily involved in union activities, but friends and family members interviewed disagree as to "Julia's" connection with politics. She obviously possessed a strong social conscience, because she chose to work in a clinic serving low-income families, but whether this conscience extended beyond health care into more radical activities is difficult to say with certainty. Her school friend Graciela concludes that because so many people were taken away "without a reason" and "Julia's" busy schedule kept her either at home or at work, she could not possibly have been involved.[36] Yet "Julia's" younger brother Manuel and a colleague at a home for mentally handicapped girls where she worked both implicate the young doctor more in political activities.[37] Finally, her first boyfriend strongly denies she had any ties to political organizations.[38] With such disparate accounts regarding "Julia's" political activities, the extent of her involvement in politics remains an impenetrable silence.[39] No one can truly claim to "know" "Julia" completely, nor did anyone interviewed witness her disappearance firsthand, thereby placing each subject's authority into doubt.

It is worth noting that these contradictions are not limited to the sections describing "Julia's" life story. The various "voices" interspersed throughout the text also offer differing interpretations of the dark years of the dictatorship. Emilio Mignone's description of the workings of state terror and the military policy of extermination (*el aniquilamiento*) is supported by Adolfo Pérez Esquivel's account of his torture and imprisonment; both speak of unlawful, immoral acts committed by the military in the name of exterminating the enemy. However, the testimony of retired General Heriberto Justo Auel refers to policies such as *el aniquilamiento* as a response to the armed guerrilla groups, "because the enemy established a model of aggression that is evasive, that lies outside of the rules of war."[40] While he recognizes that certain "errors" were committed in the course of the years of military rule, such actions receive legitimization because of the unorthodox methods adopted by the "terrorists." Although closer scrutiny of these other voices may reveal that certain explanations of the dictatorship hold up better than others—Auel's testimony in particular reads like an outlier when compared with the others—by avoiding commentary and letting each subject speak for himself, the text places each testimony on equal footing, leaving it to the reader to decide which explanation seems most accurate.[41]

These differing versions of people and events underscore the difficulty of drawing firm conclusions based on empirical evidence. The stories contradict each other, making it impossible to judge the motives of each speaker. For example, the entire testimony of "Julia's" former boyfriend Luciano is tinged with an obsessive cast. By all accounts a brilliant neurosurgeon before retiring from medicine and the world, Luciano maintains a shrine to his former lover with mementos and photographs, and his testimony is so rambling that Carlson presents very little as direct quotation. Luciano's actions reveal a man who has chosen to live frozen in the past and whose representation of "Julia" reflects more his own demons than any accurate portrayal of the young woman. Yet this rather extreme example highlights the pitfalls of re-creating a life through the memories of others. Are the people interviewed choosing to represent "Julia" as more or less involved in politics on the basis of their memories of her behavior or a conscious or unconscious desire to protect her reputation?[42] How can one account for the numerous factors informing each memory?[43] The attempts to break the overt silence of disappearance point to the central covert silence of traditional testimonial narrative: the truth.[44]

Unclear motivations and contradictory stories impede Carlson's ability to re-create the full picture of "Julia's" story. The challenges presented by those interviewed for the book represent what Antonius C. G. M. Robben has termed "ethnographic seduction," the constant negotiation of meaning and authority that occurs between the two interlocutors during an interview. Taking the literal meaning of "seduction" as "to be led astray from an intended course,"[45] Robben describes the difficulties he encountered when interviewing perpetrators and victims of the Argentine dictatorship. Placing his finger on the heart of the research dilemma, he asks: "How can we engage in constructing an intersubjective understanding with a person who either has violated or transcended the humanity we are trying to understand?"[46] In these unique circumstances where victims' stories hold claims to authenticity and actors on the political stage are described in Manichaean terms, there can be no straightforward interviews.[47]

Consciously or unconsciously, interview subjects place limits on what can and cannot be addressed, and the text acknowledges instances of reticence on the part of those interviewed. For example, after relating the testimony of Francisco, one of the senior doctors at the clinic where "Julia" worked, Carlson notes that "what is perhaps more important is what Francisco doesn't say."[48] Although Francisco and "Julia" were close friends, the doctor downplays the extent of his relationship with her or her family. Others interviewed for the book criticized the doctor for denying his friendship with "Julia," thus revealing the secret he attempted to keep hidden in his testimony. Yet Carlson's acknowledgment of overt censorship hints at other unacknowledged instances where subjects may have resisted a certain line of questioning or sought to preserve a secret more successfully. As Robben reminds us, "Ethnographic seduction reduces communication and knowledge to appearance."[49] In the case of *I Remember Julia*, the reader is left with the appearance of "objective" evidence and impartial reporting and can only wonder as to the workings of the interview process. Obviously the author feels a pull of solidarity with his subjects, the need to remember "Julia" as "someone who is not just another number in an unmarked grave,"[50] but the reader cannot know the extent to which this solidarity affected the gathering of information, as Carlson effaces any discussion of the issues of ethnographic seduction from the book.

Carlson's choice to "be silent" regarding the relationship between interviewer and subject, rather than silence the thorny issues surrounding ethnographic field work, serves to destabilize the possibility of rescuing "Julia" from anonymity. Thoughtful consideration of the delicate relationship between interviewer and subject is essential for the final text to approach a credible account of the events or life described, and scholars can develop strategies to function even with an inevitable "observer-effect."[51] Such strategies can be as simple as stating, "I am an anthropologist, this is fieldwork"—or in Carlson's case, "I am part of a forensic team identifying remains" or "I am a scholar interviewing subjects"—for that precludes the observer not only from inadvertently committing him- or herself emotionally to a situation but also from ignoring his or her disruptive presence. Carlson's role as an outsider to the community may have an effect on the type of information to which he is privy as well as the silences he identifies. The ethnographer's place in the research process is of utmost importance and must be acknowledged as part of the empirical evidence under scrutiny,[52] yet unfortunately the text does not address the issues of ethnographic seduction. Despite the variety of voices in the work, *I Remember Julia* maintains a privileged position for Carlson's "I," leaving the reader to wonder as to the author's secrets.[53]

The seductive secrets of interview subjects and undeniable observer effect that manifest themselves during the research process do not disappear from the finished product. However, more often than not, they are concealed by the editing process, which erases the authorial presence and determines the order and manner of presentation for each testimonial voice. Elzbieta Sklodowska notes that testimony is never the "pure" voice of the speaking subject but rather a collaborative project between the editor and those who witness and narrate the events; in her words, "testimony cannot—nor does it have to—avoid the mechanisms that govern other discourses."[54] Heightened attention to the role of the researcher and the construction of the text has almost supplanted questions of veracity or authenticity. Clifford Geertz emphasizes that it has become more and more difficult to defend the idea that "ethnographic texts convince, insofar as they do convince, through the sheer power of their factual substantiality."[55] While earlier researchers believed in the importance of rapport between observer and subject as determining the value of the text produced, Geertz, like Sklodowska, recognizes the importance of the editing process in any ethnographic or testimonial project and advocates an examination of how the "author-function" is made manifest in the text.

In this complex process of creating the final product, ethnographic seduction becomes replaced by what I call "narrative seduction," in which the reader is led astray by the narrative in much the same way as the investigator is taken in by the interview subject. Unlike anthropological works that emphasize the observer's role, *I Remember Julia* resembles a traditional ethnographic study that relegates explicit references to authorial presence to prefaces or conclusions.[56] While Carlson locates himself in the text in the introduction, which details the discovery of "Julia's" body and the writer's quest to discover more about the young woman, his presence effectively "disappears" from the rest of the text until the epilogue. Given his stated goal of letting the voices speak for themselves, this effaced presence is not surprising. However, borrowing Geertz's terminology, concealing the "author-function" in the text does not erase the question of how the work is "author-ized."

Questions of authorization grow more important when considered in conjunction with issues of veracity. The author's commitment to protect "Julia" and other interview subjects through the use of pseudonyms ultimately trumps some issues of truthfulness, and *I Remember Julia* suggests that it is more important to know the events than the real names of the people involved. Carlson's sense of responsibility to his subjects cannot be criticized. However, just as he is responsible to his subjects, he is also responsible to the story. After all, for most victims and their families, issues of veracity prove of utmost importance, and debates about witness reliability and the effects of extreme trauma on "truthful" testimony are mostly limited to the academic sphere. Those interviewed about their experiences of political violence rarely frame their comments by acknowledging the inherent relativity of *their* truth, or the pitfalls of witnessing trauma. "This is only my version of events and could easily be refuted by others" does not make for compelling reading. When it comes to bearing witness to trauma, the subject makes a passionate claim for truth, which is at once bolstered and weakened by the use of a pseudonym.

The decisions Carlson had to make during the process of researching and writing the book situate him between what Richard Rorty terms the "desire for solidarity" and the "desire for objectivity."[57] On the one hand, the investigator feels the need to be true to the objective facts, while on the other he or she feels the intense pull to identify with subjects who have lost so much. The language of *I Remember Julia* demonstrates a strong sense of solidarity with the interview subjects and the cause of the desaparecidos; Carlson reiterates several times the bravery of those who spoke with him regarding "Julia's" life and the dark years of the dictatorship. The author's decision to travel to Argentina and volunteer with the EAAF also implies a high level of commitment and investment. Yet the intensely personal nature of the project is complemented by the heavy burden of proof Carlson feels—solidarity with the victims in this case leads to a need for objectivity. His choice to write about "Julia" was necessarily guided by issues of truth-value: the need to find a case study that offered the strongest evidence for his work.[58] Empirical evidence that could be verified by as many sources as possible proved central to Carlson's project in order to prove the mass disappearances occurred.

In an essay about the Holocaust and history titled "Just One Witness," Carlo Ginzberg suggests, in response to Hayden White, that the truth of a historical discourse is not necessarily linked to how "effective" it is. Arguing against skepticism and relativism, Ginzberg believes that "just one witness" is sufficient to construct a truthful relation of past horror.[59] *I Remember Julia* would appear to advocate a related idea of "just one victim": if Carlson can definitively prove that just one "anonymous" skeleton in the mass grave was kidnapped, tortured, and murdered by the military, it will be impossible for people to deny the atrocities took place. The truth remains important yet always elusive.

Trapped in the morass of seduction, rhetoric, solidarity, and objectivity, what should an investigator do? Unable to attain any type of objective picture, the most one can hope for in this situation is that the investigator acknowledge the many factors that combine to create the finished product, in particular the way words can serve to cover rather than discover the truth. In the case of *I Remember Julia*, Carlson recognizes the difficulty of stitching together the fabric of a life from pieces provided by different sources. As he states in the epilogue, "Who was Julia, then? Does this collection of anecdotes and visions come close to describing her? Or are these stories merely echoes sounding against the dark wall of memory, a few scattered glimpses, and then nothingness?" He continues on to explain that the different portraits of "Julia" show how "who she is now depends on who remembers her."[60] Yet the potential effects of ethnographic seduction and the ultimate impact of issues of veracity remain largely unacknowledged. Listening to the myriad of voices in *I Remember Julia*, one cannot help but be struck by how an excess of speech does not necessarily lead to enlightenment, frustrating attempts to personalize the blank silhouette.

"Prescriptive Expectations" and Cover Stories

The empty silhouette proves a powerful symbol of disappearance—serving as a reminder of both the corpus delicti and the fraught nature of filling in the details of a vanished subject. "Julia" remains a representative of collective violence, even as Carlson attempts to reclaim her individual life; meanwhile, the challenges regarding ethnographic seduction and the pull between subjectivity and objectivity demonstrate the double process of revealing and concealing at play in testimonial narrative—breaking one silence reveals another, putting together the pieces of a story ends up "covering" another, and the amassing of empirical evidence does not always serve to enlighten. Yet these challenges are compounded by what Allen Feldman has termed the "prescriptive expectations" of testimony, how the stories in *I Remember Julia* should offer some type of moral, cathartic, or therapeutic function. According to Feldman, survivor testimonies are often packaged into legal or therapeutic frameworks that view traumatic experiences as "episodes scheduled for eventual overcoming through redemptive survival, recovery, and restorative justice."[61] Feldman believes that the idea that a testimony needs to serve some type of function actually causes further violence, because it takes a particular victim's experience and universalizes it within a framework of human rights. Such universalization "seek[s] to elevate these narratives from the particular, and from the *opaque materiality* of state, ethnicized, gendered or racialized terror."[62] Testimonies are expected to produce some type of healing, justice, or collective catharsis, when the reality underlying such violence is precisely its "opaque" nature. Feldman argues that such packaging of testimonies into "prescriptive expectations" precludes any understanding of "historical depth and complexity," for it is precisely this complexity that is lacking in the "emplotment" of testimony onto legal or therapeutic frameworks.[63]

What are the "prescriptive expectations" for a testimony of a desaparecido? Although *I Remember Julia* does not represent the first-person account of "Julia" herself, the text emphasizes the possibility of catharsis or healing. Carlson explains that the purpose of his book is both "an elegy for the dead, and a chance for the living to reclaim a memory of someone who touched their lives in a very special way, someone whom they cannot forget."[64] Many of the people Carlson interviewed had not come forward to talk about "Julia" since her disappearance, and the author emphasizes the power of reclaiming her memory to help those left behind. For example, for years, "Julia's" only surviving brother, Manuel, kept a box of her belongings stored in his closet, afraid to open it and see what memories it would release. Yet he brought the box to Carlson and opened it when he began to talk about his disappeared sister. Carlson explains: "That night, Manuel began to confront his pain, to break the unspoken taboos. . . . If Julia's story, if Manuel's story, means anything at all, it is an invitation for the rest of those left behind to begin to open the boxes, to begin to talk."[65] Carlson's words uphold a belief that a testimony to "Julia's" life will have a cathartic effect, to help those who knew "Julia" remember her and move forward.

Even those voices that provide historical context point to a somewhat redemptive function of testimony. Father Luis Angel Farinello's testimony, for example, ends with an eye toward a better future: "We're really badly off. That little light that can draw together these utopias, these dreams, cannot be seen. . . . An alternative can't be seen yet, it can't be seen. But it will come. It's sure to come."[66] The testimony of Dr. Ester Saavedra is particularly striking for its reference to the transformative nature of remembering. Referring to "Julia's" brother, Dr. Saavedra states, "I believe that Manual could say ['I remember'] because he buried Julia, and it appears to me that the burial gave him a type of forgiveness. Now he can remember her in a different way."[67] Finally, the entire project is framed in therapeutic and cathartic terms. When questioned as to why undertake an investigation that can only serve to "bring back memories of fear and pain," Carlson responds with an anecdote told by a Holocaust survivor whose life was saved by the kindness of strangers who briefly gathered around him to prevent him from freezing to death.[68] According to the author, *I Remember Julia* represents "strangers huddling in the cold, trying to preserve not a life, but the memory of one, a memory of Julia"; Carlson further notes that "these people do not gather for Julia's sake alone. They also gather for themselves," thereby highlighting the therapeutic effect the story has on those interviewed.[69] Throughout the text the reader notes the redemptive power of breaking the repressive silence: the bittersweet memories of "Julia" help the living move forward.

The packaging of the horror of disappearance into a narrative of possible redemption demonstrates how a testimonial approach—based on interviews with speaking subjects as an attempt to approach the "truth"—can unwittingly create a "cover story" that masks the depths of trauma. This is not necessarily due to the lack of objective truth—a noble concept that has nonetheless been thoroughly eviscerated—but the inability to embrace the fundamentally unknowable nature of trauma and the attempt to package and shape testimony into understandable modes that provide some type of "closure." As Feldman explains, "The authoritative and monophonic application of narrative closure can only instigate further asymmetric subject positions, *further tales left untold*, further forms of cultural violence, and further inequitable regimes of truth obtained from the condition of those who have been othered by violence."[70] Put simply, by providing any type of closure, testimony itself leads to silence, meaning that an emphasis on the cathartic effect of sharing "Julia's" story unwittingly suppresses rather than voices the tale of disappearance.

Conclusion

During the production of the *Siluetazo*, when artists were tracing the outlines of volunteers and creating the silhouettes that would eventually hang around the Plaza de Mayo, a young boy approached one of the artists and demanded: "Make my father." When asked what his father looked like, the boy replied, "He has a moustache." So a silhouette with a moustache took its place in the line of identical figures, along with several other silhouettes with some type of identifying characteristic, at the request of family members.[71] The need to fill in the details of the silhouette remains powerful, as such details provide assurance that the missing person is a member of a community that remembers and mourns, rather than simply a number, a body, material evidence of a crime. *I Remember Julia* responds to this fundamental need to rescue a desaparecida from anonymity, to give voice to a victim of trauma and break the agonizing and repressive silences surrounding the circumstances of her life and death.

Yet the task of filling in the outline proves much more complicated than the text acknowledges, for it calls attention to the limitations of empirical investigation, the "prescriptive expectations" of testimony, and the ever-present tension between a discourse of life and one of death. The philosopher Eduardo Grüner notes that the form of the silhouette itself recalls the chalk outlines of bodies found at crime scenes: the iconic language of death informs the entire project.[72] In the same fashion, although *I Remember Julia* attempts to "give voice" to a victim of violence and honor "Julia's" life, it cannot help but be rooted in the story of her death and disappearance. The silences the text attempts to break prove at once parallel and contradictory—restoring "Julia's" identity and telling her story responds to the needs of an *individual human*, while breaking the societal silence surrounding the dictatorship years by casting her as one of "the disappeared" calls attention to *collective human rights violations*. The tension between the two approaches to disappearance—"Julia" as a person, an individual; "Julia" as evidence of a collective crime, as a victim of widespread (and universal) human rights abuses—resembles an optical illusion such as the well-known Faces/Vases image, which is either two faces looking at each other, or a vase, depending on one's perspective. One cannot see both images at the same time: one vision inevitably (if temporarily) silences the other. Yet the question of whether one interpretation precludes the other ultimately cedes to a more important insight; *both* renderings of disappearance prove necessary for approaching an understanding of the silence left in the wake of disappearance, for they complement, even as they appear to occlude, each other.

I Remember Julia raises nagging issues regarding the possibility of filling in the outline of disappearance, yet the text advances a somewhat simplistic vision of the legacy of the dictatorship as a struggle for speech. It is not that Carlson does not recognize some ambiguities. As mentioned before, his epilogue raises the issue of whether the collection of testimonies approach a description of "Julia," acknowledging that she can only be remembered through others. He even engages the issue at the heart of stories of disappearance, remarking, "Question after question remains unanswered, and yet that which might seem the most obvious—who killed Julia?—is not really a question at all."[73] Such comments exhibit some understanding of the complex issues facing anyone who attempts to give voice to the victims of disappearance.

These are complicated issues that deserve consideration, yet *I Remember Julia* reduces these complexities to a simple battle between speech and silence, as if simply talking about these issues were sufficient. To Carlson, breaking the silence is the most important goal facing postdictatorship Argentina and a way to give meaning to all those who were lost during the dark years of state terror. His concluding paragraph illustrates this belief and is worth quoting in full:

> The guilty will not go to prison if this silence is broken. The murderers will not be put on trial again. But by asking these questions, memories will be released, and, so very important, lives of the dead will be remembered, while those of the living will be renewed. *The answers hardly matter.* But talk, talk, define the dark shadows that linger over every family, over every conscience that suffered during the Dirty War. Silence: there is too much silence in the unmarked graves in the cemetery of Avellaneda.[74]

With this paragraph and its especially striking phrase "The answers hardly matter," Carlson dismisses the intricacies of the interplay between silence and speech, absence and presence, by suggesting that simply talking is enough to fill in the outlines of the past. Although *I Remember Julia* acknowledges some of the nuances of disappearance, it ultimately suggests that the attempt to fill the silences with speech *in itself* is enough. Yet while the questions Carlson identifies are undoubtedly of utmost importance, his characterization of the legacies of disappearance overlooks the fact that the answers *do* matter, or perhaps more importantly, the *lack* of answers matters even more.[75]

Describing the testimonies of survivors of atrocity, Feldman claims, "These narratives of human rights violation are testimonials to the irreconcilable. They neither refract a unified speaking subject, nor readily lend themselves to unification and instrumentation from without, despite the many orderings and reductions applied to them by law, media, and medicine."[76] Testimonial narratives such as *I Remember Julia*, which cannot help but anchor themselves in empirical evidence and eyewitness accounts, convert the opaque reality of human rights violations into reconcilable accounts of violence and (possible) redemption. Such renderings expose the limits of traditional testimonial narrative, for the struggle to articulate a disappearance is not a simple battle between speech and silence. "Julia" has been silenced; this is certain. But unfortunately it proves impossible to rescue her voice, her identity, her life, or her death. The silences are painful, and they ask to be filled—the blank silhouette invites one to fill in the details—but they remain symbols of absence nonetheless. The interior of the figure does not exist without the outline. A focus on the spheres of ambiguity and silence embodied in the outline itself follows in the next chapter, which examines how a fictional representation of trauma engages the opaque reality of disappearance.

"The Shape Described by Their Absence"

Disappearance in Juan José Saer's *La pesquisa*

he power of the 1983 *Siluetazo* was its ability to represent "the presence of an absence."[1] The three visual artists responsible for its conception—Rodolfo Aguerreberry, Julio Flores, and Guillermo Kexel—proposed "creating a *graphic fact* that will create an impact due to its large size and unusual execution," a reference to the thirty thousand silhouettes they envisioned surrounding the Plaza de Mayo.[2] The initial proposal to produce identical silhouettes, without identifying characteristics, aimed to call attention to the sheer number and anonymity of the victims, yet as was seen in the previous chapter, the desire to fill in the outline with signs of each victim's unique personality proves very strong. This chapter looks at the power of the blank silhouette itself as a symbol of the aching loss of disappearance. While *I Remember Julia* represents the goal of restoring the identity of one particular victim of the dictatorship—filling in the details of the silhouette—the text under consideration in this chapter, Juan José Saer's 1994 detective novel *La pesquisa* (*The Investigation*), responds to the emptiness contained in the outline, how it both underscores the crime of disappearance and signals the impossibility of filling in the absence left in its wake.[3]

If for Carlson the silhouette of the disappeared represents an empty space to be filled through a testimonial project, Saer interprets the blank figure more as the chalk outline on the ground at the scene of a crime; *La pesquisa* is, after all, a detective novel. The philosopher Eduardo Grüner explains that to see the formal similarity between the silhouette and the police outline is "an *unconscious* gesture that accepts, at times contradicting a discourse that would rather keep talking about the 'disappeared,' that those silhouettes stand for *corpses*, bodies killed or 'absented' through violence."[4] These "absented" bodies rest at the heart of *La pesquisa*, which addresses the many silences of the postdictatorship period. Although Saer writes from a place of exile, his novel is rooted in preboom Argentina, a decade after the transition to democracy, where missing bodies, omnipresent yet often unspecified perpetrators, and an absence of any type of meaningful justice informs any attempt to relate the crime of disappearance.[5] How does one investigate and subsequently narrate a vanishing, when there are literally no traces to evidence the implied horror? This is the central question of *La pesquisa*. While *I Remember Julia* attests to the impossibility of simply combating the silence of disappearance with the speech of survivors, family members, or human rights activists, an exploration of Saer's novel—which at first glance barely addresses the issue of disappearance—demonstrates the importance of acknowledging and defining the silences themselves. Although disappearance is mentioned only fleetingly throughout the text, it remains the central—if unvoiced—mystery. Rather than tell the tale of disappearance by filling in the outline, Saer's text creates an interplay of presence and absence, speech and silence, to illuminate *how* the untold story is not told. Ultimately, *La pesquisa* highlights the importance of the silencing itself, the power of the empty silhouette.

The Absent Investigation in *La pesquisa*

As shown in the previous chapter, the silences associated with the disappeared are often interpreted as an impediment to understanding or a gap needing to be filled, rather than a way of making meaning. Carlson's work directly responds to the culture of amnesia during the Menem years—hence his urgent call to break the societal silences regarding the disappeared. Yet a parallel response to societal amnesia consists of working within the silences themselves—countering silence not with speech but with a careful analysis of the absences themselves. While the corpus of Saer's work addresses universal themes of truth, knowledge, and humanity—he once described his writing as "speculative anthropology"[6]—and *La pesquisa* may not be a direct response to Argentina's culture of silence, its engagement with issues of empirical investigation in a context of brutality, its explicit (if fleeting) references to the dictatorship and the disappeared, and its publication during the period of suppressed discourse regarding past violence invite a political reading of the novel.[7] With its focus on silence and absence, Saer's text offers an oblique look at disappearance and signals the impossibility of accessing the opaque heart of trauma.

The importance of developing a critical vocabulary to engage matters of absence and disappearance cannot be ignored, as Avery Gordon claims in *Ghostly Matters: Haunting and the Sociological Imagination*. She cites Patricia Williams's investigation into her family history as a pivotal moment in her own project. Unable to find information about her great-great-grandmother, who was a slave, Williams dedicated herself to "finding the shape described by her absence" in the written record left by her owners.[8] Similarly unwilling to conclude that a lack of facts must translate into a lack of historical presence, Gordon embraces this idea of looking for the absences left in the historical record in order to mount a critique of the social sciences' traditional empirical grounds of knowledge. Empiricist studies can only engage that which is obviously apparent in this world, yet many of the pressing questions raised in modern society can only be approached through an examination of what is hidden, what only presents itself through haunting. While earlier studies of knowledge are neatly divided between what can be "proved" through empirical analysis of existing evidence and what is absent from history and is therefore unknowable, Gordon shows how an awareness of the way in which haunting makes itself known in the world can reveal "how that which appears not to be there is often a seething presence."[9]

These ghosts haunt not only those directly involved with their story (such as family members of disappeared persons or members of minority cultures effectively "silenced" in dominant discourse) but also scholars and writers who attempt to engage these spectral presences in critical discourse.[10] Numerous writers and intellectuals of the Holocaust have written extensively about the challenges of comprehending and describing the "seething presence" of absent victims or implied horror.[11] While one cannot draw an exact parallel between the event of the dictatorship in Argentina and the Holocaust, literary representations of both events must contend with the same types of ethical and epistemological issues. By its very nature, catastrophe changes the knowing and telling of the event, in the case of the Holocaust and the Argentine dictatorship, through a double process of eliminating or intimidating witnesses on the one hand, while at the same time ensuring that any narratives of the event are insufficient to describe the incomprehensible horror.[12]

Those attempting to tell the tale of the Holocaust inevitably find themselves in the territory of what Jean-François Lyotard has termed the "differend," "the unstable state and instant of language wherein something which must be able to be put into phrases cannot yet be." Writers, historians, and philosophers must "bear witness to differends by finding idioms for them," yet without mastering the event through an easy narrative of cause and effect.[13] Lyotard objects to the way in which narrative ultimately "makes" meaning out of horror (discussed in chapters 1 and 2) and, quoting Vincent Descombes, challenges: "'You can't say everything.'—Disappointed? Did you desire it? Or at least did something—'language'—want it?"[14] Lacking the appropriate means of expression using language, the philosopher exhorts the reader to pay attention to the silences surrounding the Holocaust and the feelings they evoke.

Yet "being silent" regarding a tale of trauma does not necessarily mean that the tale itself is "being silenced." The "impossibility" of telling a tale does not doom it to oblivion, as Lea Wernick Fridman explains in *Words and Witness: Narrative and Aesthetic Strategies in the Representation of the Holocaust*.[15] Rather than simply declare that a text about historical horror somehow fails in its task of representing catastrophe, Fridman emphasizes the importance of examining *how* the rhetoric of silence and silencing operates, *how* the untold story is not told. The author notes that writers who narrate the horror brought about by events in the historical world do not attempt to reproduce that horror but rather to describe how the mind struggles to resist and master the experience. Such writing involves "strategies of silence, omission, obliqueness, and reticence which present horror in indirect ways, along with a set of strategies that seek to anchor the factuality of a horror whose first characteristic is that it can neither be believed nor put into words."[16] She structures her study around an analysis of Joseph Conrad's *Heart of Darkness*, a text whose central question is that of how we come to know catastrophic truth. Fridman contends that Conrad's narrative operates on two levels, one of "familiar and knowable" objects, in this case cannibals and rivets, and another of objects outside this familiar and knowable world, such as Kurtz's experience, where the knowledge is always "second-hand, indirect, distinctly social, and also deeply problematic."[17] Ultimately, in *Heart of Darkness*, Kurtz's story is never told but only hinted at in his hoarse whisper of "The horror! The horror!," while the reader instead receives a substitute narrative, the story of Marlow's journey to hear Kurtz's tale. Fridman emphasizes that such a substitution "leaves intact—morally, aesthetically, structurally, formally—an opacity or silence at the heart of historical catastrophe. The story that cannot be told, *is not told*."[18] By refusing to voice (or attempt to voice) a tale that resists expression, the impenetrable silence of catastrophe is preserved.[19]

La pesquisa uses a similar type of narrative substitution regarding the horror of Argentina's dictatorship. The novel tells the tale of three interrelated mysteries: the search for a serial killer in Paris, the authorship of a mysterious manuscript, and the disappearance of the protagonist's twin brother along with his lover during the dictatorship. The novel opens with the story that will dominate the text, that of the crimes in Paris, where twenty-eight elderly ladies have been brutally murdered. The absolute lack of clues and the obviously sadistic nature of the crimes prompt the police to set up a special office of investigation in the vicinity of the killings, under the direction of Detective Morvan. Morvan's search for clues to the identity of the killer is related in the style of the traditional whodunit, complete with a false ending.

This first mystery is being related by Pichón Garay, an Argentine exile visiting Argentina from his home in Paris, to Carlos Tomatis and Marcelo Soldi. The three friends have spent the day attempting to determine the authorship of a manuscript found among the papers of their late friend Washington Noriega, titled *In the Greek Tents* (*En las tiendas griegas*), and Pichón entertains them over the evening meal with the lurid details of the brutal crime spree. The third crime is the disappearance of Pichón's twin brother el Gato along with his lover Elisa from their house in Rincón Norte during the time of the dictatorship. Yet while the first two enigmas are investigated in varying degrees of intensity, the third, the historical catastrophe of disappearance, is only mentioned very briefly throughout the novel, with fleeting references to the lovers' disappearance interspersed throughout the narrative. The investigation in Paris effectively serves as an ironic substitute for the real mystery at the heart of the novel.

Saer pushes the idea of narrative substitution a step beyond its characterization by Fridman, for the replacement narrative in *La pesquisa* is not, as one might expect, the tale of Pichón's search for the truth behind his brother's disappearance but rather Pichón's story of the celebrated case in Paris. While Conrad's substitute tale directly engages Marlow's quest to discover "the horror!," *La pesquisa* instead dedicates itself to the tale of a seemingly unrelated investigation into serial killings in Paris. Yet despite (and at the same time, paradoxically, *because of*) the apparent distance between the crimes, the investigation in Paris serves to make evident and define the shape of the absences in Argentina, even as it effectively silences them through dominating the narrative. Rather than fill in the details of the silhouette, Saer's tale calls attention to its poignant emptiness.

In a perceptive study of Saer's novel, Florinda Goldberg rightly asserts that, despite the paucity of information provided about the disappearance of el Gato and Elisa, this barely mentioned mystery "constitutes the central producer of meaning in the novel."[20] Drawing parallels between the three cases, she argues that Pichón's tale of the investigation in Paris and the three friends' attempts to determine the authorship of the manuscript are actually related to the human tragedy of el Gato and Elisa's disappearance. She notes that the three cases share several superficial thematic elements, such as the presence of a ménage à trois of characters, the topic of vengeance, and the coincidence of space and time between Washington's death and the disappearance of el Gato and Elisa. In addition, the Parisian case in particular invites comparison with the specific historical period of the dictatorship through the description of innocent victims terrorized by a sadistic villain who is a member of the police force.[21] Goldberg emphasizes that the coincidences between the three stories serve to highlight the importance of the mystery that receives the least amount of direct consideration.

The "seething presence" of the silenced story of disappearance cannot be disputed. Yet while the parallels between the Parisian and Argentine cases highlight the presence of the uninvestigated and unsolved mystery, the striking differences between the investigations reveal the importance of the untold story and define "the shape of its absence." Throughout the novel Saer develops an important interplay of comparison and contrast, of presence and absence, that illuminates *how* the untold story is not told. This movement is introduced in the opening line of the novel, "There, however," which creates a distance between Argentina and Paris at the same time as it signals a comparison between the two places.[22] While the initial reading of these lines does not make explicit the exact location of the stated "there" and the implied "here," within two paragraphs the "there" is revealed to be "that place called Paris,"[23] and in the second chapter the reader discovers the "here" to be Argentina. Meanwhile, "however" suggests that while these two places will be examined in conjunction, ultimately the differences between the two will figure more importantly than the similarities. From the opening of the novel, then, the reader is primed to read the tale of crime and punishment in Paris as a foil for the situation in Argentina. With this in mind, the most important difference between the Parisian and Argentine cases is the excessively detailed investigation of the former and the almost complete absence of investigation of the latter.

The investigation in Paris exemplifies a strong belief in the empirical method of analysis, where the truth is discovered through careful investigation of physical evidence and logical ratiocination. Inspector Morvan himself stands out as the ideal detective. He is a meticulous, regimented man who structures his life in accordance with his "thirst for clarity" and "penchant for truth."[24] As a result of this impulse to discover the truth, what Pichón calls a "drive," the entire police force recognizes that if any case needs an especially careful investigation, Morvan is the only one who can "carry it through and draw from it, whatever they were, the most far-reaching consequences."[25] True to his nature, when confronted with the case of the serial killings, Morvan employs the scientific method to investigate the crimes: he examines the empirical evidence, constructs a hypothesis, attempts to prove it, and discards it when it does not explain the facts.

The investigation is nothing if not thorough. Every possible lead is pursued, extensive forensic evidence is collected at every crime scene, a complete psychological profile of the killer is developed, and suspects who match this profile are brought in for questioning. When a climate of fear develops in the neighborhood, the police force opens a special office on Voltaire Boulevard near the epicenter of the twenty-eight crimes, and policemen walk the beat each night to protect potential victims.[26] Elderly ladies are encouraged to lock their doors at night and not to interact with strangers; in short, all efforts are made to catch this "someone" or "something" who has been terrorizing them.[27]

Such excessive measures to discover the criminal and at the same time protect potential victims stand in stark contrast to the absolute lack of official investigative process following the disappearance of el Gato and Elisa. While Tomatis and Héctor (Elisa's husband) mounted a fruitless effort to locate el Gato and Elisa immediately after they were discovered missing, they finally abandon their investigation "without obtaining any result."[28] Pichón himself distanced himself from the search effort, claiming that "in any event they would not reappear,"[29] and this marks his first visit back to Buenos Aires since their disappearance eight years prior. For obvious reasons, no mention is made of any type of official inquiry into the fate of the lovers. With no bodies to evidence a crime and the generalized knowledge of the identity of the perpetrators, official channels are effectively closed.

The presence or absence of bodies marks another important difference between Paris and Argentina. Pichón describes in nauseating detail the crime scenes left by the serial killer. The bodies of the victims are left on display, more often than not carefully arranged on the dining room table as part of the remains of a gory feast: "He tore out their eyes or their ears or their breasts and left them nicely arranged on a little dish on the table." In addition, the tape over the victims' mouths and the copious amounts of blood allow police to determine that the killer began his carving when the victims were still alive. The graphic description of the systematic torture and execution of these victims recalls the untold fate of el Gato and Elisa, a comparison that is made stronger with the description of the penultimate victim. In this case, "he had opened up, with the electric knife that was still plugged in, an enormous gash that went from her throat to her pubis."[30] The use of an electric torture device on a nude victim cannot help but conjure up images of the infamous *picana* as it was employed in the clandestine torture centers in Argentina. Significantly, the only "evidence" left at the scene of el Gato and Elisa's disappearance is "a large kitchen knife and a butcher board,"[31] along with the sickening smell noted by the friend who discovered their absence. In this case, however, the horrible stench does not reveal, as it would in Paris, a body, but a piece of rotting meat. The evidence is there, the knife, the cutting board, the nauseating odor, but it does and does not point to a crime. Instead, the substitute narrative of the crime scene in Paris, with its overwhelming presence of blood, bodies, and body parts—the corpus delicti on gory display—informs the reader's interpretation of the eerily absent corporal evidence in Argentina.

Viewing the exhaustive investigation of such shockingly present evidence in Paris through the prism of the uninvestigated and untold state terror in Argentina becomes all the more poignant when one considers the victims themselves. Goldberg comments on the similarities between them, in particular their innocence and objectification.[32] Again, while such correspondences invite the reader to view both cases concurrently, the striking differences between the victims make the absence of any Argentine investigation so powerful. Pichón begins his tale of the serial killings with an extensive description of the Parisian victims, proclaiming that "in Paris there are any number of little old ladies," and proceeding to list the seemingly endless types found in the city, "the aristocracy, the middle class, the lower middle class or the proletariat, shriveled spinsters or free women who have reached old age determined not to lose their proud independence," to name only a few.[33] He continues to list their attributes, their living habits, their feelings, and their solitary existence. They have no names, no individual characteristics to distinguish them from other little old ladies; they are nothing but "an element typical of that city, a bit of local color, like the Louvre." Objects of pity or ridicule, there are so many that "when they are too far along in years, the nursing home or death whisks them out of sight, yet without their number diminishing."[34] Through his seemingly interminable description of these elderly Parisian ladies, Pichón gives the impression that they are innumerable, interchangeable, utterly forgettable, and ultimately meaningless.

Such an extensive description of these unimportant elements of society makes the amount of manpower dedicated to the investigation of the serial killer terrorizing them seem disproportionate, especially when contrasted with the few sentences in the novel dedicated to el Gato and Elisa. While detailed character sketches of the Argentine victims are not necessary in this particular case, because these two figure in earlier Saerian works (most notably in *Nadie nada nunca*), the readers know these victims as individuals with families and friends who care about them and are devastated by their loss. Pichón recalls "painful images . . . of the terrible days following the disappearance of Cat and Elisa. His two sons had seen him cry for the first time, and wander about the house with reddened eyes, insensible to anything exterior to himself, for weeks on end."[35] The elderly Parisian ladies, in contrast, come and go in an inexorable ebb and flow with no one to mourn them; when one disappears, "new graduating classes of widows, of divorcees and of spinsters [arrive] to fill the seats left vacant."[36] From Pichón's description, one can hardly imagine family members of the Parisian victims marching around a plaza with photos of their mothers or grandmothers, clamoring for justice.[37] The only ones who seem excessively concerned about the crimes are those directly affected: the elderly ladies who are potential victims, the men brought in for questioning, and the police, who are desperate to solve the case not so much because of the moral and ethical implications of the crimes, or the loss of vibrant members of society, but because it reflects badly on the force to have so many unsolved murders.[38] It is also important to note the disparity between the numbers of victims in each case compared with the official investigation. In a period of nine months in Paris, there are a total of 28 victims, while it is conservatively estimated that on average some 184 victims were disappearing monthly during the height of state terror in Argentina (1976–79), making the incredible amount of manpower in the Parisian case all the more grotesque when compared with Argentina.[39]

Finally, the fact that justice is served in Paris contrasts sharply from Argentina. Although at first the absence of tangible clues that implicate the criminal impedes the progression of the case, at an opportune moment Morvan discovers a key piece of paper implicating his colleague Lautret as the killer. Further investigation reveals an even more unexpected solution when the material evidence points to Morvan himself, yet even this surprising revelation appears credible because of the overwhelming amount of evidence supporting it. The clues implicate the criminal, and, ultimately, the detective understands that "in the material net into which he had fallen, words served no purpose."[40] Words are superfluous, because the evidence speaks for itself, and the police are able to determine a plausible motive for Morvan's crimes: his mother's abandonment when he was a child. While this neat "solution" proves untrustworthy, as will be examined shortly, of salient importance here is the fact that the police force is willing to investigate, implicate, and punish their own, another striking difference between the crimes committed by members of an official body sworn to uphold order in Paris and in Argentina.

The Untold Story

At first glance, the differences between the serial killings in Paris and the disappearances in Argentina resemble the two levels of narration described by Fridman in *Heart of Darkness*, the familiar and knowable versus the unfamiliar and unknowable. On the first level of narrative, fact translates easily into meaning and transmission of meaning, while on the second, the unreality of certain facts leads to uncertain meaning and problematic transmission.[41] Thus the replacement narrative about Paris seems to present an ideal investigation, history perhaps as it should have happened in Argentina, because it explores the "knowable world" of empirical evidence. The clues implicate the criminal, Morvan goes to jail, the case is apparently resolved without any loose ends, and the investigative process triumphs. Nevertheless, this "ideal" investigation led by the "ideal" investigator is actually undermined, and Saer's novel ultimately questions even this familiar and knowable world.

La pesquisa appears to question the traditional impulse (seen in *I Remember Julia*) to gather as much empirical evidence about the "familiar and knowable" world as possible in order to arrive at definitive conclusions. As Hayden White explains in *The Content of the Form: Narrative Discourse and Historical Representation*, since historical and fictional writing are governed by rules of narration, evidence alone cannot offer any unique clairvoyance regarding the past. The cultural desire to make meaning allows different historians to draw divergent conclusions on the basis of the same evidence, depending on which aspect of the narrative they choose to emphasize, because "any given set of real events can be emplotted in a number of ways, can bear the weight of being told as any number of different kinds of stories."[42]

Just as real events can bear the weight of numerous emplotments, the evidence in *La pesquisa* holds no intrinsic value but depends heavily on any given interpretation. Immediately after Pichón presents the tidy solution to the case, Tomatis undermines the authority of this conclusion by presenting an alternate version, equally credible, based on the exact same evidence, which reveals Lautret to be the true killer. By opting for an alternative interpretation of the same clues, Tomatis effectively uses the empirical model of investigation to question it. This alternate version of events proves that even the most straightforward of facts (Morvan, emerging from the bathroom of the last victim, covered in blood) do not necessarily translate easily into meaning. The same clues have different meanings for different people, an idea that recurs with the discovery of the key piece of paper that "solves" the case. Morvan understands that this clue only has importance within his personal investigation; while for him it "constituted irrefutable proof, [it] meant nothing to [the others]." Additionally, he recognizes that this piece of evidence implicates him as much as the three other detectives involved in the investigation, for "when the time came for proofs, all of the arguments that he was beginning to marshal against the three others, they in turn, by the same logic, could use against him,"[43] an additional realization that erodes away any inherent value of the clues.

The emphasis throughout the novel on the importance of perspective and interpretation also reveals the problematic transmission of even the familiar and knowable. Important to note here is the fact that while different perspectives are not necessarily contradictory, different interpretations are generally mutually exclusive. For example, Tomatis's perspective does not destroy the solution to the Parisian case but rather his interpretation of the facts. In other words, various points of view, although they can confuse the narration through the sheer quantity of information they offer, serve to amplify the interpretation of events, but different interpretations preclude the possibility of telling one single story.

Saer plays with various perspectives and interpretations throughout *La pesquisa*. For example, the narrative emphasizes the different perspectives between Soldi and Pichón regarding the bus station: "Soldi . . . fixes his eyes . . . on the low, flat-roofed bus terminal which, as he has noted several times, even though it was built twenty years before, Pigeon still calls the new terminal, for the sole reason that it was opened after his departure."[44] In the mysterious manuscript *In the Greek Tents*, the perspectives of the Old and the Young Soldier also reveal the importance of point of view. The old soldier has spent ten years fighting the Trojan War, but he is ignorant of the important events known to the rest of the world. He recognizes that, upon his return to Sparta, he will have to learn all the well-known incidents of the war. Pichón maintains that the old soldier has "the truth of experience" while the youth possesses "the truth of fiction," but although their perspectives differ, they are not mutually exclusive. He explains: "They are never identical but, despite their being of a different order, at times they may not be contradictory."[45] Although the "truth of experience" claims to be more "true," Pichón adds that the "Official History" that survives is the fictional one, rather than the one based on experience. In other words, while various perspectives comprise the most complete history, unfortunately only one interpretation of events reigns.[46]

La pesquisa compounds the difficulty of arriving at one solution to any mystery by highlighting the interplay between perspective and memory. When describing the three men at the table, the narrator relates with exact detail the different points of view of each diner.[47] Their different positions at the table affect what each man views, and the narrator comments: "Despite the fact that the three of them are together, sitting at the same table, because of the different position that they are each occupying at it, perhaps later on, when the night that they are sharing comes to mind again, they will not have the same memories."[48] Even those who are witnessing the same events will most likely remember them differently because of their slightly varying perspectives, introducing memory as another obstacle in the reconstruction of any chain of events.

Memory also impedes Morvan, the standard bearer for the empirical investigative model, in his reconstruction of events in the Parisian case. At first, the detective uses his powers of recollection to compensate for other senses. For example, while gazing out the window onto Voltaire Boulevard, although he can only see part of the scene, his memory fills in the rest. Pichón describes how "Morvan, in the place where he was and however far he leaned forward toward the window, could see only a part [of the street, yet] from having walked all round it in recent months, . . . he knew by heart every stretch of it."[49] Nevertheless, his experience in the case overwhelms him so completely that when he finds himself covered in blood in the apartment of the final victim, he is not even able to trust his own capacity to remember. Pichón describes Morvan's thoughts: "Though no empirical residuum of his acts remained in his memory, he would never be able to be certain that he had not committed them, just as, conversely, many other of which he had apparently real memories, once they had been diluted in the sea of events that occur, no one, himself least of all, could be certain that they had really taken place."[50] In this dark moment, he finds himself unable to trust the memories he possesses and those he does not.

After questioning the reliability of the evidence and emphasizing the way in which perspective and interpretation prevent any pure knowledge of past events, *La pesquisa* goes one step further and implies that even if one could construct a logical chain of events on the basis of the evidence, one could never accurately express that reality using language. Returning to a topic he has explored in many other novels, Saer plays with the role of language and emphasizes its artificiality and limitations.[51]

From the opening pages, Saer separates language from meaning, thereby questioning the efficacy of words to represent reality when he refers to the place "called Paris."[52] A qualification that accompanies the proper name throughout the entire text, "called" serves to draw attention to the role of language in the world ("Paris" is not a place, but simply a word, not the sign itself, but only the signifier), and also to the arbitrary quality of the act of naming. From the very beginning of the novel, the gap between words and meaning is made apparent, making it difficult for the reader to trust the narrative as a true representation of events.

With deliberate irony, the meticulous and excessive description of objects and situations serves more to destabilize than reinforce any connection between language and reality. As María Teresa Gramuglio has noted regarding Saer's narrative in general, his "obsessive description" leads to less rather than more faith in the capacity of language to describe reality with any type of precision.[53] In *La pesquisa*, Saer demonstrates the space between words and meaning by interspersing apparently innocent phrases referring to truth throughout the narrative. When describing Morvan's relationship with Lautret, Pichón explains that "Morvan had complete confidence in Lautret, who had been, *to tell the truth*, his best friend for many years."[54] A later passage describes "a combination bar, small kitchen, and grill, *strictly speaking* a long shed of whitewashed brick."[55] These seemingly innocuous phrases interrupt the narrative flow and call attention to themselves, but rather than serving to assure the veracity of the statements or clarify a description, they cause the reader to question their truth-value. In addition, the torn pieces of paper falling onto Morvan's desk that, under his fixed gaze, "turn into" snowflakes falling outside his window mark another good example of how Saer's narrative removes the value of objects in themselves through their expression using language.[56] Ultimately, this technique of minute description contradicts the usual belief that with more information comes more clarity or credibility.[57] As was seen with *I Remember Julia*, more words do not correspond to more understanding.

Perhaps the most profound effect of the inconsistency of language occurs in the simple narration of the three cases. Reflecting White's idea that the narrative quality of any tale affects its truth-value, Saer eventually equates all the versions of what happened. By showing how no single emplotting of events can approximate the truth, he winds up eliminating the authority of all versions or, inversely, privileging all equally. In Pichón's words: "By the very fact of existing every story is true, and if one wishes to extract some meaning from it, it suffices to take into consideration the fact that, in order to attain the form that is best suited to it, there is sometimes a need to produce in it, thanks to its elastic properties, a certain compression, certain displacements, and more than a few retouches of its iconography."[58] By likening the telling of (hi)story—*any* (hi)story—to writing, Saer implies that although there may be one history that occurs, in order to relate it with any meaning, it must be manipulated.

Despite the ceaseless questioning of the empirical mode of investigation, *La pesquisa* does not topple it completely. After all, while the solution to the Parisian case may be unreliable, the investigative process in itself works. As White explains, any credible version of history must rest on a solid base: "This is not to say that a historical discourse is not properly assessed in terms of the truth value of its factual (singular existential) statements taken individually and the logical conjunction of the whole set of statements taken distributively. For unless a historical discourse acceded to assessment in these terms, it would lose all justification for its claim to represent and provide explanations of specifically real events."[59] In other words, the burden of proof remains for any version of history emplotted from the events. In the case of *La pesquisa*, the physical clues, however problematic, do guide the Parisian detective to a solution, and both Morvan and Tomatis employ the same method to arrive at their different conclusions. While the novel reveals the difficulty of translating fact into unequivocal meaning through the use of empirical methods, *La pesquisa* also explores the equally difficult creation of meaning from an absence of facts. Both the problematic empirical investigation of physical evidence and the ephemeral investigation of ghostly evidence highlight the painful distance between experience and meaning.

The two Argentine cases distinguish themselves from the Parisian one in that the lack of empirical evidence impedes any investigation. In the case of the dactylogram, *In the Greek Tents*, only two facts are certain: that it is a copy and that it was written after 1918.[60] Aside from this, nothing is known about the mysterious manuscript that was found among the papers of Pichón and Tomatis's late friend Washington Noriega. Rincón Norte lacks the necessary resources to analyze the manuscript, so Pichón suggests sending it to Europe or the United States for analysis, implying that there can be no possibility of arriving at any type of scientific solution without sending the manuscript away. In the case of el Gato and Elisa, as was already mentioned, the absolute absence of evidence also serves to impede any investigative process.[61] The Argentine cases lack all elements of the first level of narrative described by Fridman, the unproblematic transmission of facts, their subsequent translation into meaning, and the eventual integration of that meaning, leaving only the exceedingly problematic transmission of "sensed reality."[62]

While it may seem counterintuitive to draw any solid conclusions based on "sensed reality," Lyotard shows how when words may fail, emotions still ring true. After proclaiming the impossibility of expressing the Holocaust using existing language, the philosopher takes issue with Wittgenstein's offhand "what we cannot speak of we must pass over in silence" at the end of the *Tractatus Logico-Philosophicus*. Emphasizing man's inability to ignore ethical and aesthetic issues, Lyotard claims, "Insofar as it is unable to be phrased in the common idioms, *it is already phrased, as feeling.*"[63] Given that for Lyotard a silence does not represent an absence but rather a possible phrase, a waiting for articulation, it follows that the lack of expression through language does not prevent the lack of expression of the Holocaust on an emotional level. Being silent does not equal being silenced.

In keeping with Lyotard's idea about how an unspoken event "is already phrased, as feeling," the only "solutions" that are not questioned in *La pesquisa* are based not on careful examination of empirical evidence but rather on a visceral reaction. For example, Pichón draws his only incontrovertible conclusion about the manuscript from his spontaneous reaction on viewing it rather than any intellectual analysis. The narrator explains that "at his first glance at the rather voluminous [manuscript], he has immediately realized that Washington cannot be the author,"[64] despite the fact that there are no physical indications on the document as to the authorship of the work.

In a similar fashion, although el Gato and Elisa's case lacks physical evidence, everyone, characters and readers alike, knows the "solution." In this case the clues are not direct but rather conditional and contextual. The repetition of the time period when the lovers disappeared immediately conjures up the context of the dictatorship for readers familiar with the recent history of Argentina. Yet even those ignorant of the details of the period can understand the description of "times of terror and violence."[65] Every single character in the novel and most readers understand that el Gato and Elisa were victims of the military dictatorship, but this understanding comes not from any analysis of the absent evidence but from an internal conviction. The Argentine solutions are visceral instead of logical, but paradoxically, although impossible to prove, they are the most certain solutions in the novel.

Despite their unequivocal nature, these ghostly truths in *La pesquisa* ultimately remain unvoiced. Pichón does not state aloud his convictions regarding the authorship of the manuscript, unwilling to provoke the ire of the work's caretaker, Washington Noriega's daughter Julia. Well aware of Julia's fierce desire to prove that the manuscript was indeed written by her father, Pichón keeps his conclusion to himself and even makes an enormous effort to control his countenance when first voicing his opinion about the work.[66] Even more reserved when it comes to the disappearance of his brother, he spends the entire novel avoiding any direct investigation into their absence and subsequent spectral presence in his subconscious. Goldberg includes a fine discussion of repression in her analysis of the novel and astutely notes that the true story about the disappearance remains in the margins both literally ("la margen del río," the banks of the river) and figuratively ("el margen de la escritura," the margins of the narrative). When their boat passes the house where el Gato used to live, Pichón can barely bring himself to direct his gaze to the structure, while the story of el Gato and Elisa is condemned to remain in the margins of the text itself.[67]

Upon viewing the house, Pichón again experiences "the hope that something within him, nostalgia, grief, memory, compassion would be set in motion, but, once again, the agglutinated layers of his being, as though they were a single compact block, have refused to come apart, or even open slightly."[68] He has repressed his emotions with such success that even when he wants to feel something, he cannot. This psychological turmoil is typical of those confronted with what psychotherapist Pauline Boss terms "ambiguous loss." Noting that "absence and presence are psychological as well as physical phenomena,"[69] Boss explains how people attempting to cope with this type of loss often find themselves in an agonizing limbo between wanting closure yet dreading the discovery or verification of one's worst fears. In her words, "Understandably, we prefer ambivalence to a resolution of grief because at least for the moment, it preserves the status quo and leaves us free of guilt. No one can be blamed because nothing is yet lost."[70]

Both Tomatis and Pichón suffer from these contradictory emotions. Soldi notes that Tomatis and Pichón seem to be "firmly settled in the present," and this decision to remain squarely rooted in the present prevents any true investigation into past events. Characteristic of those dealing with an ambiguous loss, Pichón fears discovering that el Gato "could have disappeared without a trace in the air of this world, or worse still, that in his stead he might be presented with a little anonymous pile of bones removed from an unknown plot of earth."[71] Gordon perhaps expresses it best when she writes, "Death exists in the past tense, disappearance in the present";[72] at times, it is less painful to live with the possibility contained in ambiguity than the finality associated with certainty.

Despite such attempts to remain in the present, both Pichón and Tomatis exhibit this unresolved ambiguity on an emotional level. The narrator states clearly: "So that Soldi is mistaken if he believes that Pigeon and Tomatis, monolithic and apparently at their ease in the present, are immune to the constant tug of war or the crackle that, as in the starry sky, explodes at every moment within the inner darkness."[73] They may want to avoid any "pesquisa" into the past, but despite their repression, they cannot escape the "seething presence" of their vanished loved ones. Sensed reality may present itself through ghostly evidence and be difficult to describe with words, yet it remains a very powerful presence.[74]

In the final analysis, Saer reverses the usual hierarchy of empirically knowable reality and sensed reality, prioritizing the latter as the only way to arrive at any true answers. The contraposition of an obsessively minute investigation that leads to flawed conclusions with an absent investigation that yields true results highlights the chasm between what Doris Sommer has termed "empirical 'knowledge'" and "emotional 'knowing.'"[75] The bulk of the narrative is dedicated to the substitute narrative of empirical investigation, bodies, evidence, hypotheses, conclusions, and justice, yet such excessive presence, rather than silencing the untold tale, serves to define the shape of the absences in Argentina, missing bodies, repressed emotions, miscarried justice. Yet these silences and gaps are what Toni Morrison would call "absences so stressed, so ornate, so planned, they call attention to themselves; arrest us with intentionality and purpose."[76] Throughout the novel one senses the subtle yet powerful presence of absence of the disappeared, but at the same time it is important to note that it is only through the presence of the substitute narratives that the absence is so keenly felt. The story that cannot be told, is indeed not told, yet paradoxically the deliberate *not* telling, the excessive substitution of speech, in effect does express the silenced story.[77]

Conclusion

In a provocative complement to Gordon's initial observation about absence and presence, both *La pesquisa* and *I Remember Julia* demonstrate not only "how that which appears not to be there is often a seething presence" but how that which appears to be present is actually seething with absence. The silhouettes embody a physical manifestation of the disappeared subject, the "seething *presence*" of an absence, yet they also signal an incalculable emptiness, the seething *absence* of a presence. The worthy purpose of Carlson's text, to rescue one victim from anonymity, reveals the challenges of simply combating the silences surrounding the disappeared with words, of filling in the interior of the silhouette. *I Remember Julia* attempts to assemble the missing pieces of one particular victim's life story, yet empirical evidence and answers lead to more questions and greater ambiguity. The desire to grant an identity to one blank silhouette necessarily struggles against the power of the emptiness contained in the outline. In contrast, rather than using words to fill the many silences surrounding the disappeared, Saer employs language to emphasize the presence of the gaps themselves and describe the shape of their absence, calling attention to the outline of the silhouette itself. Through the use of a substitute narrative, *La pesquisa* emphasizes the importance of the untold story and its silencing and ambiguity, resisting any attempt to master the tale.[78]

With their parallel approaches to engaging the story of disappearance, Carlson's and Saer's texts reflect to a certain extent the two strains of human rights discourse mentioned in the previous chapter, one that seeks to individualize the victims of the dictatorship, another that highlights the collective scale of absence; one that focuses on a victim's life, another that centers around his or her death. In her analysis of artistic representations of disappearance, Ana Longoni envisions the two impulses as "a series of oppositions: collective versus particular; anonymous versus named; violent disappearance versus previous biography."[79] Framed in this manner, *I Remember Julia*'s representation of "Julia's" life contrasts with *La pesquisa*'s preoccupation with the material evidence of brutal murders, yet as Longoni observes, these differing strategies "overlap, contaminate and reinforce each other";[80] as a consequence, neither text aligns perfectly within these oppositions. Although *I Remember Julia* aims for particularity, "Julia" remains part of a collective group of disappeared, and as the previous chapter's discussion revealed, a focus on her life cannot help but be grounded in her death. For its part, while *La pesquisa* emphasizes the outline rather than the interior of the silhouette, the victims of disappearance have names and identities and are not simply part of a collective and anonymous group of desaparecidos. As responses to a societal silencing regarding the disappeared, Carlson aims more to break the silences, while Saer calls attention to their presence and power, yet neither strategy can succeed perfectly in expressing the tale of trauma.

To return to the rendering of trauma in *La pesquisa*, throughout Morvan's investigation in Paris, he is plagued by recurring nightmares. In these dreams he finds himself walking through a strangely familiar city, the most striking characteristic of which is its silence. Cars, buses, and people pass through the streets in an ordinary fashion, yet "in an extraordinary silence."[81] The buildings and monuments, slightly out of proportion, defy analysis, for their physical characteristics do not reveal their function. One statue in particular is a seething mass of rugged stone that "made its meaning indecipherable." Morvan is nevertheless convinced that certain buildings are temples, although "no recognizable outward sign, least of all their dimensions, allowed one to arrive at that conclusion."[82] The detective moves through this city haunted by the sensation that he is about to discover something terrible about the inhabitants, yet he can pinpoint nothing in particular to substantiate his feelings. Everything is and is not normal about the city, and what disturbs him most of all is his absolute inability to assign any type of meaning to these dreams in his waking life.

Such dreams prove an apt metaphor for trying to capture the essence of disappearance, where the experience is at one and the same time frighteningly surreal, painfully familiar, tantalizingly close, and agonizingly silent. The disappearance, like Morvan's dream, defies empirical analysis yet allows conclusions based not on external facts but internal conviction. In short, attempting to discover the tale of disappearance is like trying to recapture the essence of a dream after awakening. The more one tries to remember specific images and explore their possible meaning, the faster the dream escapes until one is only left with vague memories that slip away when considered consciously but creep into one's thoughts unbidden when the mind is at rest. Attempts to capture the tale of disappearance in all its complexity, to surround and comprehend it, cause it to slip away and transform. Impossible to hold in its totality, ever changing and elusive, the silent story of disappearance asks not for mastery but for a patient listening to its faint call.

Silencing the Politics of Identity

From Elsa Osorio's *A veinte años, Luz* to Telefe's *Montecristo*

Among the many emotional speakers who participated in the March 24, 2004, act that converted the Navy Mechanics School (Escuela Mecánica de la Armada, or ESMA) into the Space for Memory and the Promotion and Defense of Human Rights, Juan Cabandié stood out for his powerful representation of the children born in captivity in the former detention center. Having only recently discovered his biological identity, Cabandié declared: "In this place my mother's life was stolen. She is disappeared. In this place they devised a macabre plan to steal babies. . . . But the dictatorship's sinister plan could not erase the trace of memory circulating through my veins, and I arrived at the truth. *Truth is freedom, and if we want to be completely free, we need to know the whole truth.*"[1] Cabandié's words offer a powerful call to search for the truth, no matter the consequences, in order to provide a full reckoning of the military's crimes. But in the context of crimes against humanity with profound and lasting impact, are there limits to how much truth can be told?

This chapter explores the strong taboos surrounding one of the more heartwrenching crimes of the dictatorship: the military's appropriation of children. One of the few crimes not covered by the amnesty laws (and therefore eligible for criminal prosecution), the practice of keeping pregnant detainees alive until they gave birth, giving their babies to families sympathetic to the military and subsequently killing the birth mothers, remained in the public eye despite the military's attempts to cover up their crimes. Human rights groups, especially the Grandmothers of the Plaza de Mayo, have dedicated years to locating these missing children and breaking the military's overt silence regarding this particular atrocity. Numerous publications of the Grandmothers have recounted desperate searching and recovery of stolen children, all part of a concerted effort to voice this horrific crime.[2] Nevertheless, owing to the intricate factors involved in telling the tale of the youngest victims of the dictatorship, voicing the crime often involves creating a false bottom for the well, providing easy answers to difficult questions. If, following Lawrence Langer, we should be wary of narratives that "make us feel better," rather than "help us *see* better," fictional representations of the stories of appropriated children reveal the difficulty of bearing witness to the painful living legacy of the children of the disappeared.[3] By examining Elsa Osorio's 1998 novel *A veinte años, Luz* (*My Name Is Light*) and Telefe's 2006 telenovela *Montecristo*, this chapter demonstrates the entrenched nature of certain taboos regarding stories of appropriated children.

Both *A veinte años, Luz* and *Montecristo* feature protagonists—Luz and Laura, respectively—who discover they were born in captivity during the dictatorship and given to a family sympathetic to the military. Incorporating elements of fairy tale, thriller, and telenovela, *A veinte años, Luz* depicts Luz's journey to understand her country's violent history and her true identity as an exciting yet straightforward process of discovery. In a similar fashion, *Montecristo* outlines Laura's winding path from ignorance to enlightenment regarding her origins as emotionally challenging yet unquestioningly positive. While the details surrounding Luz and Laura's situations vary, both characters embody one catch phrase of the Grandmothers of the Plaza de Mayo, "Identity cannot be imposed" (*La identidad no se impone*). Nevertheless, by romanticizing the experience of the youngest victims of the dictatorship, both works effectively silence some extraordinarily complex issues surrounding the politics of identity. On the one hand, each representation aligns with a testimonial impulse to tell the story of children born in captivity and denounce the military's actions: they serve to break the military's overt "pact of silence." Yet on the other hand, they reduce the victims' plight to a simple tale of discovery, thereby revealing a covert silence regarding the lasting effects of this particular crime against humanity.

Like *Paso de dos*, *A veinte años, Luz* and *Montecristo* also confront the ethical dilemma of representing the lived experience of victims of the dictatorship. Luz and Laura are brave women who discover their true identities despite numerous obstacles, thereby serving as heroic examples to others who may doubt their origins. By interspersing references to known clandestine detention centers, the systematic practice of torture and disappearance, and the legal aftermath of the dictatorship, these cultural texts expose the crimes of the military and function as fictional witnesses to past atrocity. Nevertheless, by choosing to portray relatively straightforward cases of identity restitution, both representations risk simplifying the complexities of the politics of identity and obscuring the tragic scope of the crime of appropriating children.

Fiction and Human Rights

A veinte años, Luz and *Montecristo* function as representative examples of portrayals of appropriated children because of the historical moment of their emergence and their popularity. Although almost a decade separates the publication of the novel from the broadcast of the telenovela, both cultural texts engage with a particular climate of openness in public discourse about the dictatorship years. Osorio's text was published in 1998, during the early years of the memory boom, characterized by increased public discussion about a topic that the Menem government had tried to suppress through amnesty laws and pardons. For its part, the broadcast of *Montecristo* in 2006 coincided with the thirtieth anniversary of the military coup and a period of renewed trials and prosecutions of perpetrators resulting from the nullification of the amnesty laws.[4]

Often described as the first novel to address the crime of appropriating children, *A veinte años, Luz* emerged shortly after a watershed moment for the Grandmothers of the Plaza de Mayo: a missing grandchild, Paula Cortassa, had taken steps to discover her biological identity because of personal doubts regarding her origins. Cortassa's case marked the first time the restoration of an appropriated grandchild's identity resulted from the *child*'s initiative rather than a process instigated by the Grandmothers. Furthermore, some of the more well-known cases of appropriated children until that time involved complicated situations of divided loyalties and difficult restitutions of identity, such as the case of the Reggiardo Tolosa twins, which made headlines during the early 1990s, and that of Mariana Zaffaroni, the subject of the moving 1997 documentary *Por esos ojos* (For these eyes). In both cases the adolescent grandchildren proved resistant to the process of restitution; press reports regarding the twins in particular emphasized their psychological trauma and suffering.[5] Thus the cases in the public eye often centered on the emotional consequences of the Grandmothers' efforts for restitution rather than the original crime committed by the military.

Cortassa became the first of a series of grandchildren to search for their own identity, as in the mid-1990s the children of the disappeared were coming of age and encouraged by human rights groups such as H.I.J.O.S. and the Grandmothers to act upon any suspicions regarding their origins. Starting in 1997, the Grandmothers launched several informational campaigns to draw young people who might have had doubts to the organization. The publication of *A veinte años, Luz* therefore coincided with the first years of the Grandmothers' public questioning regarding identity: "¿Vos sabés quién sos?" (Do you know who you are?). By addressing the issue of a young woman who doubts her identity, Osorio's novel complemented efforts by the Grandmothers and H.I.J.O.S. to break a repressive silence surrounding a particularly brutal aspect of the dictatorship.[6]

Although the story told in *A veinte años, Luz* aligned well with the multiple memory initiatives of the boom, its timing initially appeared to work against its publication in Argentina. Osorio relates that several prominent Argentine presses rejected her book; editors cited lack of public interest in the topic, deeming it "passé."[7] Apparently fearing an oversaturation of fictional representations of the postdictatorship period, these Argentine publishers chose not to print a novel concerning a child of the disappeared searching for her origins. Ironically, the memory boom seemingly impeded publication of the novel in Argentina, and consequently, *A veinte años, Luz* was first published in Spain and released a year later in Argentina.[8]

Billed as a "tale of love and revenge," *Montecristo*'s broadcast shortly after the commemoration of the thirtieth anniversary of the coup situates it squarely within the postdictatorship climate of renewed reckoning with past crimes.[9] The 2005 Supreme Court decision striking down the amnesty laws as unconstitutional supported a new wave of prosecutions and trials of military and police agents accused of crimes during the dictatorship; for those who had been protected by the Full Stop and Due Obedience laws, impunity was no longer the norm. *Montecristo* also appeared after almost a decade of the Grandmothers' campaigns designed to attract possible appropriated children to their organization. While *A veinte años, Luz* emerged at a time when few missing grandchildren were approaching the Grandmothers on their own initiative, by 2006 the Grandmothers could cite numerous success stories of individuals who had acted on their doubts and discovered their biological identities, thanks in part to collaborations such as *Teatro por la Identidad, Rock por la Identidad,* and even *Tango por la Identidad* (Theatre for Identity, Rock for Identity, and Tango for Identity), which brought renewed visibility to the Grandmothers' cause.[10] As the first telenovela to address the dictatorship and its legacy, *Montecristo* helped to further the Grandmothers' efforts by featuring the organization prominently in the story. Scenes were filmed at the Grandmothers' headquarters, and the writers Adriana Lorenzón and Marcelo Camaño consulted closely with the organization to ensure psychological verisimilitude regarding Laura's experience as an appropriated child. Like *A veinte años, Luz, Montecristo*'s overt engagement with sensitive themes of the postdictatorship such as the appropriation of children and impunity for perpetrators also helped to bring past crimes into the public eye.

Both portrayals of the legacies of the dictatorship also proved wildly popular among audiences. Since its original publication in Spain in 1998 and Argentina in 1999, *A veinte años, Luz* has been translated into sixteen languages and published in twenty-one countries, with most recent international editions released in 2012.[11] Its re-release in Argentina in 2006 also coincided with the thirtieth anniversary of the coup. For its part, in January 2007 *Montecristo* was Telefe's highest rated telenovela of all time; over forty markets had purchased the finished program, and its format had been sold to Mexico, Chile, and Portugal.[12] A further testament to its success, per-second advertising rates during the primetime broadcast cost around $1,000, compared with $65 for daytime spots.[13] The telenovela also garnered critical acclaim for its unflinching look at the dictatorship years, and critics praised its honest portrayal of recent history.[14] During the early years of the memory boom, *A veinte años, Luz* brought the plight of the children of the disappeared to a wide audience in Argentina and internationally; almost a decade later, *Montecristo* updated the story for a national audience, yet with international impact. Both cultural texts serve as highly visible fictional renderings of the living legacy of appropriated children.

Although the central plotlines differ, *A veinte años, Luz* and *Montecristo* share certain characteristics associated with melodrama, notably an intricately woven emotional storyline designed to heighten suspense. Credibility cedes to drama in both works, which place obstacles in the path of the protagonists as they search for their origins. A full summary of the twists and turns of both works is impossible in the limited scope of this chapter, but before entering into the analysis of each, I will provide a brief outline of important narrative threads.

Divided into five portions, *A veinte años, Luz* moves between time periods and geographical spaces to assemble the scattered pieces of Luz's complicated life story. The prologue takes place in Spain in 1998 and relates a conversation between Luz and Carlos Squirru, the man she suspects is her biological father. Part 1 returns to Argentina and recounts Luz's birth and appropriation in 1976. Initially Luz is promised to a mid-level official (the torturer nicknamed el Bestia [the Beast]) and his girlfriend Miriam (a former prostitute), but when

Mariana, the daughter of el Bestia's superior officer Colonel Dufau, gives birth to a stillborn son, Luz replaces the stillborn child.[15] Given Mariana's grave health after the complicated birth, the decision is made to house Luz and her mother Liliana at el Bestia and Miriam's apartment until Mariana can care for the baby. Miriam and Liliana grow close during the early days of Luz's life, and when Liliana is killed while attempting to escape, Miriam promises to help Luz know her origins.

Part 2 jumps forward to 1983 and Luz's early childhood with Mariana and Eduardo. Mariana was kept ignorant of Luz's origins, so she believes her to be her biological daughter; meanwhile, Eduardo feels wracked with guilt toward both Mariana and Luz for the deception. He vows to find the truth about Luz's history (he does not know she is a child of the disappeared), and this section recounts Eduardo's search for Luz's origins and his subsequent murder by the military (ordered by Mariana's father) when he comes too close to the truth. Part 3 covers the period between 1995 and 1998, a period of awakening for Luz as she begins to search for her origins and becomes a mother herself. Alienated from Mariana, who never really loved her, Luz finds love in Ramiro, whose parents were disappeared during the dictatorship. With his support, and the convenient return of Miriam, who reveals Luz's true identity as a child of desaparecidos, Luz tracks down her biological father. Finally, the epilogue completes the family circle by bringing her maternal grandmother into the story. Throughout the novel, portions of Luz and her biological father Carlos's conversation are interspersed into the narrative of other characters involved in Luz's life, primarily Miriam, who recounts her days with Liliana, Eduardo and Mariana, the parents who raised Luz, and Dolores, a childhood friend of Eduardo who educates him as to the horrors of the dictatorship.

The plot of *Montecristo* proves equally contorted. Loosely based on Alexandre Dumas's classic revenge tale *The Count of Montecristo*, the series follows Santiago Díaz Herrera, the son of a judge involved in the investigation of Alberto Lombardo, suspected of attending births in a clandestine detention center during the dictatorship. The story begins in 1995, when Santiago is an up and coming young lawyer working with his father and engaged to be married to Laura Ledesma, his childhood sweetheart. Santiago's best friend, Marcos Lombardo (Alberto's son), also a lawyer, is secretly in love with Laura. When Judge Díaz Herrera's investigation begins to implicate Alberto Lombardo, the latter arranges for the judge's assassination in Buenos Aires, as well as Santiago's, during a fencing tournament in Morocco in which both Santiago and Marcos are participating. After witnessing Santiago receive a bullet to the chest, Marcos returns to Buenos Aires and marries Laura, who is pregnant with Santiago's child. Ten years pass, in which Alberto and Marcos enjoy success and fortune, Laura and Marcos raise Matías as their own child, and Santiago festers in a Moroccan prison, plotting his revenge. In 2006 Santiago manages to escape from jail, and with the help of Victoria, a child of the disappeared who is searching for a sibling born in captivity, and León Rocamora, a dapper art thief, he returns to Buenos Aires to avenge the death of his father. Initially expecting Laura to be waiting for him, when he discovers she has married Marcos and is raising his son with the man who left him for dead, Santiago laments all that was stolen from him—a decade of his life, his great love, and his son—and the telenovela charts his single-minded efforts to make the perpetrators pay.

An important secondary plotline involves Laura, who is ignorant of Santiago's fate, Marcos's involvement, and even her own origins. For years she believed she was adopted by an aunt and uncle, Helena and Lisandro, after her parents died in an accident, yet as a grown woman she discovers that the adoption story was a lie. The viewers suspect long before Laura does that she is the long-lost sibling Victoria is searching for, and indeed, after many complications, Laura discovers her true identity as a child of the disappeared. Identity issues play a central role in the drama; once Laura discovers her own identity was based on a lie, she begins to insist that her son Matías know the truth about his origins, that Santiago is his biological father. Laura (like Luz) represents an adult child who awakens to the truth about her past, yet the parallels with Matías's situation serve to explore the thornier questions of identity and justice. Although drenched in melodrama and skating on the edge of credulity at times, both *A veinte años, Luz* and *Montecristo* seek to engage the difficult issues of identity politics regarding appropriated children. As this chapter will demonstrate, despite their status as popular cultural texts—a category not always associated with nuanced representation—both works acknowledge and address several important complexities of identity restitution, with one notable blind spot.[16]

Fictional Witnessing Part 1: Voicing the Crimes of the Past

Kimberly Nance's observations about the rhetoric of testimonial narrative can help illuminate how the novel and the telenovela succeed in breaking repressive silences regarding Argentina's dark history. According to Nance, authors of testimonio employ Aristotle's three categories of rhetorical strategies to tell the tale of trauma: forensic, epideictic, and deliberative. Forensic speech describes past events as just or unjust, epideictic speech categorizes present actions as either noble or shameful, while deliberative strategies employ a rhetoric of persuasion and dissuasion to compel a listener to determine whether he or she should take action.[17] Nance's analysis of testimonio reveals that many testimonial narratives (and critics of the genre) privilege the forensic and epideictic categories. Indeed, *A veinte años, Luz* and *Montecristo* align with these two strands of testimonio, for they seek to condemn the past actions of the military as well as pass moral judgment on the present actions of the characters as they define their relationship vis-à-vis the past.[18]

One strategy both cultural texts employ to call attention to past injustice is the use of representative characters to condemn the military's behavior and uphold that of the desaparecidos. In *A veinte años, Luz*, Sergeant Pitiotti, aka el Bestia, stands out for his unwavering dedication to his job as a torturer in one of the camps. He lives up to his name in many respects: prone to violent outbursts in his domestic life, he tortures with efficiency and discretion and subsequently benefits from the favors of his superior officer, Lieutenant Colonel Dufau. Dufau, the father of Luz's "adoptive" mother, firmly believes in the military cause, for "the only good subversive was a dead one."[19] El Bestia and Colonel Dufau find their counterparts in *Montecristo* in the characters of Lisandro Donoso and Alberto Lombardo. As Alberto's henchman, Lisandro solves most problems with an arsenal that includes domestic abuse, torture, and assassination. While Alberto avoids dirtying his hands with direct action, he orders the elimination of those who challenge him; powerful and ruthless, Alberto embodies the classic telenovela villain, but it is interesting to note that in this updated take on the situation of appropriated children, the villains are not military personnel (seen in *A veinte años, Luz*) but civilians with close ties to the military, thereby expanding the condemnation beyond the military to the broader society.[20]

While el Bestia and Dufau represent the military and its atrocity in Osorio's text, Liliana (and her baby) represent the human face of suffering and serve to demonstrate the worthiness of the cause of the desaparecidos. Through Miriam's eyes, the reader sees Liliana as a victim of the dictatorship's brutality, a young mother rather than a dangerous "subversive." Liliana explains to Miriam that she and other militants simply "wanted a just society,"[21] and her dying words to Miriam—"Save her, and tell her about . . . [her parents]"[22]—represent a call to remember what was done to her and her child.[23] *Montecristo* similarly emphasizes the just cause of the desaparecidos through Victoria's descriptions of her missing parents and her condemnation of the impunity enjoyed by former repressors.

Both fictional representations also seek to demonstrate the profound injustice of the military's practice of baby stealing by appealing to emotion. *A veinte años, Luz*, for example, juxtaposes the violence of the time period with the innocence of childhood. In a key scene of awakening for Miriam, Liliana recounts the horrors of the detention center, while Miriam holds the baby in her arms, singing her a soothing lullaby. The words of the lullaby are interspersed within Liliana's tales of her experience, and Miriam attempts to shield the baby from the violence and lighten Liliana's burden. As she states, "I'm trying to hide behind the nursery rhyme, . . . I want [Liliana] to keep on spewing up all that stuff I'd no idea about, . . . even if it turns my stomach, and makes me sick, and splashes all over me, and covers me in horrible stinking stuff, I just want Liliana to feel better."[24] The juxtaposition of the innocent lyrics of the lullaby with "those blood-curdling words"[25] underscores both the extent of the violence and the innocence of the victims. As a telenovela, *Montecristo* possesses a vast set of tools designed to tug at viewers' heartstrings, such as tender music when Victoria gazes at a family photograph featuring her pregnant mother, the shattered look on Laura's face when she contemplates her desperate loneliness, and the visual contrast between Alberto's remorseless impunity and Santiago's suffering.

Nance explains that the forensic and epideictic strategies rarely provoke action or social change, for they ultimately distance the reader from the text. In her words, "such modes do not actually call upon their readers to do anything beyond categorizing an act as just or unjust, or assigning praise or blame."[26] Although this is the case for the most part in *A veinte años, Luz* and *Montecristo*, both works do attempt to connect the reader and viewer more closely to the story, and even inspire direct action. For example, Osorio employs some narrative strategies that seek to bring the reader closer rather than create distance. Most strikingly, at several key moments in the text, the narrative employs second-person rather than first- or third-person narration. Although the use of "tú" (you) ostensibly demonstrates Eduardo's internal conflict, in effect these select moments address the reader directly, thereby implicating him or her in the crimes of the past.

It is no accident that the narrative begins to employ the second-person singular when Eduardo—the man who raised Luz and loved her as a daughter—begins to realize the extent of the military's violence. These moments of second-person narration often take the form of pointed questions, and in this way they situate the reader in relationship with the violence. For example, after hearing Dolores's tale of her brother and sister-in-law's disappearance, Eduardo reflects that Dolores has "good reason" to hate the military: "Wouldn't you, if Javier and Laura [Eduardo's brother and sister-in-law] had disappeared?"[27] Although the question is ostensibly addressed to Eduardo, it forces the reader to consider how he or she might feel if a loved one had been taken. These instances of second-person narration occur during Eduardo's most emotional moments: both positive, such as when he remembers his relationship with Dolores,[28] and more brutal, such as when he suspects that Luz might be a child of the disappeared.[29] Over and over the reader is brought into the text, both as a participant/witness to Eduardo's loving relationship with Dolores and as a possible unwitting conspirator in the country's pact of silence regarding the past.

Employing the second person serves to bring the reader closer to the text, yet ultimately these pointed questions or statements regarding Eduardo's inability to "see" the truth respond to the epideictic strategy of categorizing present actions as either shameful or noble. After listening to Dolores's tale, Eduardo laments, "What country, what world have you been living in while all this was going on, all these things Dolores is telling you?"[30] Eduardo suffers from "percepticide," the inability to see what is happening in front of his very eyes, and in many instances *A veinte años, Luz* emphasizes the duality between blindness and seeing in order to accentuate the gradual awakening of the characters. The name of the main character, Luz, refers to this move from darkness to light; as she states at the beginning of the novel: "I knew I had to shed light into all the dark corners of this story, to find out the truth."[31] Similarly, when Eduardo recognizes his reluctance to imagine the possibility that Luz could be the child of desaparecidos, he asks himself, "But did you really want to find out the truth?"[32] Eduardo's agonizing question—also addressed to the reader—implicates the broader society in this self-imposed blindness and encourages censure of those who choose to remain in ignorance. The use of "you" in selected moments of the text thereby serves to emphasize the reader's compromise with the epideictic—the reader must judge his or her *own* actions as either reprehensible or honorable as well as those of the characters.

While *A veinte años, Luz* seeks to engage the reader more closely in the tale through selected narrative strategies, *Montecristo* succeeded in making a measurable impact in the search for missing grandchildren, a testament to its ability to bring viewers into the story. Following Rebecca Atencio's concept of the "imaginary linkage" between cultural texts and human rights efforts in Brazil, viewers created an association between the television program and the work of identity restitution.[33] Inquiries at the Grandmothers of Plaza de Mayo tripled during the broadcast of *Montecristo*, beginning almost immediately and continuing throughout its run.[34] But the case of Grandchild 85 represents the closest link between the telenovela and the real-life search for missing grandchildren. The very day that Marcos Suárez received the news that his DNA test confirmed he was the biological child of a disappeared couple, he recognized his baby photo in a scene of *Montecristo* filmed at the Grandmothers' headquarters. Several newspapers picked up the story as a touching coincidence between fiction and real life and evidence of the wide impact of the telenovela.[35]

One final way in which both the novel and the telenovela succeed in bringing hidden truths to light is through stressing the *systematic* nature of the appropriation of children, thereby contradicting the military's claim that cases of babies born in captivity and given to more "appropriate" families were isolated instances rather than part of a standardized practice. Although the story focuses on one particular case, *A veinte años, Luz* makes clear that Luz represented simply one of many babies born in captivity and given to military families. When it turns out that Colonel Dufau will take Liliana's baby for his daughter, for example, el Bestia comforts Miriam by assuring her that she can have the next child, one of several allusions to the organized system of appropriation.[36] With numerous references to systematic appropriation and its emphasis on the work of the Grandmothers, *Montecristo* also affirms the organized nature of this particular crime.

In sum, to use Nance's terms, *A veinte años, Luz* and *Montecristo* prove most effective on the level of forensic and epideictic rhetorical strategies— depicting the repressors' past actions as unequivocally unjust, their present actions as shameful, and the present actions of characters such as Eduardo, Miriam, Victoria, and Santiago, who literally risk their lives to uncover the truth, as laudable. Both works thereby succeed in breaking the military's overt silence regarding past atrocity and, given their national and worldwide success, educating a broader public about the dictatorship's systematic appropriation of children.[37] Given these texts' imperative to tell the story of the youngest victims of the dictatorship to a wide audience, an exploration of where these fictional tales reflect the real-world complexity of issues of identity and where they opt for more simplistic renderings of past crimes reveals a strong taboo regarding the tragic consequences of the crime of appropriating children and the limits that govern any attempt to approach the "whole truth."

Fictional Witnessing Part 2: Engaging with Complexity

Both *A veinte años, Luz* and *Montecristo* fulfill the testimonial impulse to tell a silenced story, and in some respects they recognize the inherent emotional complexities of the situation of children whose identities have been stolen. Although neither work fully explores the nuance of the situations of appropriated children, and both reveal uncomfortable covert silences regarding the politics of identity, they do highlight the tension between love and politics in several ways. First, they begin to explore the complicated relationships involving the child caught between two families: in *A veinte años, Luz*, this is seen in relationship between Luz and her two "fathers," Carlos and Eduardo; in *Montecristo*, Matías negotiates the conflicting bonds with his two "fathers," Santiago and Marcos. The telenovela additionally depicts the struggle to come to terms with a new identity, seen in Laura's slow path from suspicion to enlightenment regarding her origins. Finally, both works acknowledge the complexity of the postdictatorship period by questioning to a certain extent simplistic moral codes regarding "good guys" and "bad guys" in the context of state terrorism.

The novel portrays Luz's encounter with her biological father as unquestioningly complicated and at times uneasy. Carlos exhibits a range of emotions, including surprised delight to discover that Liliana's baby survived, intense jealously regarding Luz's close relationship with Eduardo, and profound self-criticism for his negative feelings toward the man who loved Luz like a daughter. The narrative emphasizes these contradictory emotions and complicated familial relationships through the brutally honest conversation between Luz and Carlos. Her repeated lament that "No one searched for me"[38] serves both to highlight her emotional struggle and implicate Carlos as guilty of abandoning her to her fate, of not doing everything he could to help her. When he criticizes Eduardo for marrying a daughter of a military man and collaborating in the appropriation of a child that was not his, she counters: "Listen, the man who married Mariana lost his life finding out who I was. . . . But you're my own flesh and blood, and what did you do for me?"[39] Luz's sharp reproach effectively underscores the nuances of family—Carlos's position as biological father does not necessarily make him her best advocate—and also points to the challenge of making an emotional connection given the circumstances.

The way in which Carlos and Luz reflect upon the words "mamá" and "papá" also speak to the complex family relationships. Carlos is bothered by the tenderness he hears in Luz's voice when she speaks of Eduardo, and the way she calls him "papá." He reflects, "What right did he have to ask Luz to stop calling that man 'Dad' when he'd only met her a few hours ago? . . . Was it Luz's fault that she so loved the man who had stolen her?"[40] His musings demonstrate an understanding of the complexity of her situation—love and family are not simply determined by biology. Regarding her use of "mamá" to refer to her "adoptive" mother Mariana, Luz demonstrates an ambivalence that points to the loaded nature of such signifiers. When Carlos calls attention to her choice of words, Luz responds, "It's a word you only come to appreciate with time. . . . [Mariana] was the person I'd called Mum ever since I started connecting that sound with a person."[41] Such a statement implies a certain flexibility in the terms "mamá" and "papá" and prompts the reader to consider what characteristics determine the connection between the appellation and the person: biology? love? living together under the same roof?

Perhaps the best example of how *A veinte años, Luz* engages the difficulty inherent in Luz and Carlos's relationship is Luz's criticism of Carlos and Liliana's motives for having children. Speaking as the ultimate innocent victim of the dictatorship, Luz takes Carlos to task for deciding to bring a child into the world during dangerous times, accusing him of "selfishness" at best and dangerous irresponsibility at worst. As she eloquently and pointedly claims: "Children weren't given the chance to decide whether they wanted to run that risk for the sake of their beliefs, the way their parents were. . . . It was the military regime that made me disappear, but it was my own parents who exposed me to the nightmare of disappearing—and surviving."[42] By juxtaposing Carlos and Liliana's decision to have a child with the military's practice of disappearance, in this emotionally charged moment the narrative implicates the militants in the lasting effects of the violence. This bold assertion in a text that otherwise praises the revolutionary struggle responds to the complex legacy of the dictatorship.

While Carlos's efforts to understand the tangled repercussions of his new family situation serve to highlight the complicated reality of the militants, Eduardo's struggle demonstrates the equally complicated reality of the "adoptive" families. Once Eduardo begins to suspect that Luz may be the child of desaparecidos, the narrative depicts his inner conflict, his dawning awareness that what is best for Luz (finding her true identity) might have a devastating impact on his family. Like Carlos, he laments his "selfishness,"[43] his desire to pretend that Luz's presence in his life has no greater political repercussions. His divided loyalty between his family (his love for Mariana, his longing to keep Luz) and his duty to the truth clearly demonstrates the possibility for love *and* complicity to reside in the same person and makes it clear that not all of those involved in the appropriation of children base their actions on questionable moral grounds.[44]

Similar to *A veinte años, Luz*, *Montecristo* explores the intersection between love and politics, most notably in the character of Matías, the young boy who was "stolen" by Marcos.[45] Like many appropriators during the dictatorship, Marcos remains implicated in the disappearance and presumed death of Santiago, yet he raises and loves Matías as his own son. For his part, Matías adores Marcos, and the telenovela emphasizes the heart-wrenching consequences for Santiago (and Matías) as the truth is gradually revealed. Despite fortuitous circumstances that allow Santiago to develop the beginnings of a friendship with Matías, when Laura tells Matías the truth about his origins—that Santiago is his "real" father, but Marcos will always be his dad "because he loves you"—Matías initially rejects the news, accusing Laura of lying and affirming to Marcos, "You're my dad. I don't have another dad."[46] Meanwhile, Santiago expresses heartbreak and rage that Marcos has so completely stepped into the father role that is rightfully his. Yet each time he wants to force himself into Matías's life, others remind him of the delicacy and "irreparable" nature of the situation: from Matías's perspective, Marcos is his father, whom he loves deeply. An attention to how the intimacy of father and son is constructed rather than given demonstrates the tragic consequences of this particular crime: caught between two loving fathers (who hate each other), Matías exhibits contradictory emotions and divided loyalties as he negotiates the changing nature of his family.

Montecristo also demonstrates an attention to nuance in its portrayal of Laura's journey from ignorance to enlightenment regarding her origins. Although unwavering in her belief in the importance of knowing the truth—she insists to Matías that her only wish is that he not grow up with a lie, like she did—she finds it difficult to accept the truth regarding her own history, initially ignoring Victoria's suggestion that she might be a child of desaparecidos. As opposed to Osorio's Luz, who exhibits a single-minded drive to discover the truth, Laura moves more slowly, gently prodded by other characters, in particular Victoria. The contrast between Luz and Laura reflects the progression of the Grandmothers' cause. Osorio had no models on which to base her protagonist, a fact that may help explain Luz's unwavering determination; almost a decade later, the writers Lorenzón and Camaño could avail themselves of the Grandmothers' experience with adult children approaching their organization, including the complicated emotions involved with discovering a new identity. *Montecristo* thereby depicts a level of questioning and false starts to Laura's search that remains largely absent from *A veinte años, Luz.*[47]

In addition to exploring the elaborate relationship between love and politics, both cultural texts also acknowledge the nuance of the postdictatorship period by questioning facile distinctions between right and wrong, good and bad. In Osorio's novel, every time Carlos tries to judge Eduardo or Miriam, Luz demonstrates how the complicated reality precludes any simplistic moralizing. For example, after Luz insists that Eduardo too was a victim, prompting Carlos to explode, "How can you defend someone who stole your identity like that?,"[48] she fixes him with a look of rage and replies, "I would prefer it if you listened more and stopped being so judgmental."[49] Even the villains in *Montecristo* demonstrate a softer side, albeit on rare occasions; Alberto shares tender moments with his mistress Lola and their daughter, and the torturer Lisandro laments a sad childhood. Meanwhile, the "good guys" exhibit questionable behaviors at times, kidnapping and threatening members of the Lombardo family and their entourage as well as stealing the Lombardo fortune.

In *A veinte años, Luz*, the character of Miriam also serves to undermine the usual expectations regarding moral behavior. Supposedly tainted by virtue of her profession, Miriam behaves more virtuously than those who occupy a more respected position in society, in particular the military and the privileged upper class. In sharp contrast to el Bestia, who blindly parrots the rhetoric of the military regarding the patriotic duty to rid the country of subversives, Miriam makes her own decisions regarding the right course of action during this time of "war," ultimately risking her life several times in order to reunite Luz with her biological father. While on the one hand the character of the "prostitute with the heart of gold" fulfills an expected role in this sentimental tale, on the other hand it serves to question easy categorizations, thereby highlighting the complexities of the political situation.[50] Miriam's counterpart in *Montecristo*, León Rocamora, also challenges fixed definitions of "right" and "wrong." Both he and Alberto operate outside the law (Rocamora is wanted by Interpol for his role in international art theft), yet Rocamora demonstrates an impeccable moral compass regarding crimes against humanity, forcing the audience to contemplate the blurred lines between "law" and "justice" in the postdictatorship period.

Fictional Witnessing Part 3: The Limits of Complexity

Although *A veinte años, Luz* and *Montecristo* recognize the complicated situation of appropriated children and probe some of the resulting uncomfortable issues, both cultural representations silence critical elements of the story of disappeared children. The critic Marco Kunz argues that Osorio's text, like many others that treat the subject of disappeared children, chooses to profile a situation that is far from representative of the majority of cases but that allows for greater drama. Recognizing the "ethical dilemma of not straying too far from reality and at the same time satisfying the reader's expectations for suspense and emotion,"[51] Kunz believes that *A veinte años, Luz* errs on the side of too little reality. He criticizes the novel for employing "an excess of fabulation" and creating an intricate, unbelievable plot that resorts to trite stereotypes and heightened drama at the expense of verisimilitude.[52] The novel does indeed possess a large dose of sentimentality, and the central theme of "love conquers all" can easily be viewed as one of the "facile or generic narrative codes" Goldberg refers to in her consideration of an ethics of representation.[53] The use of such codes hints at the lingering taboos related to the stories of appropriated children.

Despite engaging with some of the nuance related to the crime of appropriation, both *A veinte años, Luz* and *Montecristo* reveal limits when it comes to addressing the emotional consequences of the restoration of identity, best seen in the relationship between the appropriated children and their appropriators. Although the situation of a young woman raised in a family that is not her biological one allows for a complexity of emotion, both fictional representations eschew issues of attachment or love between child and "parent." *Montecristo* makes clear that Laura did not have a happy childhood with her "uncle" Lisandro, who was physically violent toward her and her "aunt" Helena. Affective ties with Lisandro and Helena do not prevent Laura from seeking her origins; rather, her obstacles come from an internal reluctance to acknowledge a sinister past. Helena, like Eduardo, claims ignorance of Laura's origins (too afraid to question Lisandro, too in love with baby Laura) and supports Laura's search, helping clear her path toward enlightenment. When Laura finally accuses Lisandro of appropriation, the fact that Helena will also face prosecution, although somewhat troubling, does not prevent Laura from acting. In this fictional representation, Laura's search for the truth trumps any emotional attachment with the parental figures who raised her.

In a similar fashion, *A veinte años, Luz* avoids messy family politics by presenting a "mother"-daughter relationship that does not complicate Luz's discovery of her true identity; rather, it drives Luz to search for a new family. In fact, the novel portrays Mariana as an evil stepmother who never loved Luz and treats her poorly, nimbly avoiding any complications that might arise if Luz found herself caught between two loving families. Although Mariana is in a certain sense a victim of the circumstances as well—due to complications during her labor, she does not know that Luz is not her biological daughter— the narrative destroys any sympathy the reader might feel for her plight by turning her into a villain. Her characterization aligns with what Julee Tate has described as the quintessential "bad woman" in the Latin American telenovela, because of her lack of maternal instincts.[54] *A veinte años, Luz* makes clear that Eduardo was the one who wanted to have children; after Mariana recovers from childbirth and begins to care for Luz, she is almost incapable of mothering her baby, so Eduardo is the one who holds Luz, rocks her and calms her.[55] Even as Luz gets older, Eduardo proves more tender and caring toward his daughter than Mariana, and the novel repeatedly emphasizes Mariana's inability to connect with Luz as a mother should.[56] Impatient, distant, cold, and at times physically violent toward her daughter, Mariana fails the "simple maternity test," to use Tate's terms, thereby placing her firmly in the category of the "bad woman."[57]

In addition to her poor maternal instincts, Mariana also espouses unpalatable political beliefs. Although Eduardo sympathizes with her at first, owing to the fact that her family has kept her in the dark regarding Luz's origins, and he often describes her as a "victim" just like Luz, as the novel progresses Mariana's behavior negates any possible sympathy. While Eduardo experiences a gradual awakening to the political violence that had surrounded them, Mariana continues defending the military. In one particularly striking scene, when Eduardo tells her he can no longer stand to hear her defend her father's behavior, she turns into "this harpy whose face is full of rage and loathing."[58] The use of the word "harpy" seems especially apt—Mariana has become a monstrous version of a woman.

One final way in which the novel depicts Mariana as a rather two-dimensional "bad" woman is through her delight at the discovery that Luz is actually not her biological daughter. Eduardo's angst regarding Luz's origins find a sharp contrast in Mariana's happiness; the love she feels toward her father for "protecting" her by finding her a baby to replace her stillborn son mixes with her relief that certain aspects of Luz's behavior can now be so easily explained. As Luz wryly admits, "Yes, they deceived [Mariana], but she didn't care. She never protested, perhaps because she would have done the same thing herself,"[59] thereby placing the woman who raised her in the same category as the military who systematically appropriated the children. In fact, Mariana's only moments of doubt come when she fears Luz may have inherited some characteristics that will make it harder to educate her in the proper manner.[60]

While *Montecristo* initially escapes the flat characterization of the appropriator with its portrayal of Marcos as a loving father, once Santiago returns, there is no fictional space for love and complicity. Matías passes through an initial period of doubt, resistance, and confusion, but soon Marcos's behavior makes it impossible for Matías to continue to love him. A mere two episodes after discovering Santiago is still alive, Marcos orders the torture of Rocamora, thereby situating himself firmly in the camp of "depraved villain." The distancing between "father" and son continues to the end of the telenovela (Marcos imprisons Matías in a boarding school, tells him his mother is dead, and even threatens to kill him); by the time Santiago, Laura, and Matías can be together, Marcos has transformed into a psychopathic monster whose obsession with Laura ultimately destroys any love Matías might have felt for him, leaving no doubt as to who is Matías's "real" father.[61]

Through Marcos's transformation from damaged individual to depraved monster, and Lisandro and Mariana's clear characterizations as fundamentally rotten, *A veinte años, Luz* and *Montecristo* avoid undue complications that arise if appropriators truly love their "children." In popular fictional portrayals of appropriated children, any real love or kindness from the appropriators appears strictly taboo. While the placement of a stolen child in a family associated with the dictatorship allows for potential conflicts between a loving "adoptive" family and an equally caring biological one, with the child caught in the middle, *A veinte años, Luz* and *Montecristo* conveniently arrange both plot (Eduardo, Luz's loving parent, is killed when she's a young girl; Santiago develops a close relationship with Matías even before discovering his paternity) and character (Mariana is an evil stepmother, Lisandro is a monster, and Marcos turns into a psychopath) in order to avoid the potential messiness of the politics of identity.[62]

The Politics of Identity Part 1: The Rhetoric

When it comes to the politics of identity, the novel and the telenovela echo the language employed by the Grandmothers of the Plaza de Mayo. To be clear, this chapter addresses the dominant *rhetoric* surrounding the restitution of identity, seen in the organization's promotional campaigns, public statements, and publications, a rhetoric rooted in biology that emphasizes the importance of identity restitution. This rhetoric, however, should not be conflated with the organization's actions. While the language at times effaces the complexities of identity politics, the approach and actions of the organization itself toward the delicate situation of individuals who were appropriated by the military is quite sensitive. The Grandmothers recognize the profound psychological and social effects that stem from the discovery that one is a child of the disappeared, and their efforts to protect the privacy of individuals as well as provide professional support evidence a deep understanding of questions of identity.

The identification of Estela Carlotto's grandson, for example, exemplifies how the process involves a complicated blending of both biological and biographical identity. During the process of identification, the grandson was not publicly named by the organization, nor did he appear at a press conference until all parties were ready.[63] His public statements indicate the way in which he views the process as a broadening of his identity, rather than a replacement of one identity with another.[64] For example, he has chosen to maintain his adoptive name "Ignacio," but he has added "Guido" (the name given by his biological mother), as a way of acknowledging his history.[65] In this case, adopting a hitherto undiscovered biological identity implies expanding an individual's sense of self rather than denying an adoptive identity (as individuals such as Juan Cabandié chose to do), and the support the Grandmothers have provided in real-life cases reflects their sensitivity in dealing with the complexities involved.

While the actions of the Grandmothers demonstrate sensitivity toward identity politics, the public rhetoric reflected in *A veinte años, Luz* and *Montecristo* paints the issue in somewhat broader strokes, rooting the issue more firmly in biology. As the anthropologist Ari Gandsman explains, the "guiding assumption" of the Grandmothers' campaigns to draw young people who may have doubts about their identity to their organization includes two unspoken premises: "First, individuals have not only a desire but also an intrinsic need to know their biological origins, and, second, their 'real identities' are located within their biological origins."[66] One example of this premise appears in a poster campaign by the Grandmothers, which employs the slogan: "Identity cannot be imposed" (*La identidad no se impone*). The poster has a photo of the palm of a hand, with the fingertips covered by white cloths, upon which one sees the imprint of other fingerprints. Wires wrapped around the fingers hold the cloths in place, an obvious reference to the hoods prisoners were forced to wear and an indication of the way a new identity has been forced upon the individual. Across the palm the viewer reads, "Identity cannot be imposed," and at the bottom of the image a line states: "If you have doubts about your identity, call the Grandmothers," with their phone number provided. Identity, the poster suggests, is a question of fingerprints—put simply, identity is determined by biology.[67]

Biological and kinship metaphors figure heavily in human rights rhetoric regarding the disappeared. As Cecilia Sosa notes in her sociological research about the Mothers and Grandmothers, the metaphor of the "wounded family" has often been employed to describe the brutal effects of the dictatorship, and kinship relationships defined in terms of blood ties are privileged over other types of connections.[68] Gandsman similarly observes that groups based on blood relations have dominated the human rights landscape: Mothers, Grandmothers, H.I.J.O.S.[69] He further notes that among family member groups, "the Grandmothers have most explicitly embraced a biological logic," citing their advocacy of genetic identification technologies to identify their missing grandchildren.[70] In the case of appropriated children, the Grandmothers emphasize the loss of the markers of identity bestowed by their biological relatives, such as their name and extended family relationships. While the position of the Grandmothers has evolved over the years, in particular as missing grandchildren have grown from minors into adults, the importance of biological identity remains at the center of discussions surrounding appropriated children.[71]

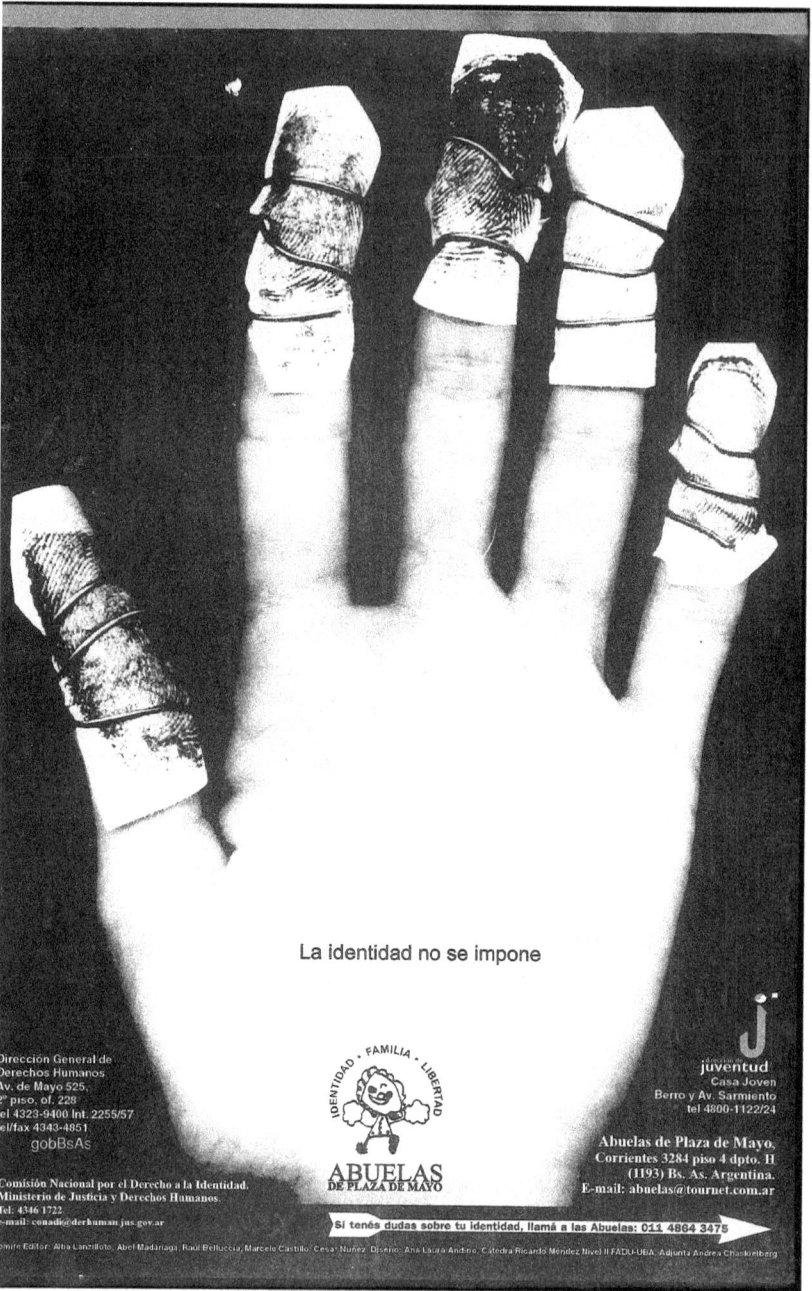

"Identity cannot be imposed" (*La identidad no se impone*). Poster campaign of the Grandmothers of the Plaza de Mayo to encourage individuals who doubted their identity to contact the organization. Courtesy of the Grandmothers of the Plaza de Mayo organization.

Both *A veinte años, Luz* and *Montecristo* uphold the suggestion that biology is destiny. As a baby, Luz suffers from nightmares stemming from the brutal transition from her biological mother to Eduardo and Mariana, and she invokes these early memories in her conversation with Carlos. Although she was taken from her mother when she was only two weeks old, the novel intimates that she preserves some recollection of that time, memories that come to the surface when she touches the artificial plastic of the baby bottle Mariana gives her to feed her own baby, Juan.[72] The touch of the plastic nipple provokes a physical reaction in Luz that catalyzes her search: her body knows what her mind has yet to understand. In the case of *Montecristo*, Laura feels a connection to Victoria the first moment they meet, in contrast to the alienation she always felt from the people who raised her. Blood proves thicker than water for her son Matías as well, as several characters comment on the resemblance between Matías and Santiago, even when ignorant of the blood relationship between the two. For example, when Sara Carruso, Judge Díaz Herrera's secretary, pulls Matías close she realizes he has the same scent as Santiago; meanwhile, Matías's fencing instructor comments on how his fighting style recalls Santiago's, much to the consternation of Marcos.

A veinte años, Luz emphasizes the importance of this "natural" type of knowing. As explained by Gema D. Palazón Sáez, much of Luz's knowing is internal—"she feels in her body the stigma of the dictatorship, because she is also a victim."[73] Examples in the text abound where Luz's intuition, intimately connected to her body, allows her to follow the path toward discovering her true identity. She always felt out of place in her home; she explains to Carlos that living with Mariana and her new husband Daniel always felt "unnatural."[74] In a similar fashion, she falls in love with her husband, Ramiro, through dancing—their bodies just "know" they are right for each other.[75] Meanwhile, in *Montecristo*, Victoria experiences a severe physical reaction when Lisandro enters a restaurant where she is dining; her body senses his involvement with her parents' disappearance. The emphasis on corporeal knowledge points to a biological determinism that aligns with the rhetoric (if not necessarily the actions) of the Grandmothers regarding what constitutes a "real" identity.[76]

A veinte años, Luz sets up a contrast between what is seen as "natural" and what is not, exemplified by Luz's relationship with her son. Luz possesses a fierce desire to breastfeed Juan, and insists upon being with him at all times, despite Mariana's insistence that she bottle feed instead. Her violent physical reaction to the touch of the bottle on one hand serves to underscore the violence of her appropriation, yet on the other hand it also serves to prioritize what is natural in family relationships: babies should not be taken away from their mothers, and the connection between Liliana and Luz (symbolized by breastfeeding) represents the most natural bond between mother and child. Any other type of connection—seen in Luz's fraught relationship with Mariana—is unnatural, and therefore a perversion of her real identity.

Both the novel and the telenovela also include many moments that directly employ the rhetoric of identity as employed by the Grandmothers. Articles 7, 8, and 11 of the International Convention of the Rights of the Child—also known as the "Argentine clauses"—explicitly refer to every child's right to "preserve his or her identity" (article 8), and at various moments in *A veinte años*, *Luz* characters allude to this fundamental right. Liliana pleads with Miriam to help her, because once she is killed Luz will have been deprived of her identity.[77] Eduardo also refers directly to the importance of identity in the greater political context when he explodes at Mariana: "So fighting for the Fatherland means decreeing whether people live or die and giving the detainees' children away and stealing their identity?"[78] In *Montecristo*, Laura insists that Matías has the right to know his identity and origins, overriding Marcos's objections that the truth will do more harm than good. The insistence on the importance of knowing one's identity closely aligns with the Grandmothers' rhetoric regarding the right to know one's biological family and origin: appropriated children have been denied their "true" (biological) identity, which must be restored, and they ideally should develop a relationship with their blood relations who have ceaselessly searched for them over the course of decades.[79]

The Politics of Identity Part 2: The Complex Reality

In these fictional accounts, like many others that treat the subject of the children of the disappeared, there is no space for a loving family.[80] Luz's (loving) adoptive father ends up dead when he tries to discover her true identity, and her (unloving) stepmother drives her away, thereby avoiding any potential conflict when Luz eventually reunites with her biological father. Meanwhile, Laura's "uncle" Lisandro is a despicable character whose violent behavior conveniently clears a path for a relatively unproblematic reunion with her family of origin.[81] While the case of Matías initially engages the nuance of a child torn between two loving families, such issues are neatly resolved through Marcos's descent into violent insanity, allowing for the reconstruction of the biological family unit of Santiago, Laura, and Matías. Nevertheless, the reality of the plight of the missing children is much more complicated, and ultimately more tragic, than most fictional narratives—or even the predominant rhetoric of the Grandmothers—allow, for it points to a crime that has both lasting consequences and, in more cases than one might want to admit, no easy possibility for reconstitution of family or identity.

The Grandmothers estimate that there are around four hundred to five hundred appropriated children: to date, around one hundred have been located.[82] Some cases of recovery indeed demonstrate a similar type of "happy ending" seen in *A veinte años, Luz* and *Montecristo*. Such is the case of Juan Cabandié, who was abused by the military man who raised him and was twenty-six years old when he discovered his true identity. Like Luz, he began to doubt his origins and worked with the Grandmothers to discover his biological family. Cabandié mentions that part of his doubt stemmed precisely from the abuse he suffered: in a 2007 documentary about the Grandmothers titled *Who Am I?*, Cabandié insists that "a person like [his "adoptive" father] couldn't be my father."[83] Cabandié's conviction of his true origin stems from a certainty that an abusive parent could not be a biological one, and he felt relief and a sense of closure when he was able to leave the lies of his past behind and embrace his "true" identity.[84]

The Grandmothers often highlight cases where the recuperation of the child is unquestioningly positive in order to promote their cause of finding these stolen children. Yet the range of responses to the work of locating missing grandchildren and restoring their identity is quite varied and nuanced.[85] Ultimately, the complexity of these cases points to some difficult (and at times irresolvable) issues regarding the politics of identity. Documentary films produced in conjunction with the Grandmothers (including Estela Carlotto's *Who Am I?* [2007]) and Daniel Blaustein's *Spoils of War* [2000]), as well as the *Spoils of War* text published by the Grandmothers, clearly show the way in which the military considered these children as "war booty" (*botín de guerra*), *things* to be distributed as they saw fit.[86] Yet it is precisely because people are *not* spoils of war that the process of recovery and restitution becomes complicated. If the actions of the military demonstrate their belief that these living beings were things that could be appropriated or given away, an emphasis on restitution unwittingly echoes this attitude.[87] Referring to the children as "stolen" or "appropriated," although true, preserves the language of ownership. This is not to say that the Grandmothers employ the language of ownership to dehumanize their missing children; on the contrary, their adoption of the term *botín de guerra* serves to underscore the depravity of the original crime, in which the military treated living beings as objects. The nature of the offense (a theft) determines the type of language used, including any attendant difficulties related to terminology. This language finds its echo in *Montecristo*, as Santiago repeats that Marcos "stole" his life, his love, and his son, but of all the crimes, the loss of Matías cuts the deepest. While Santiago desperately wants to occupy the role of father/protector, Victoria and Sara constantly caution him to be patient, precisely because Matías is not a "thing" that can be returned to a rightful owner but a living being with agency and deeply rooted affective bonds with his adoptive father.

The situation of appropriated children becomes even more complicated when one considers circumstances in which infants were placed with unwitting, well-intentioned families. While in some cases the military personnel directly responsible for the kidnapping, torture, and murder of a baby's birth parents appropriated the child, in other cases couples who adopted children had no knowledge of their origins. Although the children remain ignorant of the crime committed against them in both instances, the parents who raised them have differing degrees of culpability. The Grandmothers distinguish between appropriators and others in their rhetoric, as can be seen in Estela Carlotto's documentary film *Who Am I?* In a scene in a college classroom in 1986, Carlotto explains that eleven recovered grandchildren remained with the families that had raised them, because "they were not families that participated in the repression, in the torture and kidnapping."[88] The affective ties between children and the parents who raised them were not tainted by a criminal past. In cases involving repressors, however, Carlotto indicates that a relationship constructed from lies cannot be based on love. Referring to circumstances where "the children are in the hands of the military or police personnel who broke into houses, kidnapped, tortured and in this way appropriated the children," Carlotto declares, "Those people don't give the child love. When you steal something, you lie to the person and form a perverse relationship, one based on a lie."[89] Any bond between an appropriated child and the individuals who raised them is viewed as proof of victimization, a type of "Stockholm syndrome" in which hostages become emotionally attached to their kidnappers.[90]

The Grandmothers' position presupposes a child's desire to know what Cabandié calls the "complete truth" and suggests that once victims become aware of the "perversity" of their situation, they will distance themselves from their appropriators. Yet although some cases bear out these claims, others demonstrate the ambivalence and resistance some individuals feel toward the work of restitution, underscoring the complex politics of identity related to this particular crime. To prevent any misunderstanding, I wish to stress that my point is not to criticize the Grandmothers, with whom I sympathize, but rather to point out some of the complexities that have arisen in real-life cases and how they reveal the entrenched nature of representational taboos. Examining *A veinte años*, *Luz* and *Montecristo* within the context of identity politics reveals limits beyond which representations of children of the disappeared may

Silencing the Politics of Identity

not be able to go, even as they engage with complicated issues that challenge simplistic renderings of the restitution of identity.

The range of responses to identity restitution stands out in a 2008 collection of testimonies of appropriated children compiled by the journalist Analía Argento. Titled *De vuelta a casa: Historias de hijos y nietos restituidos* (Home again: Stories of recovered children and grandchildren), the testimonies included in the volume demonstrate that family ties are more than simply biological, and the process of appropriation does not necessarily preclude love.[91] The majority of the individuals who shared their stories with Argento felt conflicted about the process of discovering their biological identity. While some like being welcomed into another family, and others changed their names to reflect their new biological identity, several chose to maintain their given name. Some still live with or maintain very close relations with the parents who raised them, even when these individuals were implicated in the disappearance of their birthparents. Ambivalence and guilt populate each story— ambivalence toward the process of restitution, guilt that their DNA aids in the prosecution of people they consider their "parents," or a corresponding guilt for not feeling more connected to their biological families—but Argento emphasizes the importance of hearing the voices of the youngest victims, who often are represented by others (human rights groups, judges, lawyers) in the public sphere.

The story of Evelin Karina Vázquez is especially striking, for it demonstrates that the actions of the Grandmothers and those who seek the missing children are not always welcomed. Evelin refused to consider the parents who raised her as anything other than loving parents; furthermore, she considered the legal action taken against them, and the effort to restore her biological identity, as a violation in itself rather than an act of justice.[92] In fact, Evelin repeatedly refused to submit to DNA testing and hired lawyers to prevent any type of forced testing. Using the same human rights language of identity to defend Evelin's decision, her lawyer argued: "They couldn't strip [Evelin] of her identity, of the person she was and of her name because without them she would lose all of her rights. . . . She would become an NN walking the streets."[93] In this case, Evelin believed her "true" identity to be the one she was raised with, rather than her biological identity, and she categorically refused to have anything to do with her biological grandparents who had searched for her tirelessly for so many years.[94] From the perspective of the grandparents, Evelin's refusal to voluntarily submit to DNA testing and to know her birth family represented an incredible disappointment: "It was as if they had stolen her from them again, or worse."[95]

Evelin's story, as well as several others included in *De vuelta a casa*, high-lights the complications that arise precisely because children are *not* "spoils of war."[96] As living beings with agency who spent their formative years ignorant of the crime committed against them, these individuals indicate that the paths of love and biology do not always neatly intersect. The restoration of a bio-logical identity does not guarantee the reconfiguration of affective ties, and as Sosa compellingly argues in "Queering Kinship: The Performance of Blood and the Attires of Memory," the emphasis on kinship relationships based on biological identity has unexpected repercussions. Sosa examines the case of Vanina Falco, biological daughter of Luis Falco and "sister" of Juan Cabandié, whom Falco appropriated and raised as his son. While appropriated children such as Evelin struggle against a biologically determined identity because of their affection for the parents who raised them (despite their involvement in the initial crime against their biological parents), Vanina rejects a biological link with her father, precisely because of his actions during the dictatorship. Sosa notes that Vanina feels trapped by her blood ties, arguing that "biological kinship can be envisioned here as a sort of 'house arrest' that leaves her helpless and exposed to violence. Blood is Vanina's unchosen world."[97] Sosa argues for a more inclusive definition of kinship that "queers" or challenges a conven-tional understanding of blood relationships and allows individuals to choose their familial ties on the basis of factors other than biology. Yet one cannot advocate for Vanina's rejection of her biological father without also permitting Evelin to similarly choose her kinship ties, which points to the role of indi-vidual agency in the politics of identity.

Legal wrangling between suspected children of the disappeared and the Grandmothers signals a debate concerning individual and collective rights when redressing this particular crime. In his analysis of Evelin's case, Gandsman notes the Grandmothers found themselves in the unenviable position of "argu-ing for the coercive intervention of state power," against the stated wishes of the presumed victim.[98] The struggle over identity reflects the at times diver-gent needs of overlapping groups of victims, in this case the biological family (most often the grandparents) and the children themselves. While in many cases the needs of the Grandmothers and the children align, unfortunately in some cases the needs of one group are different from (or at odds with) those of the other. What the Grandmothers demand—restoring the individual's biological identity—may not be what the child wants or claims to need.[99] Although the Grandmothers' rhetoric regarding the "right to an identity" rep-resents a worthy claim and is seen as in the child's best interests, when this process encompasses mandatory DNA testing and the use of genetic evidence to prosecute the "adoptive" parents, some grandchildren have interpreted the

Silencing the Politics of Identity

experience as a further violation. Evelin describes her encounters with the judicial system in terms of persecution and victimization; to her, police entering her home to search for documents and separating her from the only people she had ever known as her parents constitutes a violation of her rights. Meanwhile, given that the grandchildren do not remember the initial crime committed against them and therefore do not necessarily consider themselves victims, the Grandmothers have been forced to advocate the overriding of individual rights in the name of justice.[100] Debates surrounding mandatory DNA analysis for suspected children of the disappeared reveal a clash between a societal need to gather proof of state terrorism (genetic evidence held inside the body of the children) and an individual's right to determine how, when, or even if one's body can be used to provide such evidence.[101] As Gandsman insightfully observes, in situations where individuals resist the work of identity restitution, the Grandmothers' "main challenge" is "to make victims of a crime understand that they are victims of a crime."[102] So, while in some cases the Grandmothers and the children work toward a common goal, in other instances the clashing needs create an agonizing situation in which nobody feels as if their rights are valued or respected.

Identity, indeed, cannot be imposed—yet this works both ways. For the Grandmothers, a "false" identity imposed on a child stolen from his or her parents can never be imposed; yet because these are living human beings and not war booty, a "true" biological identity cannot be imposed either. This tragedy is the one that needs to be told as the legacy of the systematic appropriation of children, for this particular crime against humanity has devastating, permanent effects that in many cases have no easy remedy or straightforward redress. The Grandmothers continue to suffer with the continued absence of their grandchildren—as seen in the case of Evelin, the situation may even be viewed as a second, even more devastating loss. Meanwhile, the path to restitution may cause the grandchildren some emotional pain. There is no easy way out of the labyrinth of identity politics, a testament to the tragic scope of the original crime.

The crime of appropriation remains at the heart of the politics of identity, yet both the original crime and its lasting effects are often effaced in public discourse surrounding the children of the disappeared. On the one hand, the media focus on legal battles and resistance to restitution obscures the original crime, for it emphasizes the emotional difficulties of restitution rather than the depravity of appropriation.[103] As Mariano Gaitán, a lawyer for the Grandmothers, explains, it is important to view cases of restitution *not* as a conflict between individuals and their desires but a more complicated situation of a crime against humanity that the state has an obligation to investigate.[104] The fact that the Grandmothers include a lengthy interview with Gaitán on their website defining the "right to identity" as a societal obligation rather than an individual choice responds to public debate regarding state intervention in individuals' "private" lives. A focus on current debates regarding identity politics (e.g., compulsory DNA testing) therefore silences the original crime and may even engender sympathy toward the perpetrators.

If attention on the emotional toll of the work of restitution risks silencing the crime of appropriation, the emphasis on biological determinism that understandably characterizes much of the Grandmothers' rhetoric as well as fictional interpretations of the lives of appropriated children also obscures the full extent of the offense, in this case its tragic and lasting effects. A focus on a happy reintegration of the biological family ignores the ambivalent feelings many grandchildren experience during the process of discovering their new identity. The bonds of love do not always align with the needs of justice or restitution, and to present complicated stories of identity as simple tales of discovery risks implying that this particular crime does not have painful lasting consequences, another way of silencing the crime itself.

Fiction versus Testimony

Again, as with *Paso de dos*, one can argue that fiction has the ability to transform painful reality into hopeful story—to portray history as it should have happened. Osorio states that when she wrote *A veinte años, Luz* she had not heard of any cases of missing grandchildren searching for their origins, so she was breaking new ground with her fictional portrayal of Luz.[105] The decision to depict an adult child of the disappeared finding a "happy ending" may also be viewed as a response to the case of the Reggiardo Tolosa twins; an adult protagonist would presumably have more maturity to understand the nuance of her situation and less possibility of emotional trauma. By the time *Montecristo* was broadcast, however, not only were cases of appropriated children searching for their identities more commonplace but high-profile cases such as Evelin's also demonstrated the conflicting emotions surrounding restitution of identity for adults. Yet the telenovela, like Osorio's novel, preserves the taboo surrounding the depiction of "two loving families" for appropriated children. Despite the passage of almost a decade, which saw numerous examples of the complications connected with restitution, this particular taboo appears firmly entrenched.[106] Although popular representations of complicated issues may challenge existing assumptions or beliefs—indeed, both *A veinte años, Luz* and *Montecristo* confront some uncomfortable truths regarding the legacy of appropriation—the definitive silence regarding genuine affective ties between appropriators and children speaks to the limits that govern how far such representations can go when depicting this particular trauma.

Furthermore, representing an easy way out of the labyrinth of the politics of identity, through a soothing "happy ending," can be viewed as a further violation, for by silencing the full depravity and lasting effects of the original crime, such representations undermine the goal of any type of testimonial narrative. Again, if the media spectacle surrounding high-profile cases of difficult restitutions called attention to the grandchildren's current plight at the expense of the military's original crime, the choice in fictional representations to elide the contradictions and complications related to restitution equally serves to silence the original crime and its lasting consequences. If fictional tales, much like the Grandmothers' rhetoric, do not always acknowledge uncomfortable nuances, then the stories of "incomplete" or "problematic" restorations (aside from those found in academic journals) come from the media spectacles surrounding the high-profile cases, which serve more to polarize than to educate. If the goal is to break repressive silences and tell "the truth" about the crimes of the past, one could argue that those parties committed to the victims themselves have a responsibility to tell the full truth, however painful.

Finally, one could view the "use" of these victims' tales as another form of appropriation—in this case of their stories. In the prologue to *De vuelta a casa*, Juan Cabandié states that he was initially suspicious of Argento's motives for wanting to interview these appropriated children. He complains about earlier representations of their situation, noting that often they have been "treated as *objects* of sociological study, like *the elements* of a social experiment."[107] Cabandié's use of the word "objects" is important here, as it implies again that these children need to be treated as people rather than things—and that their stories comprise part of their identity. Using their stories as inspiration for a popular novel or telenovela risks not only silencing the real tragedy of the appropriation of children but also objectifying these victims once again.

Conclusion

The attempt to bury any evidence relating to the systematic appropriation of children during the dictatorship years is referred to as a "pact of silence" on the part of the military. Yet while *A veinte años, Luz* and *Montecristo* serve to break this particular overt pact of silence, they unwittingly contribute to another, more covert silence. In her consideration of testimonial narrative, Nance refers to the power of the "socially sayable," "specific and formulaic speech acts" used by testimonial speakers "that comprise the socially acceptable channels for the narration of trauma."[108] Applying Nance's idea to the fictional realm, the socially sayable seems to affect the types of stories that can be told about past trauma. Unlike many other trauma narratives, the story of appropriation does not defy linguistic expression; rather, the inability to tell the tale reveals a reluctance to fully engage with the tragedy. In this case, the taboo regarding "two loving families" remains firmly entrenched in fictional representations of appropriated children. An aftershock of the memory boom, this crater of silence left in the wake of the explosion of memory discourse points to the limits governing which tales of horror find expression. Yet if we only tell the good stories, the ones with the happy endings, we are also contributing to a pact of silence that suppresses the really horrible tales, the ones that can never have happy endings. Furthermore, the ramifications of such silence remain and must be addressed in order to approach a full understanding of the depth of the trauma and the horror of this particular crime against humanity. Although *A veinte años, Luz* and *Montecristo* purport to help readers and viewers "see" better, ultimately they only end up "feeling" better at the end of the tale. In the final analysis, the failed witnessing in both tales implies that sometimes the obstacles to telling the whole story stem not from the impossibility of finding appropriate words but the unwillingness to articulate them.

The Memory of Forgetting in Luisa Valenzuela's *La travesía*

El olvido está lleno de memoria
[Forgetting is full of memory]

Mario Benedetti

he memory boom of the midnineties reflected a hope that formerly taboo topics would no longer remain unmentionable. If Adolfo Scilingo could talk openly about the death flights, the demands of human rights groups regarding justice and accountability should also gain traction in the public sphere. The repressive institutional silencing of the Menem years would cede to a climate of openness and accountability, as human rights groups and their allies worked to expose the military's crimes. As mentioned in the introduction, the H.I.J.O.S. group in particular embodied this hope of the memory boom, as even their name proclaimed their struggle "against forgetting and silence," the twin enemies of preserving the memory of the dictatorship and its many victims. For the members of H.I.J.O.S., the silences surrounding the fate of the babies born in captivity and given away to military families equate to forgetting the crimes of the past, while the silences regarding the militancy of the desaparecidos represent another attempt to forget the true identity of those who lost their lives fighting for a better society. The Buenos Aires chapter of H.I.J.O.S. clearly states: "Faced with the prevailing injunction—of forgetting and silence—we believe it essential to create a counterdiscourse that supports the reconstruction of the social identity of our people."[1] Speech and memory stand in clear opposition to silence and forgetting: to combat the silence of amnesia, the crimes of the past must be voiced.

Yet in contexts of trauma, memory and forgetting do not occupy mutually exclusive zones; as Benedetti's epigraph reminds us, forgetting is full of memory. This phrase captures perfectly the sometimes paradoxical relationship between memory and forgetting involved in remembering state terrorism in Argentina. As seen in the rhetoric of H.I.J.O.S., when official discourse advocates moving forward and forgetting the past in the name of democracy and progress, but the past stubbornly refuses to be silenced, the struggle of memory against forgetting becomes highly charged.[2] Nevertheless, while forgetting and oblivion may appear to be akin to silencing, they can actually be expressive in all their muteness: the silence of forgetting is never a true absence of expression but rather provokes the word. As Lyotard explains in *The Differend*, the seemingly desperate silence after trauma "is a negative phrase, but it also calls upon phrases which are in principle possible."[3] In other words, the void left in the wake of terror, the absences created by disappeared bodies, the silences contained in unasked and unanswered questions are never static absences, complete voids, but always a state of anticipation, a waiting-to-be-phrased. To return to Sommer's division between intellectual knowledge and emotional knowing, while forgetting may silence the facts on the intellectual level, at the same time it has the potential to stimulate and fortify the emotional knowing. Silence is the language of forgetting but also the means to move toward remembrance, and in this tension past violence finds its expression through a language of silence. Put simply, being silent does not mean being silenced, as seen in Luisa Valenzuela's novel *La travesía*.

Set in the late 1990s, *La travesía* centers around an exiled Argentine anthropologist living in New York City who finds herself confronted with a secret past she had hoped to forget: her brief marriage to Professor Facundo Zuberbühler and corresponding "epistolar prostitution," whereby she detailed fictitious sexual exploits to him in exchange for plane tickets to foreign destinations where she carried out field research. These letters are discovered by the Polish artist Bolek Greczynski during an exhibition he gave in Buenos Aires in 1982, and when he befriends the protagonist years later, he makes reference to these steamy missives. The letters' unexpected return force the protagonist to acknowledge her suppressed personal history as well as its relation to the violence in her country.

Tracing the protagonist's internal journey toward acceptance of her past, the novel emphasizes the impossibility of equating silence with oblivion. Although the heroine has not spoken of her past and believes it forgotten, it remains repressed inside her twenty years later. Like Freud's theory of the "return of the repressed," these memories refuse to be completely silenced and manifest themselves inside her body; in this case, the corporeal and organic nature of memory prevents its complete suppression. While *La pesquisa*, discussed in chapter 3, illustrates the gap between intellectual knowledge and emotional knowing and hints at the power of such internal conviction, *La travesía* probes further to discover its location and character: silenced memories take root inside the body and grow into a tangled emotional wilderness. By emphasizing the importance of nonverbal, bodily memories, *La travesía* suggests that a somatic language of expression—a form that recognizes both the limits of language and the ambiguous power of silence—serves best when approaching a tale of personal and national trauma, and that the silent paths of forgetting lead to memory rather than oblivion.[4] In a context often viewed as a struggle of memory "against" silence, Valenzuela's novel indicates that certain postboom silences represent not a failure to articulate the crimes of the past but a necessary means of understanding them.

The Call to Witness

The main silences in the novel correspond to the protagonist's failed witnessing of both her personal history and her country's recent trauma. Given the many challenges to witnessing horror, artistic and cultural expression can facilitate expression of atrocity, as Shoshana Felman and Dori Laub claim in their work about trauma and testimony. The authors challenge traditional notions about the act of bearing witness, in which someone views a happening and later provides an uncomplicated version of events. For Felman and Laub, the process is never so simple, for both the nature of the event and the character of the witness serve to shape the experience and determine the telling. The authors emphasize the accidental yet persistent nature of bearing witness and giving testimony: "If it is the accident [the event] that *pursues the witness*, it is the compulsive character of testimony which is brought into relief: the witness is 'pursued,' that is, at once compelled and bound by what, in the unexpected impact of the accident, is both incomprehensible and unforgettable. The accident does not let go: it is an accident from which the witness can no longer free himself."[5] Thus even accidental or unacknowledged witnessing will haunt the most reluctant of onlookers. Akin to the ghostly presence of absence Gordon addresses in her work, this silent yet persistent presence proves central to witnessing past trauma. This accidental nature of witnessing is especially important, for it includes not only those who were caught up in an experience directly (death camp survivors, former torture victims) but also those who experienced the horror only peripherally (those who lived near the clandestine camps or mass grave sites, anyone who saw someone taken from their home or off the street). Furthermore, it allows for witnesses who were not aware of what they were seeing at the time but still feel in some sense "pursued" by the past, such as the protagonist of *La travesía*. However, the protagonist's choice to "be silent" regarding her personal history and that of her country, rather than serve to "silence" the past, paradoxically leads to acknowledgment and memory.

The novel opens with a carefully scripted "accident," a blind date. The as-yet unnamed protagonist participates in a mysterious drama in the Museum of Modern Art, MoMA, in New York, in order to guide a man to his blind date with the dominatrix Ava Taurel. An anthropologist by trade, "trained to study the behavior of others, not her own,"[6] she thinks of her participation as a window into the world of those who seek excitement in the unknown, the vaguely threatening. After leaving a briefcase for the man to pick up, meeting him in one of the galleries, and passing along a message about how to find Ava, she realizes that her role in the little drama has had more serious consequences than she anticipated. Eager to free herself from the experience, because the clandestine encounter and knowledge of Ava Taurel's tastes cannot help but conjure up uncomfortable resonances with her country's recent past, she soon realizes that "it hadn't finished, no: it was just beginning. She now needed to face her own blind date with the unacknowledged part of herself that had placed her in that crazy story."[7] Her accidental (yet unacknowledged) witnessing of the dictatorship in Argentina, as well as her own complicity, begins to pursue her as a result of her participation in this "accidental" encounter in the MoMA, and the rest of the novel is spent trying to come to terms with the failed witnessing of her own personal history and that of her country during the dictatorship years.[8]

One of the more compelling images from this opening scene (appropriately titled "Sailing blindly") is that of the briefcase itself. Although she arrives at the museum early and has plenty of time to wonder as to its contents, the protagonist never once feels the temptation to look inside. The briefcase itself calls to mind the found object in the title story from Valenzuela's earlier collection *Strange Things Happen Here*, which provokes excited curiosity, soon followed by desperate fear. In the context of state terror, a mysterious briefcase can easily become an object of panic, yet in this instance, in New York City, years after the return to democracy in Argentina, the absolute lack of curiosity on the part of the protagonist is curious in itself. It is as if she knows she holds a Pandora's box of past secrets, repressed memories, and unacknowledged emotions and resolves not to open it at any cost.

The image of an unopened box of memories seems especially fitting for approaching the nature of remembering in postauthoritarian contexts. The historian Steve Stern utilizes the "memory box" as a metaphor to describe the manner in which Chileans today remember the Pinochet years. This box "contains several competing scripted albums, each of them works in progress that seek to define and give shape to a crucial turning point in life, much as a family album may script a wedding or a birth, an illness or a death, a crisis or a success." In some cases, the memory of the crucial years of the dictatorship is like a "closed box," too painful or dangerous to be considered directly.[9] Recognizing the differences between the Chilean and Argentine dictatorships, Stern's image of the memory box speaks to the remembrance of an authoritarian past in Argentina as well. For the protagonist of *La travesía*, the closed briefcase, like the closed box, aptly describes how she carries the memories of her homeland. Nevertheless, while she resists the impulse to peek inside while in the museum, her mere participation in the game as a supposedly dispassionate observer becomes a blind date with destiny, and the memories from inside her personal memory box begin to spill forth unwanted. Questions begin to emerge about her participation in the drama: "Does she even feel free? . . . Might this be a sour aftertaste from murkier times? These are the questions that begin to throb within her even if she can't formulate them yet."[10] As evidenced by the use of the word "to throb," these pulsating questions seem to comprise an integral part of her physical self. Like a beating heart, this somatic memory not only lives inside the body but also forms part of that living body, thus providing an ever-present and insistent call to witness the trauma of the past. Indeed, just as the unacknowledged event pursues the witness, these barely formulated questions begin to haunt the protagonist.

The novel emphasizes the difficulty the protagonist has in even formulating the essential questions that lie at the heart of her past. The questions themselves are important, but the narrative focuses on the way they resist articulation, describing them as "not completely formulated," "wordlessly surfacing," or "lost."[11] If asking a question with no answer is like dropping a pebble down a bottomless well, *La travesía* explores the difficulty of even grasping the pebble, for the language of these unarticulated questions, although insistent in its call, proves difficult to decipher.

Such unformulated yet insistent questions and memories are especially distressing because the anthropologist has been very successful in silencing the secrets of her past, both consciously (actively suppressing any thought or mention of her secret ex-husband Facundo) and unconsciously (never questioning the fate of her disappeared school friend Juancho). To the protagonist, the past is barely "an irritating reminder"—it is something she simply does not think about.[12] Furthermore, her silences prove both overt and covert, for just as she refuses to overtly discuss her past, she also tries to "cover" this absence with busyness and presence, distracting herself with teaching, research, and parties with her group of artist friends. These friends in New York know nothing of her ex-husband's existence, and she even keeps the relationship secret from her family and friends in Argentina. At one point she makes a halfhearted attempt to write to her friend Greta and hint as to her relationship with Facundo, but by the time the letter arrives Greta has died and her husband returns it, unopened. The protagonist realizes that "in the bottom of a purse she kept the unopened letter, just like in some part of her heart she locked away the name of the absent one who had filled her days."[13] Yet despite the protagonist's attempts to keep her personal memory box closed, these unacknowledged memories resist such artificial authority and effectively pursue her.

The interplay between overt and covert silences also highlights the slippage between personal and collective history. While the protagonist acknowledges the overt silence regarding her individual secret (the secret marriage), she is less aware that attention to her personal story serves to "cover" any reference to the collective secret (the public secret of the dictatorship's violence). The unacknowledged relationship between the personal and political therefore manifests itself as both an overt silence (her refusal to mention her ex-husband) and a covert one (using her personal secret as a foil to cover her failure to process her country's history). Echoing Idelber Avelar's discussion of the relationship between mourning and allegory, her personal story stands as a kind of allegory for the nation's violence, and it is only through acknowledging the relationship between the two (the authoritarianism of her husband and that of the nation, as well as her own tacit complicity) that she can begin the task of mourning.[14] In this case, both the overt and covert silences facilitate an understanding of trauma, as they demonstrate the intimate connection between memory and forgetting.

This constant interplay between memory and forgetting typifies the way in which trauma exerts itself on the mind, even witnessed rather than experienced trauma. As Cathy Caruth notes, "The historical power of the trauma is not just that the experience is repeated after its forgetting, but that it is only in and through its inherent forgetting that it is first experienced at all."[15] In other words, the process of forgetting is not only inevitable but also necessary in order that the trauma be remembered at all. True witnessing of trauma occurs in the unstable zone between understanding and incomprehension, the acknowledging and "listening to another's wound."[16] The eventual articulation of trauma recognizes this necessary forgetting as well; as Felman explains, before its articulation, language must "pass through its own answerlessness, pass through a frightful falling-mute."[17] The accident, the trauma, pursues the witness and demands recognition of the wound, yet silence is a natural stage in this move toward articulation. Ultimately the silencing of trauma, rather than condemning the event to the realm of oblivion, actually provokes expression. In *La travesía*, the protagonist's (c)overt silences regarding her past—her failed or unacknowledged witnessing of personal and national oppression—leads to an expression of trauma through somatic rather than verbal means.

Secrets and Lies

The latent power of suppressed memory is similarly exemplified in the concept of the secret, for its power also resides in its potential revelation. As her friend Jerome explains, the secret's object is unarticulated, but the knowledge of its silent existence gives it power; "what it conceals has no purpose unless you know there's something there, hidden." Only a certain few are privy to the secret, Jerome adds, "only those who know the secret language and understand its codes." Terrified that he may have stumbled across her own deepest secrets, the protagonist fears Jerome's claim that "the secret is an instrument of power over others."[18] The secret always contains an implicit threat—its revelation—and its tremendous power resides in this possible movement from silence to articulation.

Bolek's accidental discovery of her letters forces the protagonist into the uncomfortable position of sharing a secret with the artist and consequently feeling his power over her. These letters—written to Facundo, returned to her apartment with his name carefully removed, discovered by Bolek, and brought to her attention—denote another manner in which her repressed past (the event) pursues the protagonist (the witness). Ksenija Bilbija illustrates the unrelenting nature of these letters in her analysis of the novel. Using as a point of departure Lacan's assertion that "a letter always arrives at its destination," Bilbija suggests that the protagonist is the true recipient of the letters, rather than the stated one, and in the spirit of Lacan's statement, the anthropologist is literally pursued by the letters, for Bolek brings them back into her life and forces her to address them in all their physical reality.[19] Bilbija further likens the protagonist's secret letters to mines, "full of what 'cannot be said.'"[20] Yet these mines can be detonated at any time by a thoughtless comment from Bolek to one of their mutual acquaintances, and the protagonist lives in fear of discovery for the majority of the novel.

It must be noted that the protagonist's understandable desire to maintain a firm hold of her secrets rests upon vaguely sinister undertones. After describing the secret as an "instrument of power over others," Jerome observes that policies of secrets and centralized control of information are characteristics of totalitarian regimes.[21] As Michael Taussig explains, authoritarian regimes control the populace through the presence of "public secrets," events or practices that are "generally known, but cannot be articulated."[22] In the case of Argentina, the existence of clandestine torture centers and a centralized policy of disappearance became public secrets, information about which was carefully controlled by the military government. The protagonist herself cannot help but draw the same uneasy connection between the powerful secrets of authoritarian regimes and her personal struggles to keep her own secrets safe, noting, "Without really understanding why, she maintains an individual and self-repressive totalitarianism," most likely due to her own secret.[23] Yet the silence of her secrets and repressed memories constantly point toward articulation, compelling the protagonist to address her past.

The secret letters in *La travesía* represent more than the protagonist's shameful private history, for their discovery during Bolek's visit to what he calls "the uncanny world capital of the disappeared" suggests a relationship to the broader events of the dictatorship.[24] Tinged with blood, the letters bear the physical marks of violence, and Bolek—also an exile from a country that suffered a violent past—inevitably concludes that he must have stumbled into the apartment of one of the dictatorship's many victims. But while the protagonist, through her world travels, lived the "cover story" officials used to placate family members desperately searching for missing loved ones (the very story Facundo gave her as an explanation for Juancho's disappearance), she herself was not "disappeared."[25] The relationship between her situation and disappearance, between the letters and political violence, remains coincidental but suggestive, and the fact that her world travels coincide with the escalating violence in Argentina implies that the forgotten letters also represent the failed or unacknowledged witnessing of the terror in her home country.

Organic and Somatic Memories

When Bolek first mentions the building where he held his exhibit in Buenos Aires in 1982 and made his startling discovery of the letters, the protagonist feels "a shock so very profound that she didn't register it in the moment; her internal seismograph appeared to be broken during much of that time."[26] This image of an internal seismograph proves very appropriate to describe the somatic imprint of every experience, the impact of which may not be immediately felt. As Valenzuela has affirmed in an essay about secrets, "The

Secret resides closer to skin than clothing";[27] in other words, although the protagonist may have erased the vestiges of her marriage and her past on the surface—"covered" them with travel, work, and play—these covert silences still linger deep inside the body. Measuring Bolek's words with a seismograph also likens the internal rumblings of memory to a natural event of great proportion and lasting effect, thus foregrounding the organic quality of these memories embedded inside the body.[28] Like shock waves that can travel around the world hours and even days after a seismic rumble, the ripples of Bolek's revelation take effect after the artist leaves. The protagonist translates the internal quaking into external movement, letting her feet guide her through the city in an unconscious attempt to "sketch a map of unknown territory: her own memory,"[29] an indication that in order to recognize and understand this somatic memory, one must follow an internal trail along the body's emotional geography.[30]

The internal geography of memory does not figure in conventional atlases, as Elina Matoso explains in *The Body as Dramatic Terrain*. As part of a practice to help individuals overcome corporeal issues, Matoso envisions the body as a land that can be mapped geographically and that provides a key to understanding the images or masks that humans wear as part of their essential identities. She explains that we all possess an image of ourselves, "the Phantasmatic Corporal Map," which changes depending on each person's conception of his or her body and self.[31] Just as the protagonist in *La travesía* carries the shadow of her past inside her, all humans experience moments when "shadows, ghosts, and spirits that do not appear in any anatomy textbook reveal themselves in the body."[32] Remarking on the large number of natural metaphors used to describe the body and its functions—"cataracts, kidney stones, blood 'flow,' crying a river"[33]—Matoso further asserts that the internal markings of identity bear geographical terms, a suggestive claim in light of the connection drawn between memory, the body, and nature in *La travesía*.

Considering the fact that the majority of the novel's action takes place in the urban centers of New York City and Buenos Aires, the narrative employs a vast number of natural images, especially when describing the protagonist's inner self and the nature of memory. At one point the territory of her memory is compared to "quicksand"; in another instance the central character refers to her innermost secrets as "deeply personal items that grow covered by layers and layers of moss."[34] Yet by far, one of the most significant links between nature and memory appears when the protagonist ponders how to delve into and examine her own internal nature, for she employs a lengthy organic metaphor to describe the process: "Diving into one's imagination, occasionally coming up for air in the zones of so-called reality, only to submerge again in the underwater caves, examining phosphorescent shoals and confronting unthinkable, terrifying monsters. Being carried away by fancy in order to dive down to the deepest waters . . . there in the unfathomable depths of her own Walden Pond, in the oceanic volcanoes of her mind where monumental worms and giant larvae live off the sulfuric emissions of an unknown visceral magma."[35] Submerged caves, incalculable depths, and oceanic volcanoes with giant worms and larvae all combine to create this startling image of her interior world, her internal geography. The image of memory as a volcano seems especially appropriate, something that can lie dormant for years before suddenly announcing its existence with ferocity and disrupting the apparent calm of the surface, while the "unfathomable" nature of this inner landscape emphasizes its ambiguous qualities.

Delving into the interior wilderness of her memory requires confronting the grotesque beings of her innermost thoughts, and the process proves both complex and disturbing. As Matoso explains, approaching this unknown corporeal terrain can be complicated, as it always leads to "an enigma" that resists easy understanding yet demands attention. In her words, "Placating [the enigma] is warm and soothing, unmasking it can be cruel and shattering. To conceal, hide, or negate it means remaining trapped in one's own body, without being able to see the enigma."[36] Indeed, the protagonist's struggles to ignore and suppress her inner mysteries reveal the uncomfortable effects of keeping potentially disturbing memories trapped inside the body, as seemingly innocent conversations tinged with organic imagery often trigger emotional responses. Returning from a party, she finds herself in the middle of a conversation about lettuce, and this apparently innocuous natural image propels her thoughts inexorably to Facundo and her secret past. Unable to contain her dark thoughts, she comments on how she appears to have struck "the tip of the green lettuce iceberg. All the suppressed complaints swell her stomach and come out in burps, a complaint disguised as hissing, whistling air."[37] The natural gases that attempt to escape through her mouth seem to originate from the internal volcanoes, yet in this case, much the opposite of Valenzuela's heroine in her story "La densidad de las palabras" (The density of words), who speaks the bitter truth in the form of frogs and snakes emerging from her mouth, the protagonist struggles to keep the worms and larvae of memory imprisoned inside.

By emphasizing both the organic and somatic quality of memory, *La travesía* challenges the traditional paradigm that equates speech with memory and silence with oblivion. The interplay of natural and corporeal images to describe the interior wilderness of the protagonist in Valenzuela's text draws a clear connection between nature, the body, and memory. Unacknowledged memories embed themselves in the body and form the landmarks of the central character's interior geography. The protagonist's attempts to silence her past cause it to find corporeal pathways of expression; the relationship between memory and forgetting proves far more complicated and ambiguous than a simple dichotomy between speech and silence. Furthermore, *La travesía*'s emphasis on the importance of honoring an interior wilderness as a path toward understanding the Secret questions two discourses employed in Argentina during distinct times of authoritarian rule: first, the relationship between nature and culture manifested in Domingo Faustino Sarmiento's *Facundo: Civilización y barbarie* (including the related association between the untamed wilderness and the feminine); and second, the Cartesian division between the body and the mind emphasized in the military's rhetoric during the most recent years of state terror. By underscoring the organic and somatic quality of memory, as well as questioning traditional discourses regarding authoritarianism and its legacy, Valenzuela's novel highlights the value of nonverbal, ambiguous expression at the same time as it challenges the primacy of speech and discourse for their tendency to "fix" meaning into simplistic categories.

The novel characterizes the protagonist's struggle for remembrance as a battle to impose civilized notions on her unruly, wild memory. For example, after Bolek triggers the protagonist's internal seismograph with his startling revelation regarding the location of his exhibit in Buenos Aires, he inadvertently leaves behind an additional "organic" reminder of his visit. When he stands up to say goodnight, a red stain left on the upholstery reveals that a pen has bled through his pants. Like the pulsating questions that haunted the protagonist's participation in Ava's drama, the "bleeding" couch stands as a symbol of the as-yet-unacknowledged wounds of the past.[38] Remembering the incident later, the protagonist struggles to "immerse herself in that nothingness, swimming in the memory of an anecdote, of a stain that is so very bright and so very red, that it doesn't even look like blood, like some other stains do."[39] Denying its resemblance to blood merely invites the comparison, and both the accidental nature of the mark and its organic quality suggest the wild, uncontrolled nature of traumatic memory, a wildness the protagonist is unwilling to accept at this point in her journey. After a moment of indecision, she quickly determines that Bolek should sign the stain, thus converting the accidental mark into a work of art and imposing a civilizing force over the ominous red stain. But as the novel progresses, it becomes clear that attempts to "civilize" or control her memory through language or other means prove useless, because traumatic memory resists organized articulation or understanding.

The anthropologist's intense desire to exert a civilizing influence on her wild memory invites a comparison with Sarmiento's *Facundo*, which explains Argentina's character in terms of a fierce battle between European civilization and savage barbarism. Valenzuela's decision to name the protagonist's ex-husband Facundo further links the individual, private history embodied in the character's secret marriage to the broader social events of the dictatorship and the imagining of the entire nation. The opening line of Sarmiento's introduction—"Terrible specter of Facundo, I will evoke you, so that you may rise, shaking off the bloody dust covering your ashes, and explain the hidden life and the inner convulsions that tear at the bowels of a noble people"—echoes the struggle of the fictional anthropologist, whose personal examination of the "specter" of her ex-husband helps her understand not only her own "hidden life" but that of her country during the 1970s and 1980s.[40] But while Sarmiento's text makes it clear that the refined civilization enjoyed in the urban centers of Argentina has been cruelly corrupted by the savage influences of the interior provinces, *La travesía* responds to the urban barbarism of state terror and reveals the dangers of attempting to impose artificial control over an interior wilderness that refuses to be tamed.

The trope of *civilización y barbarie* in *Facundo* has received much critical attention and requires only a brief summary. Using the life of the gaucho bandit Facundo Quiroga as a foil for the Rosas dictatorship, Sarmiento makes explicit the connection between the bloody barbarism of Rosas and the untamed wilderness. "Savage Indians" threaten livestock and populations, while the wealth of natural resources, such as the abundance of navigable rivers, await exploitation of all their rich potential. According to Sarmiento, Buenos Aires would have the capacity to extend its civilizing influence on the interior were it not for the way in which Rosas has stifled culture in the cities. The author further explains that any type of national literature will result from "descriptions of grand scenes of nature, and above all, from the struggle between European civilization and indigenous barbarism, between intelligence and matter."[41]

In a suggestive thematic coincidence, a *travesía* itself figures prominently as one of the central natural settings of Sarmiento's text and serves to introduce the title character. The author sets the scene with the following description: "Between the cities of San Luis and San Juan there lies a vast desert, which because of its complete lack of water is given the name *travesía*. In general, those solitudes have a sad and abandoned aspect."[42] This barren landscape serves as a place of refuge for bandits running from the law, in this case Facundo Quiroga. Only the very strong make it across the *travesía* alive, and the lonely desert scene highlights not only the gaucho's comfort in the wild (he successfully survives an attack from a man-eating tiger) but also the vast expanse of untamed wilderness in the interior provinces of the country.

One final aspect of Sarmiento's text bears consideration in relation to *La travesía*: the way in which the author constructs a metaphorical relationship

The Memory of Forgetting

between woman and the wilderness. Dinorah Cortés explores how Sarmiento effectively feminizes the nation of Argentina, noting that the author describes the republic as a desirable woman he aims to "seduce, possess, and inseminate."[43] Sarmiento's lament that the Argentine Republic "has lacked a Tocqueville who . . . would have penetrated the interior of our political life as a vast field still unexplored and undescribed by science," with its image of penetrating uncharted territory, likens man's superiority over nature with male domination over the female.[44] In keeping with Sandra Gilbert and Susan Gubar's theory of the patriarchal tradition of writing outlined in *The Madwoman in the Attic: The Woman Writer and the Nineteenth-Century Literary Imagination*, whereby "the text's author is a father, a progenitor, a procreator, an aesthetic patriarch whose pen is an instrument of generative power like his penis,"[45] Cortés asserts that in *Facundo* Argentina is presented as "a desirable young woman" waiting to be "inseminated" by a civilizing man such as Sarmiento.[46]

In *La travesía*, the "feminine" wilderness of the "interior" is literally interior and feminine. Although the novel ultimately challenges the notion that this wilderness must be tamed, Valenzuela describes the protagonist's attempts to control her wild memory in terms that recall Sarmiento's text. For example, after listening to Bolek's description of how he discovered her letters, the protagonist compares her dangerous emotions to the phenomenon of a raging river: "The tumult of emotions . . . needs to find a channel, because she cannot keep living with this anxiety, as if she lacked oxygen."[47] Like the submerged volcanoes of her memory, these innermost thoughts resemble a powerful natural force in need of some form of mastery, reminiscent of Sarmiento's call to dominate Argentina's natural resources in order to become a civilized nation. In another telling passage, the anthropologist ponders the organic character of memory: "Mushrooms pop up like mushrooms, and so do memories sometimes. And they can be poisonous if you don't dig right down to the bottom. She suspects. She knows. She would prefer to be able to distance herself from the confusing, tangled forest and move through an indifferent, devitalized cellar where cultivated mushrooms grow."[48] In this instance, the contrast between the tangled forest and the "devitalized" (civilized) underground room clearly situates the protagonist's struggle to dominate her interior wilderness within Sarmiento's familiar paradigm.

Moreover, her initial notions of memory are characterized by their artificial or civilized quality. She first considers Giulio Camillo's "Theatre of World Memory," which consists of (memory) boxes that open and close to offer "total recall and the wondrous possibility to understand everything by association in order to transmit memory in shining words that shine with truth, words that produce magical effects."[49] While the defining characteristic of the theater is its ability to incorporate everything into its encapsulated memory, the protagonist's ideal image of memory, the "Memory Machine," affords complete control over which memories are saved and when (or if) they are remembered. This machine gives users the option of manipulating their memory however they choose: "Erase it, or encourage it, or awaken dormant memories, or make a file with only the happy moments, now almost forgotten, or place a set of troublesome memories in the machine in order to return to them when they can no longer hurt or humiliate us. The trick was to ask participants how they would treat their memory and what they would ask of the machine."[50] Such a device offers awesome power to those who feel in some way persecuted (or pursued) by memory, for it allows the user to decide when and how memory will be preserved and used. No wild mushrooms grow unbidden in the "Memory Machine," only their civilized counterparts in carefully cultivated beds.

While the protagonist's struggle to contain her interior wilderness echoes Sarmiento's exhortation to tame the interior provinces, a closer comparison of the two characters who share the name Facundo points to the second discourse Valenzuela challenges in *La travesía*: the hierarchical relationship between the body and the mind. The first name of the protagonist's professor links him with the gaucho bandit; nevertheless, his last name, Zuberbühler, suggests German origins and a different type of modern horror. And while Valenzuela's Facundo, like Sarmiento's, is characterized by his unquestionable authority—for example, restricting the protagonist's movements unless he can monitor them: "That was what F[acundo] said, and it was an order"[51]—Zuberbühler ultimately proves very different from Sarmiento's bloodthirsty figure who terrorized the Argentine populace. Sarmiento describes the significance of the red flag planted by Facundo after his victories as "the symbol expressing violence, blood, and barbarism."[52] Facundo Zuberbühler, in contrast, exhibits an absolute disgust with blood, especially that associated with natural processes such as menstruation. His abhorrence runs so deep that rather than share any sexual relations with the virginal protagonist, he exhorts her to find someone else with whom to share this messy experience before returning to him. For the professor, her blood provokes more revulsion than the blood shed in the practices of state terror.

In an ironic twist, despite Facundo's aversion to blood, the novel implies his connection with the military regime. Professor Zuberbühler is described as an all-powerful, shadowy character who is able to move with impunity through the streets of Buenos Aires even during the height of the political violence. The novel illustrates his connections to power implicitly (he provides the protagonist with the "cover story" regarding Juancho's disappearance) as well as explicitly (referring to him as a "victimizer" akin to repressors during the

The Memory of Forgetting

Holocaust).[53] The connection between Facundo and the dictatorship also signals complicity on the part of the female protagonist, for her participation in the "epistolar prostitution" allowed her not only to avoid the political violence but also to profit from the relationship. The anthropologist, like the female victim in *Paso de dos*, must process her intimate connection with a repressor. Viewed allegorically, the protagonist's willful forgetting of her past also implies a reluctance to confront her own complicity in the regime's violence. Although her world travels prevented her from directly witnessing the escalating violence, she remains implicated because of her continued relationship with Facundo; her fieldwork was directly funded by a man linked with the military regime. The past that haunts her thereby represents not only the unwitnessed violent past but also her tacit complicity with the violence. The protagonist's contradictory position of being both connected to and separate from the violence is mirrored by Facundo's paradoxical characterization as implicated in the regime's violent practices yet disgusted by blood.

One must note that Facundo Zuberbühler describes his personal abhorrence for menstrual blood "as if his disgust were universally accepted,"[54] and in this sense he adheres to a larger discourse that regards the woman's body as somehow unclean. As Sherry Ortner explains in her insightful examination of the question "Is Female to Male as Nature Is to Culture?," women are perceived as being more in tune with their bodies because of their reproductive role, and this association with the body adds to women's debased status in society.[55] Susan Griffin also alludes to the negative perception of the female body, in particular the reproductive organs: "At the gate of her womb is a wound which bleeds freely. It is a wound that will never heal. She is mutilated. She is damaged."[56] The professor's generalization of his personal phobia to society at large thus situates his views within an existing paradigm that considers women and the body to occupy a debased position.

So far removed from natural processes, bodily functions, or passions, Zuberbühler appears purely intellectual. Gwendolyn Díaz notes Facundo's lack of corporal desire, contrasting him with another character in the novel, the protagonist's lover Joe: "Her relationship with [Joe] is pure desire, a physical and corporal desire, not made of words (like with Facundo), but of flesh."[57] In fact, the majority of the professor's intimate encounters with the protagonist exist only in the realm of discourse: "Facundo at one end of the room and me in the other, sharing tales of lust without resorting to touch, smell, taste"; in short, "Facundo did not use all five senses, only his hearing."[58] A sharp contrast to Sarmiento's gaucho bandit, dominated by his passions and seemingly unencumbered with rational thought, Professor Zuberbühler is the epitome of Rational Man, unhindered by emotional distractions as he dispassionately listens to the protagonist's tales of her sexual encounters—what they share is literally "oral sex," or, as the protagonist terms it, "Verba, non res."[59]

Facundo's denial of the physical self calls to mind the way the military government during the dictatorship attempted to control the unruly body. Practices of kidnapping, torture, and disappearance demonstrated a widespread attempt to restrict the functioning of individual and collective bodies, and torture in particular aimed to exercise complete domination over an uncooperative or "subversive" body. Elaine Scarry makes evident how torture reduces the victim to pure corporality in *The Body in Pain: The Making and Unmaking of the World*. Emphasizing torture's effects on the victim's body and voice, she asserts, "The goal of the torturer is to make the one, the body, emphatically and crushingly *present* by destroying it, and to make the other, the voice, *absent* by destroying it."[60] The military even employed the metaphor of a diseased body to describe the spread of subversion and to justify the extreme violence.[61] Thus, not only was control over bodies practiced in a literal fashion through the systematic practice of disappearance, but the metaphorical terms in which the military defined their actions centered around control of disorderly organic processes.

The protagonist's attempts to control her wild memory also respond to this mind/body division: somatic memory can only be suppressed through denying the body. For example, during Hurricane Candy, the protagonist attempts to remain cut off from her senses in a futile effort to ignore the internal rumblings of memory. As she listens to a message from Ava on her answering machine (a different type of "Memory Machine"), she literally takes cover from nature and from her life: "I won't look at anything, don't tell me anything else, I don't want to see anything, I'm done with Ava and her silly stories, she tells the machine. And once in bed she covers her head with her feather pillow and tries not to hear the frenzied wind blowing."[62] Unwilling to listen to the wild howling of the wind, she dreams of entering into the eye of the storm, where one finds absolute silence and calm. Akin to her professor's denial of the body, the protagonist's desire to escape from her senses, from nature, and enter into a realm of absolute silence (absence of sensation, of thought, of memory) similarly aims to master the physical self.

The clear hierarchy in Sarmiento's text of culture as superior to nature and the military's discourse that devalues the body reflect the traditional interpretation of nature and the body (especially the female body) as debased concepts. Yet in *La travesía* the protagonist's attempts to tame the wild mushrooms of memory prove useless: her repressed memories of the dictatorship, of Facundo, of the letters, continue to rise unbidden from the depths of her "internal Walden Pond."[63] And in accordance with Thoreau's view of nature as a place for self-discovery and spiritual enlightenment, the protagonist's internal wilderness resists "civilizing" efforts. The somatic memory held in the body refuses subordinance to the mind, and ultimately, Valenzuela's text questions the traditional hierarchy of culture over nature, mind over body. In fact, the body (in particular, the female body) and nature, far from being devalued concepts, represent the key to the protagonist's eventual acknowledgment of her memory and the recuperation of her life. More precisely, the fundamentally ambiguous and nonverbal nature of the organic, feminine wilderness provides the only way to approach an understanding of her traumatic past.

Attempts to dominate her interior wilderness or suppress the somatic imprint of the past prove impossible precisely because the body, nature, and memory are inextricably linked, and even the wild, disturbing, or difficult-to-control elements of the self form a necessary and integral part of one's identity. As Matoso explains, a quick self-examination of one's internal geography exposes a *"strangeness"* within, that hides behind masks and gestures.[64] At one point in *La travesía*, the protagonist recalls an ethnographic informant who claimed he felt "naked" without a mask, prompting the following reflection from the anthropologist: "My body is my mask. I can't take it off, here it is—we are—joined together forever, and forever floundering."[65] The protagonist of *La travesía* lives with this fractured, masked identity in her attempt to suppress her past; on the surface she plays the part of the dispassionate anthropological observer, but inside she carries the hidden identities of secret wife and secret writer of erotic encounters.

The protagonist can only escape the seemingly endless cycle of memories springing forth from inside her body by recognizing and embracing, rather than ignoring or suppressing, her internal wild nature. Matoso emphasizes that the ultimate goal is not to rid oneself of the stranger within, for "strangeness is inherent to human nature," and that in ridding the self of one unfamiliar element, one only risks revealing another: "Beneath each mask is another mask. . . . By unmasking one strangeness I find another and another and another."[66] In the case of *La travesía*, Díaz draws a comparison between the protagonist's fractured identity and the collages of the Dadaist painter and sculptor Kurt Schwitters invoked at various points during the novel, arguing that the protagonist must recognize and embrace her dark past to reincorporate herself as a whole person.[67] Taking this idea a step further, this fractured, wild, uncontrollable nature proves powerful precisely *because of* its fractured, wild, uncontrollable nature—*La travesía* emphasizes the impossibility of truly dominating or fully understanding the strangeness within. Acceptance *without* full understanding is key to working through traumatic memory.

La travesía hails the body as the source of knowledge and memory, exemplified by the final letter the protagonist wrote to Facundo but never sent.

Reminiscent of the thesis she wrote for her professor, "Blood rituals," which examined beliefs held by different cultures regarding the purity or impurity of the onset of menarche, the letter relates a tale of pleasure in which the central character's menstrual blood plays an integral role in an erotic ritual. Far from being a source of disgust for her lover(s), in this tale the blood that flows from her womb embodies life—"For us, women's blood sows the seeds," explains one of the participants in the ritual.[68] The blood that represents creation originates in the female body, and the letter serves to break down the dualism that debases women for their relationship to the body.[69] Far from a damaged, wounded object in need of control or domination, the female body is celebrated as a source of erotic pleasure in all its messy glory, and the protagonist's appreciation of the final letter's poetic value represents her acceptance of her suppressed identity and desires.[70]

The protagonist's acceptance of *the strangeness* that lives inside her proves essential to her recovery, as does the recognition that her interior wilderness will not and should not be tamed. For the ultimate goal is not to dominate or master disturbing emotions but to acknowledge them and arrive at a point where, echoing Paul van Zyl, the executive secretary for the Truth and Reconciliation Commission in South Africa, "the past won't haunt you on its own terms, rather than your own."[71] The protagonist repeatedly finds herself caught in a position where her unconscious internal wilderness refuses to bow to the "civilizing" influence of her conscious mind; she can only move forward by finally passing through this figurative and literal wilderness in all its untamed, ambiguous essence. It seems no accident that her cathartic moment in the novel comes while visiting her sculptor friend, Raquel Rabinovich, in upstate New York. The artist's work in this natural space—rocks emerging from the earth, moving between the visible and invisible world—is an ideal metaphor for the processes the protagonist has been experiencing throughout the novel. The protagonist too has been moving between these two worlds, the visible world of her conscious thoughts—attempts to keep her past locked away, safe, forgotten—and the unconscious organic reactions in her body inspired by the memory of Facundo, the letters, and her country's bloody past.

Paradoxically, the invisible world of her interior wilderness—the zone of her memories that she is almost unable to approach, let alone understand—serves to enlighten rather than blind her. This type of knowledge resists the "civilizing" influences of language, and the protagonist is only able to approach an understanding of her past when she removes herself from the "civilizing" influences of New York City and encounters two indigenous characters, Rain Deer and Ida. While Sarmiento condemns the indigenous population of Argentina as part of the barbarous wilderness in need of domination, Rain Deer's and Ida's connections with nature are precisely what allow them to understand both the visible and invisible worlds. Rain Deer explains the indigenous way of looking at the world, which provides a key to the protagonist's journey of self-discovery: "You have to look twice, he told her, once straight on and once out of the corner of your eye, to see the perfectly defined world of clarity and the world of elusive shadows."[72] Outside the confines of the city, the protagonist becomes more attuned to this sideways manner of seeing. Rather than immediately trying to contain and control the shadows of this indirect vision, she is able to accept what it might reveal. Such indirect vision proves partial and ambiguous, but its refusal to be controlled is precisely what grants it such power of insight.

This different way of seeing responds to a natural, rather than artificial, order of things, and it affects her interactions with Rain Deer and Ida. Unable to render the poetic manner in which the indigenous man expresses himself, she comments that his words are "impossible to reproduce." Gone is the academic observer whose role is to duplicate the words verbatim and "strip them of their essence."[73] She has entered into a different way of seeing, understanding now that she must accept all her thoughts: "Join together her doubts, stack them up and try to make herself comfortable within them, as if in a nest. See the world two times. Simultaneously."[74] Without the need to suppress her thoughts, doubts can enter unbidden into her mind, like the wild mushrooms creeping through the interstices of her brain, and the protagonist takes the next essential step toward recognizing her internal wilderness: moving through an external one.

Resolved to stop running away from the past that pursues her relentlessly, the protagonist "decides for the first time to enter into the zone of the forest where there are no paths or signposts."[75] No longer following the paths of others, she begins hiking through the woods on her own, well aware that there are no trails to follow even if she should so desire. Setting her own course, she attempts to return to the place where she started, yet she only manages to lose herself deeper in the forest. A return to her previous state proves impossible (this journey, like the woman who inspired it, is an "Ida" rather than a "Vuelta"), and any hope of following others is also lost, for even the footprints lead her astray. Exhausted by hiking and the panic that begins to set in as the sun goes down and she cannot find her way, she finally decides to simply sit down and think, recognizing her own vulnerability that she has struggled to avoid for so many years. In the climactic moment when she realizes her true nature, the narration changes from third to first person, a shift that reflects the protagonist's movement from observer to participant. As her world shrinks around her, leaving everything exterior behind, she meditates: "I begin to make out numerous eyes all around me in the dim shadows of my interior forest. . . . They are animals completely made of eyes, of mouths salivating with hunger for me." These animal eyes that seem to penetrate her allow her to arrive at a great realization: "I've traveled the world so afraid that those who love me want to devour me, now I need to let myself be devoured by these beings who want to devour me."[76] Determined to give herself up to these ravenous beings, to allow the events that have been pursuing her for so many years to catch her at last, she admits, "That's who I am. A simple beating heart, without a single mask."[77] Finally able to free herself of the burden of so many unacknowledged masks in her interior geography, she is able to break free of the forest as well.

Stripped of the external masks that concealed her internal turmoil, she breaks the overt silences regarding her personal history and allows the covert ones to surface, admitting her secret marriage to her friends and resolving to finally return to Buenos Aires and confront her past. Moving across the *travesía* of her internal wilderness, the protagonist finally acknowledges the secrets that haunted her; through this recognition comes liberation from the secret's power. Furthermore, acceptance of the strangeness of her interior wilderness allows her to fully embrace her identity, which is finally revealed: Marcela Osorio. Oso. Río. Mar. Even her name embodies the natural world, no longer the debased half of an outmoded dichotomy but a personal path to remembrance and the recuperation of her identity.[78]

Although the novel charts a movement from silence to speech, repression to articulation, the mode of expression remains rooted in a world of mystery and silence. The knowledge gained is always sideways and imperfect: both interior and external wilderness ask not for mastery or full understanding but an acknowledgment of its essential impenetrable nature. *La travesía* exemplifies this fundamental ambiguity primarily through its treatment of silence and secrets as central themes of the book, which resist yet invite discovery in a maddening paradox. As her friend Rachel tries to explain when recounting a dream, "I understood. I don't know what, but I understood."[79] But while the protagonist and others note the inherent unreliability of language, the novel itself exhibits a characteristic writing style that calls attention to the limitations of language and implies that its absence can be eloquent in itself. Examples abound in the text when thoughts and sentences are simply left unfinished. For example, when considering her preference for cultivated versus wild mushrooms, the protagonist begins, "It's just that . . ."; much later, when lost in the woods, she muses, "I don't want anybody to come near me, not a bear, nor a fawn, nor an enchanted prince nor."[80] While the use of ellipses invites the reader to continue the unfinished thought, their lack calls attention to the impossibility of completing certain lines of thinking. Both techniques serve to draw the reader into the text; faced with an unfinished sentence, the reader is encouraged to fill the silence with words. Finally, a section titled "***********," and a moment when the words seem to cascade down the page like a poem also foreground the blank spaces in the text, thereby giving them weight and meaning. Yet the weight and meaning are ultimately determined by the reader, demonstrating again the ambiguity of silent expression.

Conclusion

At one point in the novel, the protagonist states, "The vacuum is intolerable and calls out to be filled,"[81] and ultimately *La travesía* shows how secrets, their counterpart lies, and repressed memories are, like the vacuum, intolerable. Attempts to artificially silence memories of unwitnessed trauma and unacknowledged complicity that throb beneath the surface fall short because of their somatic nature—held inside the body, they travel along internal pathways in search of expression. Yet such expression remains difficult to access and hard to comprehend. Rather than force the memories of trauma into comprehensible (but insufficient) dichotomies—speech versus silence, memory versus forgetting, civilization versus barbarism, mind versus body— *La travesía* indicates that the essence of trauma lies in the ambiguous and ill-defined zone of somatic knowledge, whose expression remains unruly and whose reception requires an oblique mode of seeing. Like the wild mushrooms that grow outside the boundaries of neatly cultivated beds, unacknowledged trauma (be it witnessed or experienced) spreads organically through the body in affirmation of the intimate relation between mind and body and the power of silent expression. While human rights groups such as H.I.J.O.S. struggle "against silence," *La travesía* demonstrates how the silences entwined in forgetting past violence do not bury the past under layers of oblivion but rather embody the making of memory itself.

6

Fallout of the Memory "Boom"

Seeing and Not-Seeing the Ex-ESMA in Jonathan Perel's *El predio*

n his inaugural speech to the General Assembly of the United Nations in September 2003, President Néstor Kirchner changed the tenor of official discourse regarding the dictatorship by declaring, "The defense of human rights occupies a central place in the new agenda of the Argentine Republic. *We are the sons and daughters of the Mothers and Grandmothers of the Plaza de Mayo.*"[1] By allying himself (and Argentines in general) with those who were victimized by state terrorism, Kirchner publicly declared the government's commitment to pursuing justice and working against past impunity, having matched words with actions by working to overturn the Amnesty Laws a mere eighty-nine days into his tenure as president.[2] The year 2003 ushered in an era of "Kirchnerism," marked by increased efforts to redress past human rights abuses as well as a fusion between "official" discourse and that of human rights. If the memory boom of the mid-1990s prompted a public discussion regarding the military's abuses that extended beyond human rights groups to the broader society, the Kirchner era brought the past horror to the symbolic center of the nation through overt displays of memory work and renewed trials of perpetrators.[3]

The cooperation between the government and human rights organizations took center stage with the decision to transform the notorious former clandestine detention center at the Navy Mechanics School, or ESMA, into the Space for Memory and for the Promotion and Defense of Human Rights. At the ceremony marking the transfer of the space from the military to the city of Buenos Aires on March 24, 2004, Kirchner gave a memorable address. Identifying himself as a "compañero" of those who lived through the dictatorship years but speaking as the nation's leader, President Kirchner asked forgiveness on behalf of the state for "the shame of having been silent during twenty years of democracy regarding so many atrocities."[4] Kirchner's condemnation of the official silence surrounding the dictatorship reiterated the governmental will to facilitate an open reckoning with the military's practices of violence and disappearance, and he repeatedly demonstrated his administration's commitment to truth, justice, and memory through symbolic and concrete measures designed to promote remembrance of the recent past.[5] While highly visible public displays of solidarity with human rights organizations undoubtedly facilitate a national conversation regarding the dictatorship, the use of memory initiatives for political expediency can also lead to an oversaturation of memory discourse that threatens to diminish or dilute the meaning of the initiatives.[6] The "marketing" of memory is one of the hallmarks of the Kirchner era, exemplified by initiatives such as the symbolic establishment of the Space for Memory in the ex-ESMA, yet an excess of memory discourse—the fallout of the memory boom—may mute rather than sharpen an understanding of former sites of atrocity.[7]

The preservation of the ESMA and its transformation into the Space for Memory reflects a desire to maintain a space associated with past trauma as evidence of past crimes. The massive scale of violence at the ESMA, as well as the sheer size of the grounds, makes it one of the most visible signs of past atrocity in the urban landscape of Buenos Aires. Its power as a symbol of the dictatorship years remains undisputed, and survivor testimonies, evidence presented at the ESMA "Mega-Trial," and initiatives by the Mothers and Grandmothers attest to the crimes committed at the site. Yet despite the desire of many in the human rights community that the current memorial space "voice" its past crimes, in a context of an excess of human rights discourse and "marketing" of memory, the ex-ESMA proves resistant to any authoritative interpretation of the past, as demonstrated in Jonathan Perel's 2010 documentary film *El predio* (The site).

The documentary is striking in its approach: rather than film the well-known spaces associated with the location—the iconic four-columned building that has come to stand for terror and disappearance, the Officer's Quarters where prisoners were held and tortured—it focuses in intricate detail on the various indoor and outdoor spaces that comprise the grounds of the ex-ESMA. Describing his film as an attempt to narrate "from within the silence and emptiness,"[8] Perel eschews voice-over or music, opting instead for long, still shots of selected scenes of the ex-ESMA, ranging from material items such as broken tiles and discarded toilets to human activities such as artistic interventions and film screenings. Given that the voices of the vast majority of victims who passed through the clandestine detention center are absent, and the discourse of human rights groups who lay claim to the site has proved contradictory and polemical, Perel uses a visual language of images, presumably to allow the physical space to "speak for itself." When the voices themselves have been silenced, and those that remain speak in a cacophonous debate, stripping away the dialogue can serve to "voice" the crimes of the past, for images can speak as eloquently as words. Nevertheless, rather than reveal the hidden story of trauma by means of a visual mode of expression, *El predio* demonstrates the impossibility of ever arriving at a definitive interpretation of the site through either voice or image. By rejecting a traditional documentary narrative of the site—one more authoritative voice laying claim to the ex-ESMA's story—Perel calls attention to the fallout of the memory boom, responding to an excess of memory discourse with a deliberate language of silence.

During the dictatorship years and the early 1990s, official practice served to impede the witnessing and processing of atrocity. Throughout the years of state terror, percepticide—Diana Taylor's term for the phenomenon of seeing without witnessing—prevented spectators from looking carefully at the violence that surrounded them;[9] later administrative measures such as the Amnesty Laws similarly served to close down public discussion of past horror. By using a carefully constructed visual language of silence, Perel's documentary forces the spectator to look carefully at this particular site of past horror. Yet paradoxically, although Perel's manipulation of the camera's gaze obliges the viewer to look at the site in a different and unexpected way, he or she remains unable to see. The willful blindness of percepticide (spectators who choose not to look) is therefore mirrored by an unwilled blindness (viewers who look but cannot see). By reproducing the unsettling effects of percepticide through his visual language—separating seeing from witnessing or understanding—Perel emphasizes the difficulty of actually "seeing" the site. *El predio* suggests that despite (or paradoxically, because of) a heightened awareness of issues of memory and truth, it remains impossible to "see" the ex-ESMA clearly, because sites of past atrocity cannot "speak for themselves."

Documenting Historical Reality: The Challenges of the ex-ESMA

Perel's documentary engages with the lived reality of this former detention center turned Space for Memory, a site with a long and complicated history. Originally slated for demolition, the seventeen-hectare ESMA site was transferred from the military to the city of Buenos Aires in 2004, prompting a debate regarding the future of the space.[10] Only one of the numerous buildings, the Officer's Quarters, was used for the execution of tasks related to the repressive regime, leaving many questions as to the most appropriate use of the site as a whole. Many human rights groups submitted proposals, ranging from strictly preservationist (maintaining the site exactly as it was) to transformative (converting a space associated with death to one that invited life, laughter, and growth).[11] A cacophony of voices participated in the debate, and the end result reflects this diversity of opinions. The Officer's Quarters have been preserved, particularly for their evidentiary nature, as the building stands as material proof of the junta's policies of torture, disappearance, and murder.[12] Meanwhile, other edifices have been converted into cultural centers, archives, and headquarters for various human rights groups. On any given day a visitor can peruse an art exhibit or attend a film screening; during the school break in July, both cultural centers sponsor children's activities ranging from musical performances to puppet shows. Such diverse uses attest to the multiplicity of meaning present in the current site, as well as the difficulty of "documenting" the ex-ESMA.

As a "discourse of the real," documentary film—like testimonial narrative—seeks to describe and interpret historical reality.[13] Documentary serves as "evidence" in two senses of the word: evidence as proof (used to demonstrate a particular claim) and evidence as trace (what is left behind).[14] Perel's choice of subject matter fits perfectly into this broader testimonial project: by seeking to document the ex-ESMA, a place that has generated despair and debate, *El predio* presents the viewer with evidence of the space (both as trace and as proof). Yet although *El predio* documents the site in a literal sense, the film challenges the viewer's ability to "see" the ex-ESMA in any meaningful manner, highlighting the way in which official memory initiatives can frustrate rather than facilitate an understanding of past atrocity.[15]

Despite the multiple voices clamoring for attention in the ex-ESMA, Perel's documentary eliminates them from his presentation, which suggests a lack of "informing logic" or central argument.[16] *El predio* is comprised of a series of thirty-second shots with a still camera, each revealing one particular place in the ESMA grounds: a broken window, a file cabinet, a woman singing tango on a movie screen, a conference panel, a woman planting potatoes, a drawing on a wall. The film does not immediately reveal an order or logic; rather, it falls to the viewer to attempt to put together the pieces and discover an order in the apparent chaos, an important point to which I will return later. The sound track—solely ambient sounds, with no voice-over or music—also reveals the absence of an informing logic. There is no "voice of God" narration in *El predio* to explain the images of the buildings and grounds that appear before the viewer. No music, either threatening or calming, serves to guide the viewer's emotion. Given that the sound track traditionally expresses the abstract argument and reveals the organizational principles of the documentary,[17] by eschewing any type of voice-over, Perel to a certain extent eliminates any abstract argument from his film.[18]

The absence of a central argument exposes the challenges of representing this highly charged historical space. As evidenced by the multiple voices engaged in the debate over what to do with the space, the "true" story the ESMA should tell proves both elusive and polarizing.[19] As Michael J. Lazzara has noted regarding the Villa Grimaldi detention center in Chile, such sites of memory gain meaning through the narratives given by different subjects (such as guides, visitors, or authors). In particular, the amount of narrative "closure" provided can serve to honor or ignore the fundamental ambiguities of memories grounded in ruins and absences.[20] As if reluctant to provide any type of narrative closure, *El predio* refuses to overtly add another authoritative voice to the debate, and in this sense it appears Perel is attempting to maintain some type of "neutrality" in a space that is decidedly not "neutral." In fact, the filmmaker has stated that he does not pertain to any human rights organization and that the film's purpose is to provide "a different view of how memory is constructed" as well as to encourage "more social actors to participate in the debate, so it doesn't remain restricted to human rights organizations."[21] Perel directly challenges the assumption that the human rights community has some type of special claim to the ex-ESMA. On the one hand, this may indicate an invitation for all Argentines to take part in the difficult memory work of reckoning with a violent history; on the other, implying that all voices have an equal claim ignores past imbalances of power (the historical silencing of certain groups) and may devalue to a certain extent the authority of victims of violence.[22] The filmmaker's lack of overt position can also be viewed as a response to the overuse of memory discourse: his attempt to distance himself from any existing positions regarding the ex-ESMA could be a criticism of how social actors invoke memory and human rights for political gain. Nevertheless, Perel's choice to "be silent" regarding a particular position, rather than silence the debate itself, serves to call attention to the underlying tension.[23]

But the lack of overt politics does not necessarily signify objectivity on the part of the filmmaker. Perel himself characterizes his work as "strongly political," although not in the sense of advocating a particular position. Rather, he gives the spectator the responsibility to assign or create meaning from the images presented, selected for their capacity to "make us reflect or think."[24] Keenly aware of how the world is constructed by competing discourses, Perel creates a cinematic vision that uses images geared to provoke discussion and debate while maintaining an appearance of objectivity by avoiding any direct commentary regarding his documentary subject. In *El predio*, his unstated yet implied position advocates an active creation of memory—invoking the viewer directly in its construction. Although not an "objective" look at the ex-ESMA, *El predio* challenges traditional representations of the politically charged site.

Perel's intent to create a "different view of how memory is constructed" aligns with Alison Landsberg's idea that cultural memories do not pertain to any particular group. According to Landsberg, the means of mass culture, such as cinema or experiential museums, can allow individuals to take on "prosthetic memories," whereby they experience or feel memories that do not pertain to their lived experience. Landsberg rejects the notion of identity politics, in which a group lays claim to a particular memory (such as the memory of the Holocaust as pertaining exclusively to the Jews); rather, her idea of prosthetic memory allows for the transmission of memory between individuals who do not share the same historical, ethnic, or social context. In her words, "This form of memory thus challenges, or works against, the naturalizing, essentialist tendencies of identity politics."[25] Perel's call to open up the interpretation of the ex-ESMA to those not "naturally" associated with sites of past atrocity speaks to his desire to transmit memory to a broader segment of society. Furthermore, his choice of a filmic representation of the site indicates that his documentary has the potential to allow viewers to take on "prosthetic memories" about the former clandestine detention center, even if they have not visited the site in person.[26]

The lack of authoritative voice in the documentary film and the absence of an expected human rights discourse can also be viewed as a way to call attention to the literal lack of voices of the victims. Of the five thousand prisoners who passed through the ESMA, it is estimated that around two hundred survived.[27] The majority of the people affected by the repressive mechanism that operated in the ESMA cannot lend their voices to the conversation, and any attempt to speak for them is fraught with challenges (as seen in chapter 2).[28] The silencing of voices traditionally associated with human rights (the Mothers or Grandmothers, the survivors) signals the absence of the voices of the disappeared victims. Rather than provide a "substitute narrative" to tell the tale, *El predio* highlights the absence of those who can authoritatively speak about the site. Furthermore, by "disappearing" the voices usually present in discussions of memory sites, Perel places all voices surrounding the ex-ESMA on equal footing, opening up the discussion to a broader segment of society and paradoxically highlighting the societal excess of human rights discourse through its notable absence in the film.[29]

Not only does *El predio* avoid any type of voice-over, but it also eschews another main convention of documentary film: interviews. Although people are present in the film, they do not figure prominently as speaking subjects. Perel admits: "In the editing I left out the moments where words were very present. . . . The words were left out so that only the images would speak."[30] In fact, the only words included in the documentary are signs, captions, and plaques as well as diegetic sounds of conversations or presentations. Such emphasis on a language of the visual underscores the lack of speaking subjects— both the past victims as well as the present voices involved in discussions regarding the use of the space—and it also indicates that the visual language will be more effective in "documenting" the ex-ESMA.

Speaking through Silence: The Language of Images

At first glance, a visual medium would seem to be an appropriate mode to express the inexpressible horror of a former clandestine detention center, as images also serve as "proof" and "trace" of the past. In his classic study of photography, *Camera Lucida*, Roland Barthes speaks to this relationship between words, images, and reality, emphasizing that image is more concrete than language. As Barthes explains, while an image serves as incontrovertible proof of something's (or someone's) existence, language remains more abstract.[31] By their very nature, images automatically prove their authenticity, yet "it is the misfortune . . . of language not to be able to authenticate itself."[32] Perel's choice to downplay the verbal in favor of the visual would therefore seem to respond to a desire to document the ex-ESMA more concretely. Nevertheless, the filmmaker's construction of a particular gaze, rather than allow the viewer to more completely comprehend the essence of the site, serves to highlight its fundamental inaccessibility and opaqueness and to emphasize that seeing does not necessarily translate to understanding.

El predio demonstrates a very particular and constructed gaze from the beginning. After an opening minute of black screen (a moment of silence), the scene shifts to the only shots in the entire documentary with the camera in motion. Filmed from a vehicle moving slowly down the various streets in the grounds of the ex-ESMA, the camera looks straight ahead, while the audio registers the diegetic sounds of the space itself (birdsong, distant voices, the sounds of construction). Rather than provide an establishing shot—a view of the grounds from above, a shot of entering the gate—the camera's perspective immediately transports the viewer to the interior of the site. The car never

turns, nor does it arrive at the end of a street, creating the impression of relentlessly always approaching, yet never arriving. This opening scene also finds an
eerie echo in Claude Lanzmann's well-known documentary film *Shoah*, which
uses a similar "phantom ride" shot along the train tracks leading into Auschwitz as a way to align the viewer's perspective with that of the Jews as they
arrived at the concentration camp.[33] In *El predio*, however, the phantom ride
does not mimic the arrival of the hooded prisoners but rather brings the viewer
into the space, yet without a clear point of arrival. Akin to the pebble falling
down the bottomless well, this visual moving in place prepares the viewer for
frustrated expectations. Questions abound, and perhaps a search for answers,
but the answers themselves prove elusive (or nonexistent). No obvious connection exists between one location and the next: each street looks similar to
the one before, but the shots offer no hint of how—or if—the streets connect.
After around three minutes of fragmented movement, the title of the documentary appears on the screen, in simple white letters on a black background:
El predio. Even the title conceals as much as it reveals, with no direct mention
of the ESMA or reference to the dictatorship. From the beginning, Perel's specific visual language challenges the viewer's expectations regarding the space
itself (and a documentary film about the space).

But who are the viewers whose expectations are being challenged? The lack
of direct information regarding the dictatorship appears to indicate a target
audience of viewers well informed regarding the historical context of the years
of state terrorism and the operation of the ESMA as a clandestine detention
center. Although it premiered at the 2010 Buenos Aires International Festival of
Independent Cinema, a large venue that attracts thousands of attendees, it was
billed explicitly as a film about the ESMA, an indication perhaps of the particular public it expected to attract. Yet Perel was surprised by the film's capacity to speak to a broad audience; the viewers' reaction at the festival prompted
him to observe, "It was a film for a much wider audience than I had originally
imagined. I thought it was a very difficult film to watch, and it turned out it had
the power to reach and question a much wider audience than I expected."[34] For
audience members already familiar with the history of the site, *El predio* serves
to challenge preconceived notions or assumptions regarding the ex-ESMA,
yet for others, such as a younger generation of viewers who may not have a
deep or nuanced understanding of the dictatorship, it can serve as an introduction to the topic without the overt presence of the social actors normally
associated with the transmission of memory, such as human rights organizations. Perel commented that the film inspired the audience to "question what
had happened in [the ESMA]," a testament to its ability to provoke discussion
and debate about history and historical memory.[35] For all viewers, the film

offers a profoundly unsettling experience, ideal for the transmission of a prosthetic memory regarding a time period the spectators may or may not have experienced.

After the somewhat disorienting opening sequence, the remainder of the film consists of a series of uncomfortably long takes (each one lasts around thirty seconds), shot with a still camera, of a particular detail in the ex-ESMA.[36] Scenes chosen from various areas of the site appear juxtaposed for affective rather than intellectual impact—a shot of a man drawing on a wall is followed by people hoeing the ground, then a DVD player with a blinking red light, for example—yet in each case the camera does not move. The stillness of the shots seems surprising, given the choice of medium. After all, one fundamental difference between photography and film resides in film's capacity for movement. This may explain why documentary films that rely heavily on photographic evidence add dynamism to shots by panning across or focusing in on certain elements of a photo, the "Ken Burns" effect, named after the filmmaker who developed this particular technique.[37] Yet Perel seems to employ what might be termed an "anti–Ken Burns effect"; rather than "animate" a still image, he appears to be "deanimating" a dynamic one with his choice of a still camera with no zoom or panning. The viewer is thereby forced to look at an image, object, activity, or space for a rather long time; by silencing any type of informing logic, the burden is on the spectator to make meaning.[38] The stillness of the *gaze* forces the spectator to *look*, in an effort to penetrate the meaning of the site.[39]

But the static shot also serves to unsettle the viewer and facilitate the creation of a prosthetic memory. As Pamela Colombo notes, the combination of long, still takes "is a peculiar and effective technique of disturbance, a technique for making the space itself discomfort the spectator."[40] The creation of a feeling of discomfort represents one way the documentary seeks to transmit the disorientation of the times of the dictatorship and the disquieting power of the former detention center.[41] Just as spectators who witnessed people being taken from their homes or workplaces were discomforted by their inability to witness the violence, viewers of *El predio* are unsettled by their inability to "see" the space, even while being forced to look. The intensity and duration of the camera's gaze hinders rather than facilitates an understanding of the space, and in this manner, the viewers take on (albeit partially and unsatisfactorily) part of the burden of those who were unable to connect seeing with witnessing (or knowing).[42]

Interestingly enough, the discomfort does not arise from the graphic nature of the images presented in the documentary. As opposed to a documentary such as Alain Resnais's *Night and Fog*, for example, which shocks viewers into silence with its graphic images of bulldozers pushing emaciated bodies into mass graves, *El predio* offers images of ordinary objects and events. If the perverted success of the dictatorship was its ability to make something that should be atypical (violence and atrocity) appear normal, Perel's film demonstrates how the physical evidence of such atrocity—which ought to demonstrate signs of its atypicality—appears somewhat ordinary, a fact that is profoundly unsettling. This tension arises in the contrast between what Barthes has termed the denotative (literal or descriptive) and connotative (socially constructed) meanings of an image.[43] The denotative meanings of many of the images in the documentary border on the banal: a pile of roof tiles, a collection of potatoes, people sitting in chairs. Yet the connotative meanings—"These are all part of the ex-ESMA!," "They should be somehow sinister," or "They must *mean* something"—create a tension between the ordinary and extraordinary. By calling attention to the apparent ordinariness of the site itself, Perel demonstrates both the banality of evil and the inability to "see" the past atrocity, for it remains buried under a façade of everyday existence.

Expression Through Defamiliarization

Although Perel claims to let the images of the site "speak for themselves," throughout the documentary he employs techniques of defamiliarization that prevent the images from speaking clearly, thereby calling attention to the impossibility of fully comprehending the ex-ESMA. Perel's visual language seeks to "make strange" the viewer's perception of the space in four ways: the attention to aesthetics (the role of beauty in a space associated with ugliness), the treatment of iconic images related to the dictatorship, the creation of frustrated expectations regarding any type of resolution, and the interplay between speech and silence. These techniques of defamiliarization all serve to emphasize the elusive or unstable meaning of this particular site of historical horror and the concurrent inability to present a univocal interpretation of the past.

The series of shots that comprise *El predio* reveal a strong aesthetic sensibility. By forcing the viewer to consider the role of beauty in a site associated with past atrocity, the documentary succeeds in "making strange" the site of the ex-ESMA. Careful framing and attention to lighting in certain shots is complemented by a juxtaposition of aural and visual elements that create a somewhat uncanny feeling. For example, sonorous bird song accompanies many of the outdoor shots, starting with the opening takes that move the viewer through the streets. A stark contrast from the noisy urban setting of Buenos Aires, the sound of the birds prompts a dissonance between denotative and connotative meaning—can or should there be beauty in the ex-ESMA?—discomforting the viewer from the beginning of the documentary. The aural beauty of the bird-song is echoed in some visually stunning shots of the buildings and grounds, where ruins and remains are rendered beautiful through careful framing and attention to lighting. One striking example comes early in the film, when the camera shows the interior of a bathroom or kitchen area. Piles of debris lie on the floor, yet the light filtering in through the window bathes the scene in a warm glow, almost like a still life of broken bricks. The additional contrast between the visual beauty and aural dissonance—in this case, the pounding sounds of construction—help to reveal a tension between a current, constructed loveliness in a space whose history speaks of base ugliness.

The many contrasts in *El predio* (lovely birdsong juxtaposed with scenes of construction; gorgeous lighting juxtaposed with jarring sounds of hammering) emphasize the dissonance of the site itself—Is it beautiful? Is it *supposed to be* beautiful?—yet an attention to aesthetics risks downplaying the important historical reality a documentary film purports to share. Perel's use of individual shots arranged for affective impact situates the film in the poetic rather than expository mode of documentary filmmaking.[44] Rather than explain the images presented and their significance with voice-over commentary, the poetic mode tells its story through the association of images. In so doing, it may call attention to the form of the film itself, rather than the historical referent.[45] Attention to aesthetics has often been seen as anathema to historical reality, for as Hans Richter has observed regarding the evolution of documentary film, "It became clear that a fact did not really remain a 'fact' if it appeared in too beautiful a light. . . . A 'beautiful' image could not normally be obtained *except at the expense of its closeness to reality*."[46] In the case of *El predio*, the "facts" of the space itself appear, at times, beautiful: does this indicate a distancing from the "reality" of the space?

Rather than distance the viewer from reality, I argue that the highly stylized presentation of *El predio* forces the viewer to notice the "strangeness" of referentiality itself, as in some moments the viewer is hard pressed to identify the image projected on the screen. This can be seen as a rejection of any type of authoritative discourse on the ex-ESMA, but it also risks releasing the historical referent from the film—a focus on form at the expense of content. One expects a documentary film about the ex-ESMA to demonstrate some engagement with the lived reality of the space itself; if the space is made unrecognizable or the viewer is forced to focus too much on form, the film risks communicating nothing about the site, which appears to be precisely the point of *El predio*: to document the "undocumentability" of the former site of atrocity. By compelling the viewer to note the inaccessible nature of the ex-ESMA, the documentary facilitates the viewer's understanding of the incomprehensibility of violence.

The unsettling effect of Perel's aesthetic gaze extends to his treatment of several "iconic" images related to the dictatorship. At no time during the film does the viewer see a shot of the four-columned building that has served as the face of atrocity at this particular site, nor does Perel include any shots of the Officer's Quarters, the actual site of torture. Perel explains his decision not to include the images usually associated with ESMA as part of his attempt to construct a different type of memory of the space. According to the film-maker, the images of the four-columned building or the Officer's Quarters "are images *that appear to have lost their capacity to generate debate or reflection.* I was looking for a new point of view that was a catalyst for discussions and interpretations."[47] The idea of an image losing its capacity to generate debate or reflection aligns with Marianne Hirsch's thoughts on the "iconic" nature of images of the Holocaust. In her seminal article "Surviving Images: Holocaust Photographs and the Work of Postmemory," Hirsch posits that iconic images of trauma risk either retraumatizing viewers or becoming clichéd and losing their emotive impact. Ubiquitous Holocaust images such as the entrance gate of Auschwitz, the guard towers, the bulldozers moving bodies, and the sur-vivors being liberated serve as "icons" and "have come to function as tropes for Holocaust memory itself."[48] At issue is the ability of an iconic image to repre-sent the referent of trauma, and Perel's choice to avoid any visual reference to the images associated with ESMA can be interpreted as an attempt to sidestep the thorny relationship between iconic image and historical referent.[49]

Nevertheless, while *El predio* avoids any visual reference to the iconic images related to the physical space of the ESMA, it does incorporate other iconic images related to the victims. About halfway through the documentary, the viewer sees a familiar sight: four headscarves of the Madres de Plaza de Mayo. The image of a group of mothers wearing headscarves provides an immedi-ately recognizable visual reference to disappearance and the search for justice. Toward the end of the film, another anticipated group of images appears: the photos of the disappeared. Several shots register a collection of photos hanging in a window as part of an exhibit. Displayed in vertical arrangement as moving mobiles, the photographs of the faces slowly turn in front of the camera, re-vealing the black-and-white images of the disappeared.

Despite this inclusion of iconic images of disappearance, *El predio* seeks to question or mediate the images themselves in order to emphasize their inabil-ity to communicate. The shots of the Mothers and the photos of the disap-peared are filmed in such a way as to force the viewer to consider them anew.

For example, the single shot in *El predio* of the Mothers portrays them in such as a way as to make this familiar image somewhat strange. Filmed against a dark background, the scarves stand out in stark contrast, and as the Mothers lean in to converse with each other, it almost appears as if they are floating in space. The visually striking image is at one and the same time immediately recognizable as the Mothers and somewhat disquieting as the viewer struggles to make sense of how the women occupy the space of the shot.[50]

The photos of the disappeared are also rendered strange through this technique of defamiliarization. The photos, like the Mothers, comprise ubiquitous, recognizable elements in the human rights discourse. Usually seen as part of a series (on banners or placards), *El predio* upholds one expectation surrounding the images by showing them grouped together as part of an art installation. Yet Perel's choice of shot again makes even these oft-viewed images somewhat strange and disconcerting. Three consecutive shots show the hanging photos gently rotating, the movement of the images contrasting with the still camera shot. Filmed from the outside through a glass window, at times partially obscured by large leaves, the viewer sees the images from the outside, as if to emphasize the distance between the victims and the viewer, as well as the impossibility of ever accessing their true experience—the photos remain remote and distant. Noisy bird song and other ambient sounds provide the

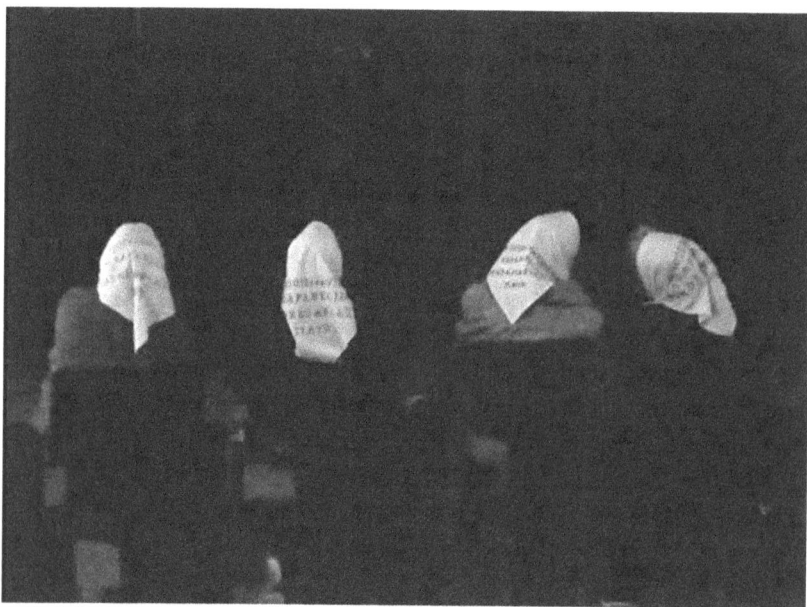

Mothers of the Plaza de Mayo attend an event at the ex-ESMA. (*El predio*)

Fallout of the Memory "Boom"

background noise for these particular images, making the next shot even more striking in its silence. This time the camera is looking from the inside of a building, through the glass, at the natural world outside, and the sounds are almost completely muted. The contrast in soundscape proves striking, as does the haunting possibility that this particular shot might represent the impossible gaze of the photos themselves looking out. The documentary does not make use of the shot/reverse-shot sequence during the rest of the film, but the striking juxtaposition of the photos of the disappeared (from the outside looking in) with a subsequent shot of the world outside the buildings (from the inside looking out) perhaps implies an attempt to access the inaccessible perspective of the victims themselves.[51]

On the one hand, situating the viewer in the position of the victims of violence—to the extent possible—may facilitate the creation of a prosthetic memory. Yet on the other hand, the sequence of shots around these particular images of disappearance suggest an impossibility of approaching the victims of violence, both on the part of the viewer (whose access is mediated by glass) and the victims themselves (whose voices are muted by such mediation).[52] Again, Perel renders this iconic image of disappearance disquieting and strange. Unable to process the images of the Mothers and victims in an unthinking

Photos of the disappeared displayed at the ex-ESMA, shot from the outside looking in. (*El predio*)

View from the inside looking out onto the grounds of the ex-ESMA. (*El predio*)

manner, the viewer must contemplate these iconic visual representations in a new fashion. Nevertheless, the essence, truth, or meaning of the images remains obscure. As viewers, we *look*, but the *gaze*, rather than providing illumination, makes it harder to *see*. The desire to look carefully at the signs of past violence emphasizes the inherent instability of meaning.

Perel further thwarts the viewer's ability to connect seeing with understanding by frustrating any desire for resolution. While at first glance the scenes do not appear to have an "informing logic," closer observation reveals patterns of shots that do acknowledge what Bill Nichols terms the viewer's "need to know."[53] *El predio* both fulfills and frustrates this expectation, for at certain moments the viewer's initial confusion regarding a particular shot or image is resolved; at others, the needed resolution remains absent. To choose one example, early in the film the camera records a close-up of a hand drawing on a wall. The subsequent take reveals the same wall, shot from farther away. At this point the viewer notes that a wall shown earlier in the film—marked with holes—is being used as a canvas for some type of drawing. Images of the wall and the drawing populate the rest of the film, and at various points during the documentary the viewer sees more and more of the wall as it is filled up with pencil drawings resembling bones and fossils. A final concluding shot shows

Fallout of the Memory "Boom"

the end result of the artistic endeavor: Perel has documented the creation of Javier Barrio's art installation "Museo del gliptodonte" (Museum of the Gliptodon), a pencil drawing taking up an entire wall, accompanied by a resonant sound track describing the connection between past and present. In this case, the viewer's initial confusion is neatly resolved, as the "big picture" becomes clear. Perel starts with the smallest detail—the hand drawing—then moves back to reveal, demonstrating how a change in perspective (a wider view) can change one's interpretation or understanding.[54]

Other moments in the film also fulfill this "need to know," as initial establishing shots that may seem confusing (a blinking red light, a person hoeing the ground) later become clear (a DVD player preparing to project a movie, an artistic intervention involving the cultivation of potatoes on the ESMA grounds). Like an impressionist painting comprised of tiny dots that requires a distant view to see the picture, little pieces of the visual puzzle do come together in a very deliberate way—the language of images constructed by Perel allows at least some areas of the ESMA to "speak."[55] Yet these little resolutions serve more to call attention to the lack of resolution on the grander scale—as viewers, we see some little pieces, but the greater significance of what the ex-ESMA "means" remains frustratingly out of reach. The moments where a "story" comes together (such as Barrio's art installation), rather than reveal a "grand narrative" of the site, signal the elusive and unstable nature of meaning. The numerous scenes that do not pertain to any type of narrative—such as the many shots of construction, the street signs on the grounds, or the exterior shots of buildings—frustrate the viewer's "need to know." Overall, despite the small resolutions in *El predio*, the whole picture of the ESMA remains fuzzy, as if the impressionist painter left the work half-finished.[56] Such lack of closure is especially striking for a documentary film; as Nichols explains, "Permanent uncertainty and unresolved suspense . . . seem anathema to a tradition devoted to telling what it knows."[57] The creation of small moments of meaning makes the larger ones more striking for their impenetrable nature. By alternately revealing and concealing the "evidence" of the ex-ESMA, *El predio* signals an opaqueness regarding the interpretation of the site, the impossibility that the viewer could ever "see" beyond the fragmented multiplicity.

Finally, *El predio*'s deliberate use of silence serves as the final technique of defamiliarization that maintains the site's meaning in a state of permanent instability. As mentioned earlier, the lack of voice-over commentary—the decided absence of words in general—serves to engage the viewer. Perel's visual language forces the viewer to look, thereby involving him or her in the task of making meaning. But the silence in the documentary also serves to lend weight and meaning to the few words that are present. At several key moments the documentary does provide some words. In particular, the first shot after the opening title shows a sign outside the ex-ESMA that designates the site as a memory project sponsored by President Kirchner, part of the "Work Plan for All Argentines," with the slogan "Argentina somos todos" ("Argentina is all of us" or "We are all Argentina") displayed at the bottom. Yet the sign is filmed from behind, from the inside looking out, meaning the viewer has to read the words through the banner, backward. Leaving aside for a moment the way in which the viewer is already primed to "make strange" (read backward) a common image (a sign), these phrases gain a certain import as the first—and some of the only—words in the entire documentary. When juxtaposed with the next shot—a sign reading "Danger: Construction Zone"—the viewer is left to draw his or her own conclusions. The "danger" of a construction zone—that somebody might get hurt—is thereby linked to the earlier idea of the ex-ESMA as a memory project. Memory is under construction. Somebody might get hurt.[58]

Other moments where Perel includes words in the documentary prove equally evocative. A medium shot of sheets of paper plastered on a wall is followed by a close-up revealing the papers as Rodolfo Walsh's famous "Carta abierta de un escritor a la junta militar" (Open letter to the military junta). Immediately recognizable as a symbol of both resistance to the military regime and the junta's power (since Walsh lost his life shortly after publishing the epistle), these words have a resonance in the context of dictatorship and disappearance that affords them special significance on the ESMA grounds. In a similar fashion, the words describing the purpose of the artist Marina Etchegoyhen's potato planting project Cosechar/Multiplicar (Harvest/Multiply) also provide the viewer with some interpretative text: "Artistic action / To build a memory and create a future / Sowing potatoes into the soil of ESMA / Reproducing and harvesting energy." The selective use of written language compels the viewer to take a closer look and meditate on meaning. In terms of the visual language Perel cultivates throughout the documentary, a paucity of words means that those that are present speak louder than they otherwise might.

A lack of voice-over commentary also grants importance to the spoken word, as seen in the final scene of Barrio's "Museo del Gliptodonte," which features a booming recorded voice. Although it remains a diegetic rather than extradiegetic voice, the words that accompany the viewing of the drawing call attention to their power. Amid an eerie pounding of drums, blowing wind, and clanking of chains, a sonorous voice proclaims: "I am the gliptodon" (a prehistoric armored mammal), followed by a description of this beast's origin ("before what we know as ancient") and desire ("Get me out of here!"). The

Fallout of the Memory "Boom"

voice asks the listener, "Do you bellow with pain? Or is everything silence? A solemn silence," before the scene abruptly cuts to another shot of the growing potatoes. The overt mention of silence in a documentary whose most striking characteristic is its absence of voice contributes to the overall effect of highlighting the role of nonverbal expression in the ex-ESMA.

Perel additionally plays with the idea of nonverbal expression through multiple shots that emphasize the contrast between emptiness and fullness. Several sequences in the documentary show a space filling up, an auditorium filling up with people, for example, followed by a subsequent shot of the space being emptied—people getting up after a film showing, or workers taking down chairs after a panel. The number of shots that feature spaces without human presence also attests to a quality of "emptiness" in the site itself. The contrast between filling and emptying the spaces of the ex-ESMA recalls one of the central debates regarding the use of the space, in particular whether the emptiness of the space could sufficiently express the past horror or whether it could only communicate by being "filled." Some, like Marcelo Brodsky, emphasize that the emptiness (el vacío) is not sufficient for transmitting memory, advocating populating the space with verbal and visual clues to help visitors understand the tragedy of the dictatorship. Others such as Leonor Arfuch counter that part of ESMA's reality is this very absence of interpretation or answers, and thereby the space should be preserved in its evocative emptiness.[59] By focusing on the moments of filling (auditoriums, walls) and emptying (rooms), El predio highlights the give-and-take between offering and withholding some type of interpretative framework, yet ultimately it refuses to take an overt position in the debate, at times providing guidance, at others not, again frustrating any expectation that the space will "speak" to the issue.[60] Nevertheless, this movement of filling and emptying suggests a question regarding the remains of the ESMA: the prisoners and repressive apparatus no longer occupy the space; what has taken its place? Multiple scenes of objects that have been removed—radiators, roof tiles, toilets—invite the viewer to meditate more generally about removal and replacement: What is being taken out of the ESMA? What is being put in?[61]

The final manner in which El predio speaks through silence is seen by the moments of blackness that open and close the film. While the majority of the shots in the film have a duration of thirty seconds, the opening shot of a black screen, with no sound whatsoever, lasts for a full minute. The uncomfortably long duration adds to the effect of disturbing and discomforting the viewer but also encourages some type of reflection. Akin to the ubiquitous "moment of silence" at commemorations of past violence, these silences engage the viewer by calling attention to themselves. At the beginning, the silence serves to prepare the viewer for a documentary that will question ways of seeing an all-too-familiar yet still opaque site of past atrocity; meanwhile, the final shot gives the viewer a chance to reflect on what he or she has just seen without the distraction of image or sound. In both cases, the transition between scenes of the ESMA and the silence is shatteringly abrupt, emphasizing the unsettling effect silence can have owing to its apparent lack of meaning. But at the same time these moments of silence offer a needed response to a site that resists fixed meaning and interpretation; faced with incomprehensible horror and atrocity, the most appropriate response seems to be a fall to silence rather than a rush to speech, and *El predio* honors this need in a deliberate and overt manner. Beginning and ending with a discomforting silence, *El predio* invites the spectator to look carefully at the ex-ESMA, yet ultimately demonstrates that no single vision of the space can encompass the truth of the site, given the unstable relationship between seeing and knowing.

Conclusion

The final scene of the documentary depicts the open gates of the ex-ESMA, with a steady stream of traffic and people passing by. A full minute in duration, the shot positions the viewer from the inside looking out, observing the motorists and pedestrians as they go about their business. Critics have read this final scene as an invitation to extend the dialogue regarding the dictatorship to the broader society or a comment on how the ESMA seems to exceed its boundaries.[62] I posit that this scene, along with the opening shots of slowly moving through the grounds, perfectly captures the attempts to understand a traumatic past. While the opening scenes provide the sense of always approaching, yet never arriving, the final shot suggests a corresponding inability to leave. Despite the open gates, the viewer remains situated firmly inside the ex-ESMA, trapped, perhaps, in an endless loop: always approaching, never arriving, yet at the same time never leaving. The percepticide at play during the dictatorship is mirrored by the inability to comprehend the ESMA's current story, and the viewer is stuck in a continuous moment of frustrated approximation to past violence.

In short, if the walls and grounds of the ex-ESMA do speak, it is incredibly difficult to understand what they are saying. By constructing a highly stylized visual language of silence, Perel's documentary calls attention to the impossibility of arriving at a definitive interpretation of the space, for this particular site of past atrocity appears unable to "speak for itself." Even while *El predio* constructs a world of images without commentary, it demonstrates the impossibility of unmediated communication about the ex-ESMA, suggesting that the site ultimately proves if not an empty signifier, at least a flexible one, able to be filled with a variety of interpretations and functions. By silencing an authoritative discourse, Perel's documentary responds to an oversaturation of human rights discourse, the use of memory for political purposes.[63] Refusing to offer a definitive interpretation of the ex-ESMA honors the unresolved tensions that occur when one can only approach, but never arrive at, the full story.

President Néstor Kirchner's condemnation of the official silence regarding the dictatorship's crimes represents a vociferous extension of the memory boom, as concrete and symbolic memory initiatives mushroomed in the legal and societal spheres. The dictatorship and early postdictatorship practices designed to prevent the witnessing of atrocity ceded to highly visible memory work aimed at encouraging the public to look more closely at the past. Yet a loud explosion of memory ironically can serve to deafen rather than enlighten, as Perel demonstrates in *El predio*. His carefully constructed cinematic gaze forces the spectator to look at the former site of atrocity, yet in a maddening paradox, such intense looking, rather than lead to greater understanding, calls attention to the inability to contain the former clandestine detention center within existing interpretive frameworks. And the unsettling feeling of incomprehension, rather than lead to despair, may encourage the creation of a prosthetic memory. On the one hand, the discomfort one experiences when viewing *El predio* serves to highlight the opaque reality of the violence committed in the grounds of the ex-ESMA; on the other, it may help the viewer take on the burden of an unexperienced and unwitnessed act of atrocity.[64] By refusing to articulate a definitive story of the ex-ESMA, *El predio* compels the viewer to take the plunge into the bottomless well, for only by experiencing the vertiginous drop can one begin to approach an understanding of past violence.

Conclusion

Always Approaching, Never Arriving

On the twenty-fifth anniversary of the coup, a commemorative act was held in the Memory Park in Buenos Aires. At the close of the event, the names of 110 disappeared victims were read, followed by a minute of silence. The moment of silence is a powerful instrument for provoking emotional consideration of atrocity and has become an almost ubiquitous element of commemorations to past trauma. However, such acts of remembrance seem one of the few places where silence is welcome. Human rights organizations have understandably focused on breaking the repressive silence of the military, condemning institutional silencing, and denouncing a culture of amnesia—recall the H.I.J.O.S. group's mandate "against silence"— yet the link between silence and memory extends beyond the "moment of silence." As this book claims, attention to the silences left in the wake of dictatorship reveals the challenges of truth-telling and the lingering taboos surrounding representations of violence (the fallout of the memory boom), as well as the fundamental role silence plays in the expression of trauma (how silence comprises an essential element of the boom itself).

Two general categories of conclusions arise from this examination of silences in cultural production pre- and postboom. The first concerns the association between human rights discourse and the stories that come to the fore regarding the dictatorship. A focus on the way in which cultural works that seek to expose the crimes of the military engage with silence highlights tensions and debates in the human rights community and also demonstrates how the discourse of human rights informs the narratives of past violence. The second relates to the expressive nature of silence itself when voicing trauma. Approaches to the past that honor the fundamental ambiguity of silent expression best respond to the paradoxes and ambiguities of the postdictatorship period itself. The use of the word "approaches" is deliberate, as it echoes Perel's evocative image of "always approaching, yet never arriving" at the meaning of violence, which embodies the central paradox of the expression of past trauma.

Silence and Human Rights:
The Fallout of the Memory Boom

Although the struggle against institutional silencing represents a worthy goal, the push to break repressive silences can often reveal tensions and taboos in the human rights community regarding the expression of the dictatorship's violence. A consideration of the silences surrounding representations of torture or stories about the appropriation of babies brings the limits governing the tales of trauma into sharp relief, signaling the way in which certain interpretations of the postdictatorship period can dominate cultural representations of trauma. As seen in Pavlovsky's play *Paso de dos*, the only way for the victim to maintain her humanity is through her stubborn silence under torture (chapter 1). Yet the powerful overt silence of the torture victim exposes a more disturbing covert silence regarding the public's tolerance of "betrayal" and militancy. Osorio's novel *A veinte años, Luz* and Telefe's *Montecristo* similarly adhere to the conventional story of identity restitution as relatively straightforward and unquestioningly positive (chapter 4). However, by breaking one overt pact of silence surrounding the children of the disappeared, both works unwittingly suppress the complexities of identity politics. The covert silences in all these cultural texts signal an "authoritative" discourse emanating from the human rights community: the interpretation of torture victims as heroes (*Paso de dos*) or the suggestion that love and appropriation are mutually exclusive (*A veinte años, Luz* and *Montecristo*).[1] Representations of torture victims who "break" or individuals who exhibit extended resistance to the process of identity restitution do not align with the established narratives regarding these crimes against humanity.

Furthermore, the taboos regarding tales of trauma shift according to the story being told. One striking example concerns the portrayal of the repressor, which differs between torture narratives and tales of identity restitution. In *Paso de dos* the torturer is a normal, if corrupted, individual rather than an inhuman monster, yet the humanizing of the repressor—considered an essential element for the accurate representation of torture—proves taboo for the stories of appropriated children. In *A veinte años, Luz* and *Montecristo*, the repressors are depicted as evil individuals incapable of truly loving the stolen child in order to avoid the messy politics of identity.[2] However, the caricatured representation of repressors in stories of appropriated children undermines the crucial message of torture plays regarding the average person's capacity for evil. Dramas such as *Paso de dos* strive to emphasize the audience members' potential for carrying out violent acts, thereby preventing the comfortable distancing that allows the viewer to consider the torturers as unlike "us." With stories of the children of the disappeared, on the other hand, there exists a desire to distance the appropriators from "normal" people in order to allow for an unproblematic reintegration of the biological family unit. Placing these two representations in dialogue demonstrates that the nature of taboos governing tales of past violence shifts depending on the story being told. When the story is about torture, characterizing the repressors as normal if corrupted individuals serves to lessen the distance between "us" and "them"; when the story is about stealing children, the repressors must be cast as pure villains. Attention to these shifting taboos reveals the entrenched nature of prevailing representations as well as the uncomfortable or unpalatable aspects of the dictatorship that remain suppressed: the fallout of the memory boom.

Listening to the silences in cultural representations of the postdictatorship also facilitates an understanding of the tension in human rights discourse regarding who gets to speak for the victims of violence. Carlson's *I Remember Julia: Voices of the Disappeared* exhibits the challenges of seeking to rescue one victim's voice from an anonymous grave (chapter 2); meanwhile, Saer's *La pesquisa* hints at the impossibility of accessing any of the voices of the missing victims of violence (chapter 3). Both renderings of the story of disappearance embody the struggle to tell the story of an absent victim: Can "Julia" speak through others? Can a deliberate *not*-telling of the story of violence actually "speak" in all its eloquent silence? Looking at Carlson and Saer's differing responses to the aching silence of disappearance reveals the central opposition between considering victims as individuals (focusing on their lives) or as part of a collective (focusing on their deaths). At the same time, following Thomas Laqueur, the corpus delicti of human rights discourse still informs both tales.

But what happens when the victims of violence are not dead bodies but living beings with agency? Considering works that address the desaparecidos alongside the stories of appropriated children exposes the complications that arise when determining who should speak for victims who *can* articulate their own stories. Placing *A veinte años, Luz* and *Montecristo* within the larger framework of identity politics displays the tensions that emerge when cultural representations reinforce the established discourse of a human rights organization, but not all the victims of violence follow the script. Here the fallout from the memory boom encompasses the lingering effects of the dictatorship's violence, as even attempts to articulate the depravity of appropriation unwittingly silence the tragic scope of the original crime.

The disquieting and prescriptive aspects of human rights narratives and the tension regarding who should speak for victims of violence also come to the fore in Perel's documentary of the ex-ESMA (chapter 6). In this case, the oversaturation of memory discourse regarding the site represents the fallout from the boom, and the excess of voices vying for interpretive hegemony leads to Perel's deliberate construction of a visual language of silence (image without overt commentary). *El predio* resists the homogenizing interpretation of human rights organizations regarding the Space for Memory, in which certain parties lay claim to the "truth" of the site. Rather, the film raises the question of who is (or should be) speaking for the victims of the dictatorship's established practices of torture and disappearance: Can everybody have a voice? Are all voices equal, or should the voices of actors in the human rights community command more authority? Listening to the silences present in representations of the postdictatorship calls attention to the central importance of agency and the conflicting factors that shape any attempt to articulate a victim's story.

Arriving

As a way to understand the challenges of expressing the atrocity of the dictatorship, this book advocates exploring the interplay between overt and covert silences, between obvious absences of speech and silences that are "covered" by excessive or misleading talk. Several of the works considered present a "cover story" that masks the real tale in some way. In *Paso de dos*, *A veinte años*, *Luz*, *Montecristo*, and *I Remember Julia*, these covert silences conceal the uncomfortable realities surrounding the legacies of the dictatorship. Tales of torture, the appropriation of children, and disappearance are rendered through placating "cover stories" that allow the reader or spectator to ignore the complicated, painful reality of the issues. Emphasizing the powerful silence of the martyr, the happy reunification of a biological family, or the uncritical breaking of the silence of disappearance risks a dangerous oversimplification of the extraordinarily complex phenomena embodied in the legacies of authoritarianism. By providing a false bottom for the well, such representations of past violence ultimately leave the most difficult aspects of the postdictatorship unexamined, to the detriment of those who would seek fuller understanding of past atrocity.

Yet cover stories are not always protective or placating; they can also serve to unsettle. Like the aforementioned works, *La pesquisa* also crafts a substitute narrative that obscures the tale of trauma. The reader never arrives at the story of el Gato and Elisa's disappearance but wanders instead through the complicated psychological tale of serial killings and mysterious manuscripts. Rather than a soothing cover story that indicates the unproblematic resolution of complicated issues, the covert silence of Saer's tale calls attention to the unresolved nature of disappearance. In this case, the cover story serves not to settle but to unsettle any notion that one can access the opaque heart of trauma.[3]

The twin faces of covert silence—either settling an issue with a protective narrative or unsettling it through a lack of resolution—demonstrate the fundamentally ambiguous nature of silent expression. Yet such ambiguity can be difficult to face, especially during the postauthoritarian period's search for concrete answers. Like the vacuum, silence proves somewhat intolerable, and the temptation to assign a fixed interpretation (either positive or negative) can be very powerful for authors and critics alike. There is a tendency to want to ascribe meaning to the silences left in the wake of the dictatorship, which often leads to rather essentialist interpretations: silence is either a powerful expression of resistance (the stubborn silence of the torture victim) or a sign of utter annihilation or absolute powerlessness (the repressive silences that need to be broken).[4] The fact that so many representations choose to assign a specific value to the silences addressed speaks to a discomfort with ambiguity. Yet the power of silent expression comes not from its ability to align with one of the extreme positions (either power or powerlessness) but its position in the middle ground. Silence calls attention to the tension between both extremes because of its ability to represent power and powerlessness at the same time.

The pull to assign either a positive or negative interpretation to silence appears linked to the aforementioned inclination of human rights discourse to "dictate" meaning regarding the past violence. Significantly, the same works that expose the entrenched taboos regarding the expression of state terrorism— *Paso de dos, A veinte años, Luz, Montecristo,* and *I Remember Julia*—are also those that assign a fixed interpretation to silence. Carlson's project to reclaim "Julia's" identity, along with the two cultural works that address the legacy of appropriation, seek to break repressive institutional silencing: silence here is unequivocally negative. Meanwhile, *Paso de dos* creates a powerful and unquestioningly positive overt silence in the space of the torture chamber. An essentialist rendering of silence—silence as power, silence as powerlessness—signals a univocal interpretation of the past, effectively closing down other options. To return to Perel's image, cultural representations that interpret silence in an essentialist manner suggest an arrival at definitive meaning rather than an approach to understanding past violence.

Approaching

It is precisely the ambiguous nature of silence—its refusal to neatly align with either pole of a dichotomy—that allows it to more fully express the ambiguity of the postdictatorship period. Akin to the human rights paradox outlined by Stern and Straus, silent expression encompasses both the universal inexpressibility of extreme violence—the opaque heart of trauma—as well as particular taboos that govern cultural representations of the legacies of the dictatorship. Listening to silences reveals the perpetual tension between the impulse to bear witness to atrocity (in the name of universal human rights) and the challenges to articulating the crimes of the past, in particular the paradoxical pull between universal barriers to expression (the challenge of representation) and local factors that suppress unpalatable or inconvenient stories (taboos within the human rights community). Representations of torture such as Pavlovsky's *Paso de dos* therefore wrestle with both the inexpressibility of the brutal practice as well as societal taboos regarding betrayal and militancy, and this tension informs the knowing and telling of the tale. When employed to express the central human rights issues of the postdictatorship, silence helps illuminate the complicated and ambiguous aspects of such critical matters as torture, disappearance, and the crime of appropriation.

Furthermore, cultural works that employ silence as a successful mode of expression demonstrate that the memory boom does not stand in complete opposition to silence. Silence in fact embodies an essential element of the construction of memory itself: being silent does not equate to being silenced. A novel such as Saer's *La pesquisa*, which ostensibly does not address disappearance, rather than relegating the tale of trauma to oblivion actually calls attention to absent bodies and miscarried justice. Valenzuela's *La travesía* exemplifies the intimate connection between silence and remembering through its exploration of organic, somatic memories that resist repression (chapter 5). The untold secrets and unvoiced memories the protagonist holds inside do not equate with forgetting; rather, the silences themselves prove essential to her eventual reckoning with the past. Meanwhile, Perel's refusal to add another authoritative voice to the debate surrounding the use of the ex-ESMA serves to highlight the questions and debates regarding appropriate use of a site of past horror as well as the constructed nature of memory. The silences in these works do not cover the past; instead, they call attention to themselves as essential elements of an always partial understanding of trauma.

The use of ambiguously insistent silences in cultural works also engages the reader or spectator to make meaning (or recognize the impossibility of arriving at a definitive interpretation). Just as the unresolved questions at the end of *The Official Story* compel the viewer to conclude the tale, the truncated sentences and unfinished thoughts in *La travesía* invite a more active engagement with the story. In a similar fashion, the absent investigation in *La pesquisa* compels the reader to ponder both the inexpressibility of trauma and the consequences of miscarried justice. Meanwhile, *El predio*'s language of fragmented images forces the viewer to create the story of the ex-ESMA (or acknowledge its fundamental opaqueness). These works do not let the reader or viewer off the hook regarding the implications of past violence; rather, they prevent any type of detached observation. As opposed to representations of trauma that provide easily digestible interpretations of violence, those that employ silent expression draw the audience into direct engagement with the incomprehensibility of past horror, forging a link between cultural representations of violence and society's understanding of the past.

Renderings of trauma that employ ambiguous silence honor the fundamental incomprehensibility of violence, the unfathomable depths of the well. Literary and cultural works are especially suited for sounding these bottomless depths, as they are not bound by the same "prescriptive expectations" of traditional testimonial narrative (to return to Allen Feldman's useful term). Loosed from strictly empirical terms of analysis, artistic representations of violence have the capacity to respond to paradox and ambiguity in all their complexity. Although not all literary treatments of the dictatorship live up to the promise of the medium (see chapters 1 and 4), cultural production in particular can recognize and probe the many silences left in the wake of state terror in all their messy ambiguity, thereby testifying to the limits of our understanding. When it comes to events that challenge our comprehension, such as the massive scale of human rights violations during the Argentine dictatorship, arriving at any type of closure or understanding betrays the heart of the experience. The salient characteristic of "incomprehensible" or "unspeakable" violence is its very incomprehensibility or inability to be voiced. Like the "dream-tale of disappearance," naming or explaining it causes it to slip away—the essence of trauma remains inaccessible. Expressing the trauma of the past through silence will never allow arrival at definitive closure. Yet it serves to nurture the tension of "always approaching yet never arriving," which remains the best option for engaging with a traumatic past.

I offer one final observation regarding the importance of honoring ambiguity. It seems no accident that of all the works under consideration in this study, the one that most overtly engages with ambiguity and silence is the most recent: Perel's documentary of the ex-ESMA (2010). As Andreas Huyssen has posited regarding the interplay of memory and forgetting in the aftermath of state repression, to move forward with important memory work, certain unpalatable realities often must be "forgotten," at least temporarily. Citing the convenient suppression of the militancy of the Argentine victims as a necessary element to move forward with societal repudiation of governmental violence, Huyssen suggests that a nuanced accountability with the past is often only possible after the passage of time, an idea that this study upholds.[5] Following the human rights paradox, local conditions (the need to unambiguously condemn the military's violence in the immediate aftermath of the dictatorship) determine the limits of universal concepts such as "truth" and "justice" (a portrayal of victims that downplays the inconvenient truth of their militancy). In a similar vein, Carlson's insistence on the importance of breaking silences—whatever the cost to nuanced understanding—makes sense given the context of repressive silencing and impunity in which it was written (early 1990s); meanwhile, the era of repealed amnesty laws and further prosecutions of perpetrators facilitates Perel's use of ambiguous silence as *the* mode of expressing a past that resists simplistic interpretation. Yet despite the factors from different eras that impact the narrative of past trauma—what Lazzara refers to as "open" versus "closed" structures—the attention to silences remains critical for a deeper understanding of the dictatorship years.[6]

Questions and Answers

One of the biggest unanswered questions during the dictatorship years was the poignantly simple *¿Dónde están?* (Where are they?). The nature of disappearance made this particular question especially fraught, as the initial impulse to locate the missing victims alive gradually ceded to the realization that they probably had been murdered by the military. Yet the persistence of the group of Mothers of the Plaza de Mayo led by Hebe de Bonafini to demand the "reappearance alive" of their children led to a rejection of exhumations of mass gravesites, monuments to the disappeared, or other "proof" of their death.[7] These mothers did not want to find the answers at the bottom of the well; they refused to explore the painful truths regarding their loved ones' fates. Rejecting the remains of their sons and daughters allowed them to honor the lives and ideas of their missing children rather than accept the tragic finality of their deaths. The silence connected to disappearance thereby proved both an agonizing question—*¿Dónde están?*—and a source of solace, an "ambiguous loss" in every sense of the term.[8]

This anecdote reveals the final insight regarding the knowing and telling of state terrorism in Argentina: when it comes to reckoning with the past, nobody appears to want to explore the "whole" truth.[9] The military's refusal to account for the victims of the repressive mechanisms of torture and disappearance finds an uncomfortable echo in the Mothers' resistance to seek answers or the lingering taboos that shape tales of torture and appropriation. Facing the stark brutality of the tragic legacies of the dictatorship can be too difficult to bear; when it comes to voicing the trauma of the past, some stories resist expression on many levels. The silences that populate the postdictatorship landscape represent a persistent presence of absence, and the responses to such silences demonstrate the complicated legacies of authoritarianism: the troubling fallout of the memory boom and the inability to arrive at a full understanding of past violence. An attention to the silences illuminates both what remains inaccessible along with what is articulated through silent expression, and careful listening reveals how cultural representations are always approaching yet never arriving at a full reckoning with the past.

Notes

Introduction

1. I employ the term "Dirty War" to orient the reader to the specific time period under consideration, because this is the phrase that has come to dominate studies concerning these years. However, I share Frank Graziano's reluctance to employ a term invented by the military to justify their policies of state terrorism as some form of legitimate (if unorthodox) military engagement. Frank Graziano, *Divine Violence: Spectacle, Psychosexuality, and Radical Christianity in the Argentine "Dirty War"* (Boulder: Westview Press, 1992). While Graziano chooses to maintain the term within quotation marks in order to expose and emphasize its euphemistic nature, in the remainder of the study I shall refer to the period 1976–83 as the years of military rule, state terrorism, or simply the dictatorship.

2. For an excellent discussion of how Argentina's innovative responses to the dictatorship's abuses established the nation as an exporter of human rights tactics, see Kathryn Sikkink, "From Pariah State to Global Protagonist: Argentina and the Struggle for International Human Rights," *Latin American Politics and Society* 50, no. 1 (2008): 1–29.

3. Ibid.

4. For a discussion of the memory "boom" as part of the history of memory in Argentina, see Gabriela Cerruti, "La historia de la memoria," *Puentes* 1, no. 3 (2001): 14–25. For a closer look at the way in which Scilingo's televised confession related to the proliferation of memory initiatives and the creation of H.I.J.O.S., see Claudia Feld, *Del estrado a la pantalla: Las imágenes del juicio a los ex comandantes en Argentina* (Madrid: Siglo XXI de España Editores, 2002).

5. For the purposes of this study, the preboom era refers to the early years of President Carlos Saúl Menem's government, between 1989 and 1995. The postboom begins after Scilingo's confession and the subsequent explosion of memory initiatives and extends to the present day.

6. I employ the adjective *cultural* to refer to the aesthetic realm, works of literature, film, theater, physical memorials or monuments, and so on, rather than a shared set of attitudes, beliefs, or values (such as a "culture of amnesia" or "Argentine culture").

7. The concept of the "inexpressibility of trauma" is rooted in Holocaust and trauma studies. While at first glance the sheer number of cultural works that address torture and disappearance in Argentina may appear to belie any claim of the impossibility of representing violence, incorporating trauma as a theme or topic of a particular work does not equate to a representation of the violence itself. The "inexpressibility of trauma" refers to the obstacles that arise when finding appropriate words to render extreme violence, including both the incapacity of language to fully capture horror as well as the notion that any representation risks changing the fundamental nature of the event (e.g., sanitizing the experience). For more on the limits of representing horror, see Saul Friedlander, ed., *Probing the Limits of Representation: Nazism and the "Final Solution"* (Cambridge, MA: Harvard University Press, 1992); Dominick LaCapra, *Representing the Holocaust: History, Theory, Trauma* (Ithaca, NY: Cornell University Press, 1994). For an examination of the limits of language to represent physical pain, see Elaine Scarry, *The Body in Pain: The Making and Unmaking of the World* (New York: Oxford University Press, 1985).

8. For more on how the escraches constitute a performance of cultural memory, see Diana Taylor, *The Archive and the Repertoire: Performing Cultural Memory in the Americas* (Durham, NC: Duke University Press, 2003).

9. In broad terms the postdictatorship period reveals a tension between attempts to silence the past by moving forward and efforts to work toward accountability and full reckoning with past violence. In her seminal work *State Repression and the Labors of Memory*, Elizabeth Jelin notes the contrast between institutional silencing and human rights and artistic work in the public sphere. As she states, "Those directly affected by repression bear their suffering and pain, which they translate into various types of public action," affirming the place of dissident groups struggling against institutional efforts to silence the past. *State Repression and the Labors of Memory*, trans. Judy Rein and Marcial Godoy-Anativia (Minneapolis: University of Minnesota Press, 2003), xv.

10. Michael T. Taussig, *Defacement: Public Secrecy and the Labor of the Negative* (Stanford, CA: Stanford University Press, 1999), 5.

11. Diana Taylor, *Disappearing Acts: Spectacles of Gender and Nationalism in Argentina's "Dirty War"* (Durham, NC: Duke University Press, 1997). Numerous other critics comment on this interplay between visibility and invisibility, or presence and absence. See in particular Manuel Antonio Garretón, "Fear in Military Regimes: An Overview," in *Fear at the Edge: State Terror and Resistance in Latin America*, ed. Juan E. Corradi, Patricia Weiss Fagen, and Manuel Antonio Garretón (Berkeley: University of California Press, 1992), 13–25. For another discussion of the public yet secret quality of repression, see Patricia Weiss Fagen, "Repression and State Security," in *Fear at the Edge: State Terror and Resistance in Latin America*, ed. Juan E. Corradi, Patricia Weiss Fagen, and Manuel Antonio Garretón (Berkeley: University of California Press, 1992), 39–71. Finally, Graziano outlines this process of revealing and concealing the spectacle of power in *Divine Violence*.

12. Andrés Avellaneda describes two basic types of censorship: official decrees prohibiting certain forms of expression and the more subtle censorship seen in kidnappings,

suspension of human rights, and emigration. Andrés Avellaneda, *Censura, autoritarismo y cultura: Argentina 1960–1983* (Buenos Aires: Centro Editor de América Latina, 1986), 10.

13. The *Nunca Más* report was not the only venue for sharing the experience of victims of military rule. Starting in 1982 and reaching its peak in 1984, the press broadcast sensationalist coverage of the dictatorship's crimes. These exposés, later dubbed the "horror show," featured gruesome details of exhumations and tortures but little historical context. Although highly visible, this coverage did not serve to enlighten the public regarding the reasons underlying the violence. See Feld, *Del estrado a la pantalla.*

14. The Full Stop Law (Ley de Punto Final) designated an endpoint to prosecutions of suspected repressors, while the Law of Due Obedience (Ley de Obediencia Debida) declared that subordinate officers who were following orders were exempt from prosecution. One crime not covered by these amnesty laws was that of the appropriation of minors.

15. For a closer analysis of how Menem sought to construct a culture of oblivion regarding the dictatorship, see Cerruti, "La historia de la memoria."

16. "World Report 2015" (New York: Human Rights Watch, 2015).

17. The former torture victim disappeared from his home in September 2006 and remains missing to this day.

18. Steve J. Stern and Scott Straus, eds., *The Human Rights Paradox: Universality and Its Discontents* (Madison: University of Wisconsin Press, 2014).

19. Ibid., 9.

20. For an exploration of the flexible concept of "truth" within the H.I.J.O.S. organization, see Noa Vaisman, "'Memoria, Verdad y Justicia': The Terrain of Post-Dictatorship Social Reconstruction and the Struggle for Human Rights in Argentina," in Stern and Straus, *The Human Rights Paradox*, 125–47.

21. Stern and Straus, *The Human Rights Paradox*, 10.

22. Current scholarship includes individual articles or chapters that address silence in a particular work, or silence related to women's writing. Examples include: D. Jan Mennell, "(Im)penetrable Silence: The Language of the Unspeakable in Manuela Fingueret's *Hija del silencio*," *Revista Canadiense de Estudios Hispánicos* 27, no. 3 (2003): 485–507; Z. Nelly Martínez, *El silencio que habla: Aproximación a la obra de Luisa Valenzuela* (Buenos Aires: Ediciones Corregidor, 1994). For a nice exploration of how silence dialogues with memory making in Argentine testimonial novels by Alicia Kozameh and Nora Strejilevich, see Ana Forcinito, "Testimonial Narratives in the Argentine Post-Dictatorship: Survivors, Witnesses, and the Reconstruction of the Past," in *Post-Authoritarian Cultures: Spain and Latin America's Southern Cone*, ed. Luis Martín-Estudillo and Roberto Ampuero (Nashville: Vanderbilt University Press, 2008), 77–98. Forcinito notes that Kozameh's *Pasos bajo el agua* suggests "the impossibility of a complete and perfect account of the past," while the fragmentary nature of Strejilevich's *A Single, Numberless Death* also points to testimony's "incompleteness." "Testimonial Narratives in the Argentine Post-Dictatorship," 86, 87.

23. Michael J. Lazzara, *Chile in Transition: The Poetics and Politics of Memory* (Gainesville: University Press of Florida, 2006), 154. See in particular his chapter on art and disappearance, which provides an insightful overview of the two central (and intertwined) strategies artists employ to render disappearance: "*marking the presence and marking the absence.*" Ibid., 104.

24. According to the philosopher Bernard P. Dauenhauer, "Each aspect of silence can be as distressing and misery-laden as it can be consoling and peace-bearing." *Silence: The Phenomenon and Its Ontological Significance* (Bloomington: Indiana University Press, 1980), 23. The linguist Adam Jaworski refers to silence as "probably the most ambiguous of all linguistic forms." *The Power of Silence: Social and Pragmatic Perspectives* (Newbury Park: Sage, 1993), 24.

25. I am grateful to Rebecca Atencio for calling my attention to the way in which silence facilitates this shared production of meaning.

26. The final scene eerily echoes Alicia's memory of sitting in a rocking chair, waiting for her own (deceased) parents to return, and the abandonment she felt. The visual linking of Alicia and Gaby's situations indicates a measure of ambiguity regarding Gaby's fate. What type of parental or familial relationship awaits Gaby?

27. I do not mean to imply that the ending is completely ambiguous, as the film definitively resolves certain questions. For example, it is clear Alicia has decided to leave Roberto and reject her former complicity with the repressors. Nevertheless, the film does not provide similar resolution regarding Gaby. While Alicia obviously has established the beginnings of a relationship with Sara, it is unclear what the next steps might be, where they will lead, or what the legal or emotional ramifications might be.

28. The lack of impartiality proves especially loaded in contexts of justice (or its lack). There exists a strong social mandate to see true justice as emerging from an impartial location, yet the very ambiguity of silent expression negates the possibility of establishing such objective grounds. I am grateful to Kristin Dykstra for noting how silent expression's negation of neutrality relates to broader issues of justice.

29. As Lazzara argues in the Chilean case, "Absence (even more than presence) characterizes post-dictatorial experience." Lazzara, *Chile in Transition*, 103.

30. The field of transitional justice, for example, has begun to recognize the importance of including literary texts as objects of study. Rebecca Atencio has identified how cultural works in Brazil both contribute to national debates regarding the dictatorship and impact the transitional justice processes. See Rebecca J. Atencio, *Memory's Turn: Reckoning with Dictatorship in Brazil* (Madison: University of Wisconsin Press, 2014). See also Siphiwe Ignatius Dube, "Transitional Justice Beyond the Normative: Towards a Literary Theory of Political Transitions," *International Journal of Transitional Justice* 5, no. 2 (2011): 177–97.

31. For more about the debate regarding definitions and the question of whether testimonio can provoke action, see Kimberly Nance, *Can Literature Promote Justice? Trauma Narrative and Social Action in Latin American Testimonio* (Nashville: Vanderbilt University Press, 2006).

32. For a discussion of the autobiographical pact of truth, see Nancy Miller, "Facts, Pacts, Acts," *Profession* (1992): 10–14.

33. Jacques Derrida, *Demeure: Fiction and Testimony*, trans. Elizabeth Rottenberg (Stanford, CA: Stanford University Press, 2000), 29.

34. Ibid., 30.

35. Berel Lang, "The Representation of Limits," in *Probing the Limits of Representation: Nazism and the "Final Solution,"* ed. Saul Friedlander (Cambridge, MA: Harvard University Press, 1992), 316.

36. For more on the way in which cultural and artistic production can bear witness to authoritarianism, see Ksenija Bilbija et al., eds., *The Art of Truth-Telling about Authoritarian Rule* (Madison: University of Wisconsin Press, 2005).

37. Shoshana Felman and Dori Laub, *Testimony: Crises of Witnessing in Literature, Psychoanalysis, and History* (New York: Routledge, 1992).

38. Cathy Caruth, *Unclaimed Experience: Trauma, Narrative, and History* (Baltimore: Johns Hopkins University Press, 1996), 5.

39. Nance, *Can Literature Promote Justice?*, 7. Although one could argue that the victims of violence in Argentina represent "extraordinary" rather than "ordinary" speaking subjects (if one categorizes the military's practices as a "genocide"), I employ Nance's ideas to emphasize the distinction between *purpose* and *mode*, a difference that does not discriminate between types of testimonial subjects.

40. For a close examination of the way in which fiction contributes to the testimonial project, see Jessica Murray, "Tremblings in the Distinction Between Fiction and Testimony," *Postcolonial Text* 4, no. 2 (2008): 1–19. Murray's analysis of a non–Latin American text helped me see how this slippage between fiction and testimony might operate in a Latin American context of historical atrocity. For further discussion of the blending of story and history, especially in Latin America, see Ksenija Bilbija, "Story Is History Is Story . . . ," in Bilbija et al., *The Art of Truth-Telling*, 112–17. Bilbija notes that the Spanish language makes no distinction between the terms "story" and "history," as both concepts are encompassed in the term "historia."

41. Lazzara, *Chile in Transition*.

42. Cynthia E. Milton, ed., *Art from a Fractured Past: Memory and Truth-Telling in Post–Shining Path Peru* (Durham, NC: Duke University Press, 2014), 17, 18. Milton compellingly advocates for an examination of the "aesthetic pursuit of truth," given not only art's ability to express the inexpressible but also its capacity to allow traditionally marginalized groups to have a voice. Ibid., 17.

43. Atencio, *Memory's Turn*.

44. *Nunca Más: Informe de la Comisión Nacional sobre la Desaparición de Personas (CONADEP)* (Buenos Aires: EUDEBA, 1984), http://www.desaparecidos.org/nuncam as/web/english/library/nevagain/nevagain_001.htm.

45. Jacobo Timerman, *Prisoner without a Name, Cell without a Number*, trans. Toby Talbot (New York: Knopf, 1981); Alicia Partnoy, *The Little School: Tales of Disappearance and Survival* (Pittsburgh, PA: Cleis Press, 1986).

46. Sommer explains that rather than expect a full revelation, the reader of any testimonial narrative must be attuned to such silences in order to approach minority writing in a respectful manner. Doris Sommer, *Proceed with Caution, When Engaged by Minority Writing in the Americas* (Cambridge, MA: Harvard University Press, 1999).

47. Nance, *Can Literature Promote Justice?*, 106.

48. See chapters 1 and 4 for more on how the socially sayable affects the types of stories that can be told after the return to democracy.

49. For more about the general concept that one must have one's voice heard for a particular experience to be remembered, see Vera L. Zolberg, "Contested Remembrance: The Hiroshima Exhibit Controversy," *Theory and Society* 27, no. 4 (1998): 565–90; Shaunna L. Scott, "Dead Work: The Construction and Reconstruction of the Harlan Miners Memorial," *Qualitative Sociology* 19, no. 3 (1996): 365–93; James Young, *The Texture of Memory: Holocaust Memorial and Meaning* (New Haven, CT: Yale University Press, 1993); Robin Wagner-Pacifici and Barry Schwartz, "The Vietnam Veterans Memorial: Commemorating a Difficult Past," *American Journal of Sociology* 97, no. 2 (1991): 376–420.

50. Jelin, *State Repression*, xviii.

51. Steve J. Stern, *Remembering Pinochet's Chile: On the Eve of London, 1998* (Durham, NC: Duke University Press, 2004); Steve J. Stern, *Battling for Hearts and Minds: Memory Struggles in Pinochet's Chile, 1973–1988* (Durham, NC: Duke University Press, 2006); Steve J. Stern, *Reckoning with Pinochet: The Memory Question in Democratic Chile, 1989–2006* (Durham, NC: Duke University Press, 2010).

52. Jelin, *State Repression*, xviii.

53. Stern, *Remembering Pinochet's Chile*, 104.

54. Jelin, *State Repression*, 17.

55. These range from "deep" or "definitive" silences that represent a complete erasure of a past event to deliberately created silences, "the results of explicit policies furthering forgetting and silence" (Jelin, *State Repression*, 18). In keeping with the essentialist interpretation of silence as negative, most of the silences addressed represent a lack of power, with the exception of "liberating" forgetting, which allows a person or group to shift focus from the past to the future (ibid., 20). Yet in general, the silences Jelin identifies represent the total annihilation of a past event, or an attempt to bury a shameful past. Even "liberating" forgetting finds its dark counterpart in Argentina's policies of protective amnesia, which touted forgetting as the key to moving forward.

56. Stern, *Remembering Pinochet's Chile*, 133.

57. Ibid., 149, 213.

58. Jelin, *State Repression*, 23.

59. For more on the making of memory and silence in Pinochet's Chile, in particular how one history can be used to cover another, see the third book in the trilogy, Stern, *Reckoning with Pinochet*, 265–72. For a discussion of the connection between silence and dignity, refer to pp. 293–97 of the same volume.

60. As mentioned before, the choice to eschew a comprehensive taxonomy of silence represents an attempt to respond to the multilayered complexities of the phenomenon.

61. Robyn Fivush, "Speaking Silence: The Social Construction of Silence in Autobiographical and Cultural Narratives," *Memory* 18, no. 2 (2010): 94.

62. Vered Vinitsky-Seroussi and Chana Teeger, "Unpacking the Unspoken: Silence and Collective Memory and Forgetting," *Social Forces* 88, no. 3 (2010): 1104.

63. Although published in 1996, Carlson's investigative work took place during 1990–91. For this reason, this text is considered part of the preboom cultural production, as it directly addresses the climate of silencing and fear that characterized the early years of the Menem administration.

Chapter 1. Tortured Silence and Silenced Torture in Eduardo Pavlovsky's *Paso de dos*

1. Marta Platía, "En peligro de muerte permanente," *Página/12*, July 30, 2013, 8. Unless otherwise noted, all translations in this book are my own.

2. At the time of the performance, Menem's pardons of the officials convicted in the 1985 trial were imminent. Given the antiauthoritarian themes of Pavlovsky's earlier works (such as *El Señor Galíndez* [1973], *El Señor Laforgue* [1983], and *Potestad* [1985]), *Paso de dos* was expected to comment on issues of violence and human rights.

3. I use the term "unsettle" in terms of complicating or disrupting existing interpretations, in keeping with Leigh A. Payne's analysis of how perpetrator confessions serve to "unsettle" the past. *Unsettling Accounts: Neither Truth nor Reconciliation in Confessions of State Violence* (Durham, NC: Duke University Press, 2008).

4. The playwright has asserted that the female character's silence is her "singular trait," one indication of the importance attributed to this particular aspect of the work. Marguerite Feitlowitz, "A Dance of Death: Eduardo Pavlovsky's *Paso de dos*," *The Drama Review* 35, no. 2 (1991): 69.

5. This chapter addresses the 1990 performance of the play, directed by Laura Yusem, which chose to divide She's character into mind/body, with Susana Evans playing the role of She's body, onstage with Pavlovsky in the role of He, while Stella Galazzi voiced She's lines from a seat in the audience. It must be noted that not all performances of *Paso de dos* choose to employ two actors for the role of She. Other stagings have one actor playing the part.

6. See Feitlowitz, "A Dance of Death"; and Taylor, *Disappearing Acts*. Other analyses of the play that focus on gender include Estela Patricia Scipioni, *Torturadores, apropiadores y asesinos: El terrorismo de estado en la obra dramática de Eduardo Pavlovsky* (Kassel: Edition Reichenberger, 2000); and Philippa J. Page, *Politics and Performance in Post-Dictatorship Argentine Film and Theatre*, Colección Tamesis, Serie A, Monografías 301 (Woodbridge, Suffolk, UK: Tamesis, 2011).

7. The dilemma of fictional portrayals of torture has been seen in the debates surrounding the 2012 movie *Zero Dark Thirty*, which has received criticism for its portrayal of torture as an effective means for gathering information. Critics contend that by exaggerating (or inventing) the role torture served in leading to the capture of Osama Bin Laden, the movie helps justify and perpetuate its use. Of further importance is the

fact that in fictional portrayals of torture, the victim's silence often aligns with their role as "good" or "bad." The bad guys can be "broken" by torture and made to reveal important information, while the good guys maintain their heroic silence.

8. Elizabeth Swanson Goldberg, *Beyond Terror: Gender, Narrative, Human Rights* (Princeton, NJ: Rutgers University Press, 2007), 14. Interestingly, Goldberg notes that while literary representations are not immune to ethical questions, such questions have remained relatively unexamined in literary studies (16–17).

9. Herbert Lindenberger explains that drama that takes its theme from historical events makes "a greater pretense at engaging with reality than do writings whose fictiveness we accept from the start." *Historical Drama: The Relation of Literature and Reality* (Chicago: University of Chicago Press, 1975), x. Playwrights must consider not only the nature of the history on which they base their work and the way in which theatrical conventions affect the portrayal but also "the influence of our present situation on our interpretation of the work." Ibid., 10. Diana Taylor further emphasizes that theater that represents torture is particularly answerable to real life, for while the act itself may bear some resemblance to a performance, torture is not theater. The make-believe suffering portrayed by actors on stage mirrors the actual torture and murder of countless victims of military regimes, and any attempt to re-present torture inevitably raises questions about the relationship between on-stage representation and off-stage reality. While witnessing this spectacle of violence, the audience is forced to consider their role in the practice of torture in society at large, for "the very existence of torture, whether one openly confronts the practice and its implications or denies them, threatens to undermine one's sense of well-being, one's comfortable moral and ethical principles, one's easy assumptions about human nature and the civilization we live in." Diana Taylor, *Theatre of Crisis: Drama and Politics in Latin America* (Lexington: University Press of Kentucky, 1991), 143.

10. Eduardo Pavlovsky, *Paso de dos* (Buenos Aires: Ediciones Ayllu, 1990), 26, 27.

11. Ibid., 27, 28.

12. Ibid., 27.

13. Ibid., 29.

14. Feitlowitz, "A Dance of Death," 67.

15. Taylor, *Disappearing Acts*, 7.

16. In an interview with the playwright, Marguerite Feitlowitz mentions this disconnect between the fictional space of the play and the broader political context. See "A Dance of Death."

17. The script of *Paso de dos* lacks stage directions. Feitlowitz attended the play and describes this final scene in her article "A Dance of Death." This additional absence in the work brings up interesting issues regarding authorial control that lie outside the limited scope of this chapter, including the fact that Pavlovsky not only wrote but also starred in the production in Buenos Aires. While the lack of stage directions could grant complete artistic liberty to any other director who chose to stage the play, the script's ambiguity may also imply a desire on the part of the playwright to maintain control over its production, in effect silencing alternative performances.

18. Marguerite Feitlowitz explains in *A Lexicon of Terror: Argentina and the Legacies of Torture* (New York: Oxford University Press, 1998) how the Mothers of the Plaza de Mayo protested the presentation of *Paso de dos* because of the play's message and its "salaciousness" (3). These women do not see the positive (or feminist) interpretation that Yusem and Pavlovsky maintain are present in the work. It should also be noted that at the time of performance, the amnesty laws were in full effect, meaning that torturers enjoyed society's tacit approval. Not until much later would *escraches* and challenges to the amnesty laws change the tenor of societal acceptance.

19. Pavlovsky, *Paso de dos*, 12.

20. Ibid., 26, emphasis added.

21. Ibid., 20.

22. Ibid., 20–21.

23. Ibid., 21–23. It should be noted that She does provide some names and addresses, but in the context of the interrogation it is clear that they are meaningless. The questions do not correspond with the answers ("He: Who? / She: Having lunch with the one who smiles on the right / He: On the right of whom? . . . She: They met at a barbecue of a young woman with the name Ocampo"; ibid., 21). Meanwhile, the names appear either invented or random ("She: A good person, somewhat shy, who went to the Northland High School in Olivos where the Sury Hockey player Lea Fate came from"; ibid., 22). This scene serves to demonstrate She's ability to manipulate the interrogation sessions rather than offer proof of her giving away information.

24. Pavlovsky, *Paso de dos*, 27.

25. "Por algo será" is a phrase used by many Argentines to justify the military violence. Loosely translated as "there must have been a reason," it serves to explain away disappearance by implicating the victims in their fate, for example, "If Fulano was taken away, there must have been a reason."

26. Feitlowitz, "A Dance of Death," 71.

27. Scipioni, *Torturadores, apropiadores y asesinos*, 279.

28. There have been a few confirmed cases of torturers and prisoners developing love relationships. For information about relationships that developed in the ESMA, see Darío Gallo and Olga Wornat, "Amores clandestinos," *Noticias* 21, no. 1107 (May 14, 1998): 24–29. Laura Yusem refers to these relationships in her interview with Feitlowitz, claiming that the play forces spectators to confront difficult realities. Nevertheless, as Fernando Reati notes, these relations are much more prevalent in fictional representations of the dictatorship than in real life. Fernando Reati, "Historias de amores prohibidos: Prisioneras y torturadores en el imaginario argentino de la posdictadura," *Insula* 711 (2006): 27–32.

29. Ana Longoni, *Traiciones: La figura del traidor en los relatos acerca de los sobrevivientes de la represión* (Buenos Aires: Grupo Editorial Norma, 2007). Longoni's text considers three novels that treat the figure of the survivor: Miguel Bonasso's *Recuerdo de la muerte*, Rolo Diez's *Los compañeros*, and Liliana Heker's *El fin de la historia*.

30. Longoni, *Traiciones*, 151.

31. For more on how *Paso de dos* occupies an ambiguous zone between Manichaean extremes, in particular regarding gender, see Page, *Politics and Performance*.

32. Brenda Werth, *Theatre, Performance, and Memory Politics in Argentina* (New York: Palgrave Macmillan, 2010), 76.

33. The "love affair" between a torturer and a former victim raises numerous psychological issues that lie outside the scope of this chapter. For a thorough consideration of the subject, see Taylor, *Disappearing Acts*; Feitlowitz, "A Dance of Death"; or Scipioni, *Torturadores, apropiadores y asesinos*.

34. Pavlovsky, *Paso de dos*, 17.

35. Ibid., 15, emphasis added.

36. Edward Peters, *Torture* (Philadelphia: University of Pennsylvania Press, 1996), 184.

37. Pilar Calveiro, *Poder y desaparición: Los campos de concentración en Argentina* (Buenos Aires: Ediciones Colihue, 2006), 34.

38. Pavlovsky, *Paso de dos*, 11.

39. Ibid., 16–17.

40. Ibid., 18.

41. Ibid., 19.

42. Ibid., 25.

43. The ambiguities regarding She's position are even clearer in the performance, as the actress portraying She (Susy Evans, Pavlovsky's wife) alternates between resisting and willingly participating in the sexual acts with He. "I react differently each time," Evans states. "Sometimes it's erotic, sometimes it's torture. . . . What I never forget is that I'm going to die, that these are the last moments I have with him. And I don't want to die, I want to keep being with him." Feitlowitz, "A Dance of Death," 69–70.

44. For an examination of how wide ranging taboos regarding torture and "betrayal" prove in torture plays in the Southern Cone, see Nancy J. Gates-Madsen, "Tortured Silence and Silenced Torture in Mario Benedetti's *Pedro y el capitán*, Ariel Dorfman's *La muerte y la doncella* and Eduardo Pavlovsky's *Paso de dos*," *Latin American Theatre Review* 42, no. 1 (2008): 5–31.

45. On one end of the spectrum are works such as Jorge Andrade's *Milagre na cela* (Miracle in a prison cell, 1977), which moves beyond the suggested spirituality of Benedetti's play to depict the divine martyrdom of a nun who steadfastly refuses to grant her tormentors any type of victory, whatever the personal physical cost. Augusto Boal's *Torquemada* (1971) includes a striking scene in which seven sons are tortured consecutively in front of their mother, in order to discover the location of a resistance leader. In each case, their mother exhorts them to stay firm in their silence, believing they should die for the cause rather than reveal any information. The other plays Albuquerque examines similarly represent the interaction between interrogator (torturer) and victim as a continual battle of wills to elicit a "confession," depicting the frustration of the victimizers or the strength of the victim. Of all the works under consideration in Albuquerque's chapter, only one, Oduvaldo Vianna Filho's *Papa Highirte* (1968), mentions a victim who "broke" under torture, yet even in this case the torturers are

"exasperated by their victim's tenacity." Severino João Albuquerque, *Violent Acts: A Study of Contemporary Latin American Theatre* (Detroit: Wayne State University Press, 1991), 186.

46. The fictional portrayal of heroic torture victims is not limited to Latin America. As Darius Rejali explains, most torture narratives emphasize resistance rather than betrayal, and fictional works such as George Orwell's *Nineteen Eighty-Four* as well as nonfiction accounts such as Jean Améry's *At the Mind's Limits: Contemplations by a Survivor on Auschwitz and Its Realities* remain the exception for their description of utter and complete betrayal. Darius Rejali, "Whom Do You Trust? What Do You Count On?," in *On Nineteen Eighty-Four: Orwell and Our Future*, ed. Abbott Gleason, Jack Goldsmith, and Martha C. Nussbaum (Princeton, NJ: Princeton University Press, 2005), 155–79.

47. This is not to imply that the practice of torture is justified, or that it does not constitute a violation of human rights. I am calling attention to how the specific politics of torture victims can be supplanted by a broader discourse of human rights. For more on how the discourse of universal human rights came to dominate the discussion of the victims of the dictatorship's violence, see Emilio A. Crenzel, *Memory of the Argentina Disappearances: The Political History of Nunca Más*, trans. Laura Pérez Carrara (New York: Routledge, 2012).

48. Stern and Straus, *The Human Rights Paradox*.

49. Marcelo Brodsky, *Memoria en construcción: El debate sobre la ESMA* (Buenos Aires: la marca editora, 2005), 200.

50. Scipioni notes that the lack of political justification for torture marks *Paso de dos* as different from Pavlovsky's earlier works. *Torturadores, apropiadores y asesinos*, 247.

51. Eugenio Di Stefano, "From Revolution to Human Rights in Mario Benedetti's *Pedro y el Capitán*," *Journal of Latin American Cultural Studies* 20, no. 2 (2011): 121–37.

52. Pavlovsky, *Paso de dos*, 28.

53. Longoni, *Traiciones*, 181.

54. Longoni observes that the rhetoric of militant revolutionary groups considered that the militant's death served to give life to the revolutionary struggle. Ibid., 182.

55. Lindenberger, *Historical Drama*, 40.

56. Ibid., 39.

57. Ibid., 48.

58. Darius Rejali, "Movies of Modern Torture as Convenient Truths," in *Screening Torture: Media Representations of State Terror and Political Domination*, ed. Michael Flynn and Fabiola F. Salek (New York: Columbia University Press, 2012), 219–37. Rejali's examples of convenient truths in film include the use of Abu Ghraib photos to blackmail prisoners, or the misrepresentation of the effects of electrotorture. I employ his term to identify different convenient truths in *Paso de dos*.

59. Scarry, *The Body in Pain*, 29. It should be noted that torture's early origins do lie in extracting information as part of a judicial process (see Peters, *Torture.*). However, its contemporary use reveals an anachronistic understanding of this historical reality.

60. The "ticking time bomb" argument remains quite prevalent in more recent debates regarding the use of torture in the United States' "war on terror." Harvard law professor Alan Dershowitz has argued that since torture is (and will continue to be) practiced, it should be regulated in some way. He suggests issuing some type of "torture warrant" only in such instances where the infliction of pain on a limited number of individuals (the terrorist and the ticking time bomb) would prevent the suffering of many. Alan Dershowitz, "Tortured Reasoning," in *Torture: A Collection*, ed. Sanford Levinson (Oxford: Oxford University Press, 2004), 257–80. Elaine Scarry's response in the same volume counters, "An accurate understanding of torture cannot—in my view—be arrived at through the ticking time bomb argument, which (quite apart from what any one advocate may intend) opportunistically provides a flexible legal shield whose outcome is a systematic defense of torture." "Five Errors in the Reasoning of Alan Dershowitz," in *Torture: A Collection*, ed. Sanford Levinson (Oxford: Oxford University Press, 2004), 281. Recognizing the prevalence of such arguments in the post 9/11 world, she notes that one must always respond to the hypothetical case of the ticking time bomb, "even though the arguments (both for and against it) provide a false location for achieving a genuine understanding of torture." Ibid. I agree with Scarry's characterization of the ticking time bomb argument as at best insufficient for understanding the practice of torture and at worst a dangerous justification for its practice. More recently, *Screening Torture* also criticizes the prevalence of the "ticking time bomb" argument in cinematic representations of torture, which have become more prevalent post 9/11. Flynn and Salek, *Screening Torture*.

61. Scarry, *The Body in Pain*, 29.

62. Page duBois, *Torture and Truth* (New York: Routledge, 1991), 150. Taking issue with Scarry's claim that torture separates the individual from the ability to produce meaning, Ñacuñán Sáez asserts that the words uttered during torture possess a meaning that has measurable effects in the world outside the torture chamber. Nevertheless, the emphasis on the real-world consequences of information extracted during torture risks leaving the burden of responsibility with the victim; after all, his or her words provoke such terrifying consequences. Yet the key element of the torture victim's speech is not the meaning of the words themselves (in the sense of their real-world application) but the responsibility for that meaning. The words screamed out during a torture session may indeed mean something, but is the victim who produces the words from the depths of his or her pain responsible for that meaning? And who is in a position to judge? Ñacuñán Sáez, "Torture: A Discourse on Practice," in *Tattoo, Torture, Mutilation, and Adornment: The Denaturalization of the Body in Culture and Text*, ed. Frances E. Mascia-Lees and Patricia Sharpe (Albany: State University of New York Press, 1992), 126–44.

63. Scarry, *The Body in Pain*, 29.

64. Ibid., 35.

65. Ibid., 30. Idelber Avelar takes issue with Scarry's characterization of torture as unmaking the world, arguing that "Scarry's thesis presupposes that what is destroyed by torture—'civilization,' 'world'—is somehow completely uncontaminated by torture

itself." "Five Theses on Torture," *Journal of Latin American Cultural Studies* 10, no. 3 (2001): 259. Nevertheless, the central thrust of Scarry's argument, that in the torture chamber the victim loses all connection to exterior referents, remains sound whether those exterior referents stand completely outside of the torture experience or are somehow implicated by it.

66. Quoted in Feitlowitz, *A Lexicon of Terror*, 67.

67. Taylor, *Theatre of Crisis*, 111.

68. Feitlowitz describes watching the play as "a punishing experience." "A Dance of Death," 64.

69. Feitlowitz, *A Lexicon of Terror*, 3.

70. Longoni, *Traiciones*, 14.

71. Pavlovsky, *Paso de dos*, 19.

72. This relationship between powerful fictional overt silences and uncomfortable societal covert ones reveals the ethical issues at play regarding the representation of torture in works such as *Paso de dos*. Debates regarding the circulation of images from Abu Ghraib prison and the justification of torture in the "war on terror" underscore the importance of an ethics of representation. As Elizabeth Dauphinée argues regarding the use of photographs from Abu Ghraib by human rights activists, "there is no ethically pure way to circulate those images," for they remain within the "economy of violence" in which they were produced. "The Politics of the Body in Pain: Reading the Ethics of Imagery," *Security Dialogue* 38, no. 2 (2007): 149, 150. Dauphinée explores the "irresolvable ethical dilemma" posed by the use of violent imagery, despite the good intentions by those who show the photos. Because the use of the images always ends up somehow explaining the violence (either condemning or excusing it), the author notes that refusing to reproduce them represents an ethics in itself, thereby suggesting that silence is a viable alternative, perhaps the lesser of two evils. Ibid., 148–50.

73. As Taylor explains, "The violence at work in genocide and other kinds of victimization is difficult if not impossible to represent; it works on the real rather than the symbolic order. It does not *mean* or *signify* anything else." Taylor, *Theatre of Crisis*, 123.

74. Lawrence L. Langer, *Versions of Survival: The Holocaust and the Human Spirit* (Albany: State University of New York Press, 1982), 12.

Chapter 2. Filling in the Space of Disappearance

1. Ana Longoni notes that this tension between individual and collective aims was present in the original happening. The initial plan was to create individualized silhouettes for each victim, but since the list of victims was incomplete, the Mothers of the Plaza de Mayo advocated creating identical silhouettes to represent the victims as a collective whole. Nevertheless, some silhouettes did have defining characteristics, as people requested figures that resembled a particular loved one. Ana Longoni, "Photographs and Silhouettes: Visual Politics in Argentina," trans. Yaiza Hernández, *Afterall Journal* 25 (2010), http://www.afterall.org/journal/issue.25/photographs-and-silhouettes -visual-politics-in-the-human-rights-movement-of-argentina.

2. This tension complements the human rights paradox articulated by Stern and Straus. In this case, rather than a pull between the local and the universal, one sees a tension between the individual and the collective, within a particular local context. Stern and Straus, *The Human Rights Paradox*.

3. President Menem's tenure is not known for advances in human rights work. While he did collaborate with the Grandmothers of the Plaza de Mayo, facilitating their quest for justice regarding the children of the disappeared, the Menem government did not collaborate with other human rights organizations, many of which turned to international courts to further the cause for justice. Cases brought before the Inter-American court led to a law of financial reparation, first for ex–political prisoners, and later extended to family members. Prosecutions in Italy regarding Italian citizens who were disappeared prompted a mixed response from the Menem government. While the government provided airfare for one witness to testify in a trial that began in 1987, when Italian judges attempted to obtain evidence for a different trial in 1994, Menem passed an executive decree prohibiting collaboration with foreign judges. Michelle D. Bonner, "Defining Rights in Democratization: The Argentine Government and Human Rights Organizations, 1983–2003," *Latin American Politics and Society* 47, no. 4 (2005): 65–66.

4. Both texts tackle the challenge of telling the story of disappearance within the postamnesty period of silencing, which is why I have chosen to consider them in conjunction.

5. The Equipo Argentino de Antropología Forense (EAAF) was established in 1984 to respond to judicial orders to exhume mass gravesites. Existing methods, which included the use of bulldozers, were unscientific and often led to destruction of the remains, so a team of forensic scientists including Clyde Snow, a leading international expert in forensic anthropology, traveled to Argentina to train EAAF members in traditional archeological and forensic anthropology techniques. The group is entirely supported by international grant money, and during the years following the return to democracy it worked at several gravesites attempting to categorize and identify remains. Although the organization was able to positively identify remains and bring closure to some families during the early 1990s, its work definitely benefited from the postboom climate of openness, and the 1996–97 Biannual Report notes a marked increase in the number of family members approaching the organization for help identifying missing loved ones. Increased access to police documentation in 1997 and 1998 also allowed the EAAF to more accurately identify remains, and their work significantly expanded in scope during these years. "1996–97 Biannual Report" (Equipo Argentino de Antropología Forense [EAAF], 1997).

6. Eric Stener Carlson, *I Remember Julia: Voices of the Disappeared* (Philadelphia: Temple University Press, 1996), xiii–xiv. Issues of identity are of central importance when telling the story of the disappeared. Since "Julia" is not the real name of the victim whose remains were discovered in the graveyard, I preserve the name within quotation marks throughout the chapter in order to call attention to the paradox of telling "Julia's" story without revealing her name.

7. A report on the early years of the work of the EAAF details the way in which the military took great pains to hide the bodies of their victims by falsifying death certificates, disposing of bodies under cover of darkness, and burying individuals whose identities were known in anonymous graves under the label N.N. Mauricio Cohen Salama, *Tumbas anónimas: Informe sobre la identificación de restos de víctimas de la represión ilegal* (Buenos Aires: Catálogos Editora, 1992), 38. The work of the EAAF arose as a means to positively identify individuals who were suspected to be desaparecidos. One stated goal of the organization is "to contribute to the reconstruction of the recent past, which was often distorted or hidden by the government institutions who are themselves implicated in the crimes under investigation," a clear indication of the testimonial nature of the EAAF's activities. "1992 Annual Report" (Equipo Argentino de Antropología Forense [EAAF], 1992), 2.

8. Carlson, *I Remember Julia*, xiv.

9. Ibid., xiv–xv.

10. A discussion of the possibility of accessing a truly "unmediated" account of any event lies outside the scope of this chapter. Carlson obviously serves as mediator in *I Remember Julia*, but his efforts to quote his interviewees in the first person speak to a desire to share their words without external commentary or judgment.

11. The exception to this is the chapter titled "The Clinic," in which Carlson attempts to interview doctors and directors at the clinic where "Julia" worked and from where she was taken. Rather than provide direct testimony of employees, Carlson relates his fruitless efforts to glean information.

12. Thomas W. Laqueur, "The Dead Body and Human Rights," in *The Body*, ed. Sean T. Sweeney and Ian Hodder (Cambridge: Cambridge University Press, 2002), 75–93.

13. Allen Feldman, "Memory Theaters, Virtual Witnessing, and the Trauma-Aesthetic," *Biography: An Interdisciplinary Quarterly* 27, no. 1 (2004): 170.

14. Carlson, *I Remember Julia*, 68.

15. Ibid., xii. Carlson explains that the lack of X-rays or dental records makes positive identification challenging in the majority of cases, and he refers to the identification of murder victims as "the rare exception rather than the norm." Ibid., xii–xiii.

16. Carlson, *I Remember Julia*, xvii.

17. Ibid., xiii, xv.

18. Laqueur, "The Dead Body and Human Rights," 77.

19. Ibid., 81, 92.

20. For more on the history of EAAF and its international work, see eaaf.typepad .com/founding_of_eaaf/, accessed April 15, 2014.

21. Ari Gandsman, "The Limits of Kinship Mobilizations and the (A)politics of Human Rights in Argentina," *Journal of Latin American and Caribbean Anthropology* 17, no. 2 (2012): 197. The most extreme position, expressed by Hebe de Bonafini, president of the more radical branch of the Mothers of Plaza de Mayo, rejects any exhumations at all, thereby rejecting the notion of the missing as dead bodies.

22. Carlson, *I Remember Julia*, 3.

23. Such contextualization is understandable given the North American audience for the book and Carlson's aim to educate a wider public regarding the silenced story of disappearance in Argentina.

24. Carlson, *I Remember Julia*, ix.

25. Ibid., x.

26. I have chosen to preserve the replacement identity within quotation marks in order to highlight the importance of this displacement. One must note that the practice of using a pseudonym is not particular to Carlson.

27. The suppression of personal information also occurs in the 1992 EAAF collection *Tumbas anónimas*. The EAAF clarifies that although they changed certain names at the request of family members, the use of false names to a certain extent maintains the victims' status as N.N., and they emphasize that their principal objective is to "restore a name and a history to those who were stripped of both." Cohen Salama, *Tumbas anónimas*, 13.

28. Again, the perception of "Julia" as representative of the collective group of victims furthers Carlson's goal of educating a broader public regarding the horror of the Argentine dictatorship, yet at the same time it inevitably diminishes a consideration of "Julia's" individuality.

29. Gandsman, "The Limits of Kinship Mobilizations," 198.

30. Ibid., 199.

31. For a consideration of the importance of agency in testimonial speaking subjects that builds on Gayatri Spivak's well-known essay "Can the Subaltern Speak?," see John Beverley, "Testimonio, Subalternity, and Narrative Authority," in *Handbook of Qualitative Research*, ed. N. K. Denzin and Y. S. Lincoln (Thousand Oaks: Sage, 2000), 555–65. While "Julia," a middle-class doctor who works at a clinic serving low-income patients, cannot be considered a member of a subaltern group, the testimonies of victims of political violence struggle with some of the same types of issues, such as resisting the authoritarian impulse to fix meaning or trying to find an audience for their stories. In this case the actors are not marginalized because of race or class but because of their political situation.

32. As Mark Roseman notes in the case of the Jewish Holocaust, "The survivor's testimony is often *all* there is: friends and relatives have been murdered; the family property, family letters, everything that belonged to the survivor's past life has been destroyed." "Surviving Memory: Truth and Inaccuracy in Holocaust Testimony," *Journal of Holocaust Education* 8, no. 1 (1999): 2.

33. Carlson, *I Remember Julia*, 25.

34. Ibid., 47.

35. Ibid., 66.

36. Ibid., 43.

37. Ibid., chapters titled "Manuel" and "Laura."

38. Ibid., chapter titled "Luciano."

39. The tendency by many who knew "Julia" to downplay or deny any type of militancy may also indicate the way in which the dominant human rights discourse

advanced by the *Nunca Más* report had been internalized by those attempting to process the violence. As explained by Emilio Crenzel in his analysis of the emergence and narrative of the CONADEP report, the document legitimized the characterization of victims as apolitical (effacing any mention of political affiliations in favor of generic characteristics such as gender or age), thereby establishing a dominant discourse regarding the victims as "innocents." Following Steve Stern, Crenzel claims that the *Nunca Más* report introduced an "emblematic memory" regarding the disappeared that dominated discussion and analysis of the dictatorship years. *Memory of the Argentina Disappearances*, 95–96.

40. Carlson, *I Remember Julia*, 148.

41. This is not to say that all testimonies are equal in terms of truth-value. I simply note that Carlson chooses to include voices from differing sides of the political spectrum; whether these testimonies hold up under closer scrutiny is not considered in his project. One reviewer of Carlson's book notes that these particular competing explanations for the dictatorship prove "especially significant" given that initially the coup was welcomed by large sectors of Argentine society as a way to control escalating violence on the left and right; these voices speak to the type of violence that was seen as acceptable at the time. Myriam Yvonne Jehenson, "Book Review: *I Remember Julia: Voices of the Disappeared*," *Humanity and Society* 23, no. 4 (1999): 389.

42. Again, for a detailed discussion of the way in which the CONADEP *Nunca Más* report came to establish an "emblematic memory" of the disappeared as apolitical, see Crenzel, *Memory of the Argentina Disappearances*.

43. For a discussion of competing versions of the memory of a life, see William Zinsser, *Inventing the Truth: The Art and Craft of Memoir* (Boston: Houghton Mifflin, 1998). The introduction in particular talks about his mother being saddened by his representation of his childhood as more melancholy than she remembered it. He asks, "Had I subconsciously reinvented it to make it more lonely than it really was? Had she subconsciously never noticed?" Ibid., 7. In this case, at least the subject of the life is a vocal participant in the creation of the story, making the ambiguous re-creation of "Julia's" life story even more problematic.

44. I use the word "truth" carefully, as issues of veracity regarding testimonial narrative prove thorny. The reliability of the witnessing subject combines with the possibility of language to ever represent trauma, and issues of accuracy versus urgency abound in testimonies of violence. For more on the reliability of the witness, see Beverley, "Testimonio, Subalternity, and Narrative Authority." For a thorough discussion of testimony and veracity, see the controversy surrounding David Stoll's assertion that Rigoberta Menchú's emblematic testimonio may not be the eyewitness testimony it purports to be. Two key voices in the debate include John Beverley, "The Real Thing," in *The Real Thing: Testimonial Discourse and Latin America*, ed. Georg M. Gugelberger (Durham, NC: Duke University Press, 1996), 266–86; and Doris Sommer, *Proceed with Caution*. Numerous other voices could be added to this scholarly sampling; suffice it to say that very few remained neutral in the debate. For a good discussion of trauma and language, see Leigh Gilmore, *The Limits of Autobiography: Trauma and*

Testimony (Ithaca, NY: Cornell University Press, 2001). Finally, for opposing arguments regarding the relationship between accuracy and urgency—should issues of truth play a role in testimonies about trauma?—see Lawrence L. Langer, *Holocaust Testimony: The Ruins of Memory* (New Haven, CT: Yale University Press, 1991); Roseman, "Surviving Memory"; and Patti Lather, "Issues of Validity in Openly Ideological Research: Between a Rock and a Soft Place," *Interchange* 17, no. 4 (1986): 63–84. Langer argues that the human element in Holocaust testimonies precludes issues of truth-value; meanwhile, Roseman argues that a concern with accuracy is useful for understanding the processes of memory itself. Finally, Lather asserts that sympathy with a victim or identification with a cause does not preclude truth standards, and that even scholars who engage in "openly ideological research" must pursue "rigor as well as relevance" (67).

45. Antonius C. G. M. Robben, "The Politics of Truth and Emotion among Victims and Perpetrators of Violence," in *Fieldwork under Fire: Contemporary Stories of Violence and Survival*, ed. Carolyn Nordstrom and Antonius C. G. M. Robben (Berkeley: University of California Press, 1995), 98.

46. Ibid., 86.

47. According to Robben, the complex relationship between those touched by trauma and those attempting to "give voice" to their stories revolves around the mutual manipulation or preservation of secrets. Faced with victims and families of victims whose stories underscore the barbarity of the military and former officers who defy demonization, Robben became well aware of the extent to which each party in the interview struggled to persuade. Yet he also notes that such seduction or manipulation is not always intentional. Like many scholars, Robben was reluctant to doubt the veracity of victims' statements. After all, "it is much easier to acknowledge manipulation by victimizers than by victims." Ibid., 84. However, victims too manipulate interview situations, and often Robben would find himself listening to tales that were so moving that he was unable to ask any questions. While he does not accuse his informants of deliberately manipulating his emotions, he notes that such charged accounts obscured his ability to recognize what he calls "the discourse behind the conversation." Ibid., 94.

48. Carlson, *I Remember Julia*, 131.

49. Robben, "The Politics of Truth and Emotion," 87.

50. Carlson, *I Remember Julia*, xvii.

51. For an excellent exploration of the interview/subject relationship, see Ruth Behar, *The Vulnerable Observer: Anthropology That Breaks Your Heart* (Boston: Beacon Press, 1996). Behar advocates clearly articulating the observer's methods and personal involvement in the subject studied. For a detailed look at how Behar highlights her role and relationship with her subject in the text, see Ruth Behar, *Translated Woman: Crossing the Border with Esperanza's Story* (Boston: Beacon Press, 1993).

52. Sandra Harding, *Feminism and Methodology: Social Science Issues*, Readers Notes edition (Bloomington: Indiana University Press, 1987).

53. The reference to Carlson's "I" comes from Behar's discussions of "resisting the 'I' of the ethnographer as a privileged eye, a voyeuristic eye, an all-powerful eye." *The*

Vulnerable Observer, 21. This is not to imply that Carlson hides any sinister motive or goal, simply that he speaks quite little of himself, apart from retelling how moved he was to investigate "Julia's" story. His role as investigator remains outside the text; the book jacket explains he conducted interviews during two years, one of them as a Fulbright Scholar, and that at the time of publication he was a Fellow for Physicians for Human Rights, and the text explains his volunteer work with EAAF, perhaps leading to one reviewer's erroneous identification of Carlson as "an American anthropologist." Michael Whine et al., "Book Reviews, Terrorism and Political Violence," *Terrorism and Political Violence* 11, no. 1 (2007): 142.

54. Elzbieta Sklodowska, *Testimonio hispanoamericano: Historia, teoría, poética* (New York: Peter Lang, 1992), 181.

55. Clifford Geertz, *Works and Lives: The Anthropologist as Author* (Stanford, CA: Stanford University Press, 1988), 3.

56. For more on the authorial presence in traditional ethnographic study, see Geertz, *Works and Lives*.

57. Richard Rorty, "Solidarity or Objectivity?," in *Post-Analytic Philosophy*, ed. John Rajchman and Cornel West (New York: Columbia University Press, 1985), 3–19.

58. Carlson explains that his choice to write about "Julia" was guided by practical considerations, stating that "there was a great deal of forensic evidence available that positively identified her as a murder victim of the Argentine military." Carlson, *I Remember Julia*, xiv.

59. Carlo Ginzberg, "Just One Witness," in *Probing the Limits of Representation: Nazism and the "Final Solution,"* ed. Saul Friedlander (Cambridge, MA: Harvard University Press, 1992), 82–96.

60. Carlson, *I Remember Julia*, 181.

61. Feldman, "Memory Theaters, Virtual Witnessing, and the Trauma-Aesthetic," 165.

62. Ibid., 169, emphasis added.

63. Ibid., 170. It should be noted that Feldman's analysis deals with first-person testimonies of violence; nevertheless, his critique of the way in which testimonies are emplotted to fulfill particular functions is equally applicable to *I Remember Julia*, as Carlson's organization of the voices fulfills expectations regarding the function of telling the tale of disappearance: a hope for some type of catharsis or therapeutic effect.

64. Carlson, *I Remember Julia*, xvii.

65. Ibid., 183.

66. Ibid., 33.

67. Ibid., 50.

68. Ibid., xv–xvi.

69. Ibid., xvi.

70. Feldman, "Memory Theaters, Virtual Witnessing, and the Trauma-Aesthetic," 194, emphasis added.

71. This incident is related by Julio Flores, one of the artists responsible for the *Siluetazo*. Julio Flores, "Siluetas," in *El Siluetazo*, ed. Ana Longoni and Gustavo Bruzzone (Buenos Aires: Adriana Hidalgo, 2008), 83–107.

72. For this reason, the Mothers insisted that the silhouettes be hung vertically, rather than pasted on the ground. Eduardo Grüner, "La invisibilidad estratégica, o la redención política de los vivos: Violencia política y representación estética en el siglo de las desapariciones," in *El Siluetazo*, ed. Ana Longoni and Gustavo Bruzzone (Buenos Aires: Adriana Hidalgo, 2008), 285–308.

73. Carlson, *I Remember Julia*, 182.

74. Ibid., 183, emphasis added.

75. Part of the lack of nuance could be explained by Carlson's age at the time of investigation and writing—he was still a college student when he volunteered with the EAAF, and he conducted his research during his last year of college and the year after graduation.

76. Feldman, "Memory Theaters, Virtual Witnessing, and the Trauma-Aesthetic," 194.

Chapter 3. "The Shape Described by Their Absence"

1. Flores, "Siluetas," 100.

2. Ana Longoni and Gustavo Bruzzone, "Introducción," in *El Siluetazo*, ed. Ana Longoni and Gustavo Bruzzone (Buenos Aires: Adriana Hidalgo, 2008), 28.

3. At first glance it may seem strange to compare an obviously invented tale of disappearance with the real-life efforts of a forensic team member to piece together a portrait of a victim, yet both works address the fundamental question of how to write the story of a person who has been erased. Placing these works in comparison helps illustrate the parallel responses to the pre-1995 period of silence and silencing: breaking the silences through empirical investigation or working within the silences themselves to tell the tale of trauma.

4. Grüner, "La invisibilidad estratégica, o la redención política de los vivos," 298.

5. It must be noted that Saer was not a political exile—he moved to Paris in 1968 to pursue his studies and remained there until his death in 2005. Nevertheless, the corpus of his work remains intimately linked with his homeland, and several of his novels address the tumultuous political times of the 1970s and 1980s. Both he and Carlson approach the crime of disappearance as "outsiders" in a sense, Carlson as a North American academic and Saer as an exile.

6. Gustavo Valle, "La incertidumbre elocuente (entrevista con Juan José Saer)," *Letras Libres*, June 2002, accessed November 8, 2015, http://www.letraslibres.com /revista/convivio/la-incertidumbre-elocuenteentrevista-con-juan-jose-saer.

7. By proposing a political reading of the novel I align with Florinda F. Goldberg's rather than Philip Swanson's interpretation of the text. While Goldberg emphasizes the centrality of disappearance in *La pesquisa*, Swanson argues that a political reading rests on "a removal or neutralization of the ambiguity and indeterminacy that

seems so crucial to Saer's literary universe." Philip Swanson, "The Detective and the Disappeared: Memory, Forgetting, and Other Confusions in Juan José Saer's *La pesquisa*," in *Investigating Identities: Questions of Identity in Contemporary International Crime Fiction*, ed. Marieke Krajenbrink and Kate M. Quinn (Amsterdam, Netherlands: Rodopi, 2009), 292. In this chapter I argue that it is precisely this ambiguity, rooted in silence, that fortifies the political reading—the two are not mutually exclusive. Saer may not be an overtly political author (unlike Carlson, he does not define his text as a response to societal amnesia or silencing), yet his text addresses the legacy of disappearance in Argentina. A focus on universal themes such as the nature of knowledge does not preclude a focus on a particular geographical location and historical moment. See Florinda Goldberg, "*La pesquisa* de Juan José Saer: Alambradas de la ficción," *Hispamérica: Revista de Literatura* 26, no. 76–77 (1997): 89–100.

8. Quoted in Avery F. Gordon, *Ghostly Matters: Haunting and the Sociological Imagination* (Minneapolis: University of Minnesota Press, 1997), 6.

9. Ibid., 8.

10. Numerous critics have remarked on the need for a different type of narration for the years of state terror. In fact, Florinda F. Goldberg begins her study of *La pesquisa* by citing various intellectuals who have commented on this problem in Argentina, implying that the central issue facing any writer attempting to engage the recent past in Argentina is not just the imperative to tell the story but the challenge of finding appropriate words and modes of telling. "*La pesquisa* de Juan José Saer."

11. See, for example, Friedlander, *Probing the Limits of Representation*. See also Felman and Laub, *Testimony*.

12. This is perhaps best exemplified in Elie Wiesel's oft-quoted paradox, "A novel about Auschwitz is either not a novel or it is not about Auschwitz," which underscores the seemingly immense gap between language and experience. This dual effect of catastrophe is also examined in Felman and Laub, *Testimony*.

13. Jean-François Lyotard, *The Differend: Phrases in Dispute*, trans. Georges van den Abeele (Minneapolis: University of Minnesota Press, 1988), 13.

14. Ibid., 80.

15. Lea Wernick Fridman, *Words and Witness: Narrative and Aesthetic Strategies in the Representation of the Holocaust* (Albany: State University of New York Press, 2000), 6.

16. Ibid., 13.

17. Ibid., 19.

18. Ibid., 20.

19. The ability to preserve the opaque heart of catastrophe sets fictional representations of trauma apart from their traditional testimonial counterparts. By using a language that honors the silences of trauma, fictional tales are able to avoid the "prescriptive expectations" Feldman bemoans in traditional testimonies, for such expectations are not mapped on top of fiction in the same way they are for texts that stake a closer claim to approaching the truth. Freed from the burden of responding to a particular set of expectations, fiction can push the limits of what is considered a "truthful" rendering of historical horror such as torture or disappearance.

20. F. Goldberg, "*La pesquisa* de Juan José Saer," 91.

21. Ibid., 94–95.

22. Juan José Saer, *The Investigation*, trans. Helen Lane (London: Serpent's Tail, 1999), 1.

23. Ibid.

24. Ibid., 11.

25. Ibid., 10.

26. It seems no accident that Saer locates the police station on a street named after a thinker whose name evokes confidence in progress through reasoning and scientific investigation. Such detail adds to the creation of the image of an ideal investigation, where even the location of the office itself inspires confidence.

27. Saer, *The Investigation*, 22.

28. Juan José Saer, *La pesquisa* (Buenos Aires: Seix Barral, 1994), 117.

29. Saer, *The Investigation*, 118.

30. Ibid., 30, 101.

31. Ibid., 69.

32. F. Goldberg, "*La pesquisa* de Juan José Saer," 95.

33. Saer, *The Investigation*, 2.

34. Ibid., 4–5, 3.

35. Ibid., 119–20.

36. Ibid., 3.

37. One should also note the disparity in ages between the victims. Most victims of the dictatorship were much younger than the Parisian ladies, as young as high school age in some cases. While I am reluctant to offer any judgments as to the relative value of the victims' lives, Pichón's description implies that the Parisian victims were well past their prime, in stark contrast to the desaparecidos in Argentina.

38. Saer, *The Investigation*, 79–80.

39. These estimates are based on the 11,061 victims cited in *Nunca Más* (assuming that around 80 percent of the disappearances occurred during the first few years of the dictatorship). Many human rights groups place the number of victims much higher, at around 30,000, or almost three times the numbers listed in the CONADEP report.

40. Saer, *The Investigation*, 159.

41. Fridman, *Words and Witness*, 21.

42. Hayden White, *The Content of the Form: Narrative Discourse and Historical Representation* (Baltimore: Johns Hopkins University Press, 1987), 44. This is not to say that any set of real events can be emplotted in any number of ways—a sort of "anything goes" type of history. Each version does hold true to the rules of evidence and must base its validity upon the events themselves. Thus while there may be various explanations for a certain set of events, some explanations will be more compelling than others.

43. Saer, *The Investigation*, 109.

44. Ibid., 117.

45. Ibid., 127.

46. Taking her cue from the characters' discussion of the two orders of truth depicted in the mysterious manuscript, "the truth of experience" and "the truth of fiction," Florinda Goldberg concludes that the story of el Gato and Elisa's disappearance cannot be told, because to do so would cheapen it by turning it into "the truth of fiction," an object of consumption. In her words, "Ethically, when faced with disappearance, either one relates what is known or one doesn't relate anything." "*La pesquisa* de Juan José Saer," 99. While I agree that there are ethical issues at play with attempting to represent any disappearance, such as the ones treated in other chapters about torture and the children of the disappeared, I believe that Saer is in effect telling the tale of the disappearance through so ostensibly *not* telling it, through the nature of the substitute narrative. The story that cannot be told is not told, but it is ultimately sensed.

47. Saer, *The Investigation*, 82–85.

48. Ibid., 85.

49. Ibid., 7.

50. Ibid., 158.

51. Saer's corpus of work is characterized by such preoccupations with language and perspective. *Nadie nada nunca*, for example, relates certain scenes more than once, in greater and lesser detail, in order to call attention to the relationship between language and point of view. Juan José Saer, *Nadie nada nunca* (Mexico City: Siglo XXI, 1980). Similarly, *Glosa* and *Lo imborrable* also treat this topic of the ability or inability to capture what is real through language. Juan José Saer, *Glosa* (Barcelona: Destino, 1988); Juan José Saer, *Lo imborrable* (Madrid: Alianza, 1993).

52. Saer, *The Investigation*, 1.

53. María Teresa Gramuglio, "El lugar de Saer," in *Juan José Saer por Juan José Saer* (Buenos Aires: Editorial Celtia, 1986), 294.

54. Saer, *The Investigation*, 25, emphasis added.

55. Ibid., 83, emphasis added. The original phrase is "en rigor de verdad," a clear allusion to "truth."

56. Ibid., 88.

57. For a detailed discussion of how Saer's narrative undermines mimetic representation, see Daniel Blaustein, "Estrategias narrativas en *La pesquisa* de Juan José Saer," *LLJournal* 2, no. 2 (2007).

58. Saer, *The Investigation*, 15.

59. White, *The Content of the Form*, 45.

60. Saer, *The Investigation*, 50.

61. This is not to say that the evidence does not exist—el Gato's and Elisa's bodies lie somewhere. The lack of official impetus remains the central obstacle to any type of investigation of this crime. Nevertheless, the absence of bodies or physical evidence of a crime impacts the ability to mount any type of exploration into their disappearance.

62. Fridman, *Words and Witness*, 21.

63. Lyotard, *The Differend*, 80, emphasis added.

64. Saer, *The Investigation*, 58.

65. Ibid., 68.

66. Ibid., 61.

67. F. Goldberg, "*La pesquisa* de Juan José Saer," 97–98.

68. Saer, *The Investigation*, 67–68.

69. Pauline Boss, *Ambiguous Loss: Learning to Live with Unresolved Grief* (Cambridge, MA: Harvard University Press, 1999), 14.

70. Ibid., 71. Boss explores two central types of ambiguous loss in her eponymous book, the physically absent yet psychologically present (disappeared victims of oppressive regimes) and the physically present yet psychologically absent (such as victims of Alzheimer's). While obviously the first type is most pertinent to this discussion of disappearance, in a way the substitute narrative demonstrates this second type of ambiguity, as it is physically present (populated with clues, criminals, justice) yet psychologically empty (ultimately unresolved).

71. Saer, *The Investigation*, 181, 119.

72. Gordon, *Ghostly Matters*, 113.

73. Saer, *The Investigation*, 120.

74. Morvan also experiences these visceral sensations during his empirical search for truth, but he is unable to utilize them as proof in his system of investigation. For example, when he enters the bathroom of the penultimate victim, Morvan "had the sensation of proximity and imminence that made him so anxious." Ibid., 102. Nevertheless, the same sentence notes that only the lab will be able to determine who used the shower and under what circumstances. Morvan's instincts are present, but he chooses to ignore them, only arriving at visceral conclusions in his subconscious mind. He suffers from a recurring dream, in which he is convinced certain buildings are temples, despite a complete absence of supporting evidence, a conclusion he never could draw in his waking life. Morvan thus experiences visceral emotions and is capable of drawing conclusions from them, but, at least while awake, he is unable to proceed beyond his emotional reactions to any conclusions.

75. Sommer, *Proceed with Caution*, 162. Sommer makes this distinction in her analysis of the silences and absences in Toni Morrison's *Beloved*. In this case, however, the gap between knowledge and knowing is present only for the characters in the novel. While Sethe refuses to share her story with Paul D, the reader learns of her terrifying experience through the omniscient narration. In *La pesquisa*, however, the reader is also denied the full story of disappearance, for neither the characters nor the narrator articulate the fate of el Gato and Elisa.

76. Toni Morrison, "Unspeakable Things Unspoken: The Afro-American Presence in American Literature," *Michigan Quarterly Review* 28, no. 1 (1989): 11.

77. An unexpected result of telling a silenced story through narrative substitution is that readers or critics may miss the subtle clues. In his analysis of *La pesquisa*, Julio Premat lists four central mysteries of the novel, yet the disappearance of el Gato and Elisa does not figure among them. Admittedly his article chooses to focus on aspects of writing in the novel (how Saer equates the guilt of committing a crime to the guilt of writing) rather than political themes, yet the failure to acknowledge the centrality of the story of disappearance in the novel effectively condemns the story to silence once

again. Julio Premat, "El crimen de la escritura: La novela policial según Juan José Saer," *Latin American Literary Review* 24, no. 48 (1996): 19–38.

78. Interestingly enough, both Saer and Carlson provide a type of "cover story" that conceals the true tale of disappearance. Yet while Carlson's tale provides a protective narrative that looks toward an eventual triumph of language and clarity, Saer's cover story serves to unsettle the reader and call attention to the profoundly unresolved nature of disappearance.

79. Longoni, "Photographs and Silhouettes: Visual Politics in Argentina."

80. Ibid.

81. Saer, *The Investigation*, 18.

82. Ibid., 19, 20.

Chapter 4. Silencing the Politics of Identity

1. Asociación de Abuelas de Plaza de Mayo, *La historia de Abuelas: 30 años de búsqueda* (Buenos Aires: Abuelas de Plaza de Mayo, 2007), 185, emphasis added.

2. Publications by the Grandmothers include Julio E. Nosiglia, *Botín de guerra*, 3rd ed. (Buenos Aires: Abuelas de Plaza de Mayo, 2007); and Asociación de Abuelas de Plaza de Mayo, *La historia de Abuelas*. For a history of the Grandmothers' search published outside of Argentina, see Rita Arditti, *Searching for Life: The Grandmothers of the Plaza de Mayo and the Disappeared Children of Argentina* (Berkeley: University of California Press, 1999).

3. Langer, *Versions of Survival*, 12.

4. According to Adriana Lorenzón, one of the writers for *Montecristo*, 2006 "was a particularly apt year to make the telenovela because of a public openness to the theme. On one hand, because of the thirtieth anniversary of the coup and the creation of the Grandmothers of Plaza de Mayo. On the other, because, with the overturning of the amnesty laws and the reopening of trials of those responsible for the horror, the way was cleared for the search for truth and justice." Adriana Schettini, "El fenómeno Montecristo," *La Nación*, November 26, 2006.

5. According to the Grandmothers, most media outlets characterized the restoration of the twins to their biological families as "damaging," with no mention of the original crime committed against the children's parents or the crime of appropriation. Asociación de Abuelas de Plaza de Mayo, *La historia de Abuelas*, 103.

6. One should note that Osorio rejects the characterization of her novel as "testimonial," claiming she did not set out to "do politics" with the book. Verónica Abdala, "La apropiación de bebés, un nuevo tópico literario," *Página/12*, June 20, 1999. Nevertheless, its choice of subject matter and the timing of its publication engage it in the larger testimonial project of breaking the repressive silences of the regime. Furthermore, the website of the Grandmothers includes the novel in its list of "recommended reading," further indication of its implied connection to their human rights cause. See http://www.abuelas.org.ar/areas.php?area=historias_abu.php&der1=der1_mat.php&der2=der2_mat.php, accessed November 8, 2015.

7. Silvina Friera, "No toda la sociedad es culpable," *Página/12*, October 24, 2006.

8. *A veinte años, Luz* was originally published by Alba Editorial (Barcelona) in 1998. It was released in Argentina in 1999 by Mondadori.

9. The opening episode was broadcast on April 25, 2006.

10. These "For Identity" events incorporate entertainment strategies to educate the public regarding appropriated children. The pioneer event, Theatre for Identity, was a collaborative project between the Grandmothers and playwrights, actors, and directors, who wrote and produced plays that centered on themes of appropriation. The collaborative model of Theatre for Identity informs the other "For Identity" events.

11. The 2012 publications include re-releases in French, Italian, Polish, and Chinese. For a list of versions and editions, see elsaosorio.com, accessed November 8, 2015.

12. Italy, Spain, and Colombia also made *Montecristo* adaptations; in 2007 the finished telenovela was sold to Albania, Bulgaria, Israel, Macedonia, Serbia, and the Philippines, adding to the forty-plus markets that had already purchased the program in 2006. Charles Newbery, "Telefe Extends 'Montecristo' Sales," *Variety*, February 19, 2007.

13. Dom Serafini, "Argentina: Domestic Recovery Fuels International Boom for Telefe," *Video Age International* 27, no. 1 (2007), http://www.videoageinternational .com/articles/2007/01/telefe.html.

14. In 2007 the program was a finalist in the drama category of the New York Festival, and it won the Martín Fierro de Oro award. For a discussion of *Montecristo*'s strengths as a representation of the dictatorship years, see in particular Nora Mazziotti, "La venganza de Montecristo y la máquina novelesca," *Tram(p)as de la comunicación y la cultura* 47 (2006): 60–64. Elizabeth Jelin also praised the telenovela's "complexity of character development, nuance, ambivalent situations and moral dilemmas." Schettini, "El fenómeno Montecristo."

15. The English-language translation of the novel refers to el Bestia as "Animal." For the purposes of this chapter, I preserve the Spanish for this character's name. All other quotes from the novel are from the translation, unless otherwise indicated.

16. As Rebecca Atencio notes in her discussion of *Anos rebeldes* (Rebel years), the first Brazilian miniseries to address the legacy of the dictatorship, genres such as telenovela have "a proven ability to help empower citizens to enter the circle of witnessing and reinvent memory." *Memory's Turn*, 81.

17. Kimberly Nance, *Can Literature Promote Justice?*, 23–31.

18. Although Nance does not include fiction in her analysis of testimonio's rhetorical strategies, given the broader definition of testimonio outlined in the introduction, her categories prove useful when thinking about the novel and the telenovela.

19. Elsa Osorio, *My Name Is Light*, trans. Catherine Jagoe (New York: Bloomsbury, 2003), 230.

20. As befits the genre of telenovela, the characters in *Montecristo* are necessarily drawn in broad strokes, yet despite the lack of nuance regarding the villains, they fulfill the forensic function of testimonial works.

21. Osorio, *My Name Is Light*, 69.

22. Ibid., 95.

23. Other characters also serve to educate the reader as to the goals of the militants, including Pablo, who rejects his upper-class background to fight for the working poor, and Dolores, Eduardo's friend.

24. Osorio, *My Name Is Light*, 69.

25. Ibid.

26. Nance, *Can Literature Promote Justice?*, 30.

27. Osorio, *My Name Is Light*, 155.

28. Ibid., 147.

29. Ibid., 167.

30. Ibid., 159.

31. Ibid., 8.

32. Elsa Osorio, *A Veinte Años, Luz* (Buenos Aires: Grijalbo Mondadori, 1999), 192, translation mine.

33. Atencio, *Memory's Turn*, 6.

34. Schettini, "El fenómeno Montecristo."

35. See Emanuel Respighi, "Una foto en 'Montecristo,'" *Página/12*, September 24, 2006; Schettini, "El fenómeno Montecristo"; Mercedes Halfon, "Los nietos de 'Montecristo,'" *Perfil*, October 2, 2006. Both Suárez and the Grandmothers comment on the incredible coincidence of timing. The Grandmothers had selected a few photos to include as part of the program, chosen more for their high quality of preservation rather than any singularity related to the missing child, and Suárez's image happened to broadcast the night of his discovery. According to the article in *Perfil*, several media outlets incorrectly reported that Suárez had recognized himself in the program and *then* pursued DNA testing, further evidence of the imaginary linkage of human rights efforts with cultural production.

36. Osorio, *My Name Is Light*, 112.

37. The writers of *Montecristo* in particular emphasize that one of their central goals was to bring the story of appropriated children to a wider public. As Adriana Lorenzón explains, "In Argentina much had been written about the disappeared and appropriation of children, but the message did not go beyond the sector already interested in the topic. The genius of Montecristo was addressing the theme in a popular genre such as telenovela. This allowed us to reach many citizens for whom the work of the Grandmothers didn't form part of their daily life. As a result of the program, those people included this reality in their conversations." Schettini, "El fenómeno Montecristo."

38. Osorio, *My Name Is Light*, 111.

39. Ibid., 283.

40. Ibid., 153.

41. Ibid., 186.

42. Ibid., 84. The original Spanish refers to being "desaparecido . . . con vida" (disappeared . . . alive), a reference to the calls for "aparición con vida" (reappearance alive) by the family members of the disappeared.

43. Ibid., 251.

44. Eduardo's good intentions should not obscure the fact that he remains implicated in the crime of appropriation by failing to ask questions when his father-in-law finds a baby to replace his stillborn son.

45. While not technically a child of the disappeared, Matías serves as a parallel to Laura, for both are raised believing a lie about their origins and must come to terms with a new identity. Furthermore, the parental figure in Matías's life is directly implicated in the violent disappearance of his biological father.

46. *Montecristo* (Buenos Aires: Telefe, 2006).

47. This is not to imply that Luz's encounter with her biological family lacks complications—as mentioned above, her reunion with Carlos demonstrates nuance regarding love and biology—I only note that, unlike Laura, Luz does not demonstrate a reluctance to explore her origins.

48. Osorio, *My Name Is Light*, 159.

49. Ibid., 160.

50. The novel in particular is very critical of those characters who view the world in terms of black and white, and there are many mentions of the importance of "shades of gray" in this complicated postauthoritarian society. Once he becomes aware of the truth regarding the disappearances, Eduardo criticizes Mariana's "infantile" world view that categorizes people as either "good guys" or "bad guys." (Mariana's insistence that they raise Luz with the "correct" ideas about right and wrong also serves as a critique of such dogmatic thinking). For her part, Dolores (as the counterpart to Mariana) recognizes that she must avoid making extreme judgments; after telling her story to Eduardo and noting his absolute shock and surprise that such things could have been happening in Argentina without his knowledge or understanding, she meditates, "She shouldn't judge everything in black and white; there are shades of grey." Ibid., 156. The narrative's insistence on the importance of these shades of gray serves to roundly critique the military's rhetoric of subversives who needed to be eliminated and speaks to the complexity of the postdictatorship context.

51. Marco Kunz, "Identidad robada y anagnórisis: De *Nunca Más* a *Quinteto de Buenos Aires*," in *Violence politique et écriture de l'élucidation dans la bassin méditerranéen*, ed. Claude Ambroise and Georges Tyras (Grenoble: Université Stendhal, 2002), 181, 180.

52. Ibid., 187. Kunz goes so far as to discredit any testimonial value the novel may possess, a position I find too extreme.

53. In her analysis of the novel, Gema Palazón Sáez emphasizes the importance of the love story amid the violence. To her, the novel suggests that love is one of the only forms of resistance that the dictatorship cannot crush. "Reconstrucción identitaria y mecanismos de la memoria: *A veinte años, Luz*," *Río de La Plata* 29–30 (2004): 475–85.

54. Julee Tate, "The Good and Bad Women of Telenovelas: How to Tell Them Apart Using a Simple Maternity Test," *Studies in Latin American Popular Culture* 26 (2007): 97–111. Tate explains that "good" and "bad" women in telenovelas are easily distinguishable by their desire (or not) to have children. "Good" women seek to fulfill

their roles as mothers, while "bad" women will either constrict their own fertility (through birth control and abortion) or use maternity as a way to "trap" a man (through a false pregnancy test).

55. Wracked with guilt when Mariana's labor begins to put her life in danger, Eduardo recalls, "She wasn't very enthusiastic about having a child." Osorio, *My Name Is Light*, 41. As opposed to other characters whose names exemplify their identity, Mariana does not fit into the Marianist model, as defined by Evelyn Stevens: the self-sacrificing soul for whom motherhood is the ultimate actualization of her role as a woman. See Evelyn Stevens, "Marianism: The Other Face of Machismo," in *Confronting Change, Challenging Tradition: Women in Latin American History*, ed. Gertrude M. Yeager (Wilmington, DE: Scholarly Resources, 1994), 3–17. Mariana's name is the only one that seems to run counter to her personality; while Luz does seek to bring her hidden past to light, el Bestia displays savage behavior, and Dolores has indeed suffered, Mariana's name appears only for ironic effect.

56. After Eduardo is killed, Mariana becomes even more despicable, remarrying a man with close ties to the military and distancing herself even more from Luz. Mariana takes every opportunity to criticize or insult her daughter, and Luz recalls the numerous arguments that ended "with her slapping me." Osorio, *My Name Is Light*, 267.

57. Tate, "The Good and Bad Women of Telenovelas," 110.

58. Osorio, *My Name Is Light*, 197.

59. Ibid., 208.

60. Ibid., 209.

61. The words "monster" and "psychopath" are used with more and more frequency as the telenovela progresses to refer to Marcos, Lisandro, and Alberto, the three central villains; any shred of humanity they may have possessed toward the beginning of the series is completely destroyed by the end.

62. It is worth noting that Mariana is not the only character who is portrayed in a rather flat manner in *A veinte años, Luz*. Most of the military characters, or those who sympathize with the military, are equally two dimensional. Colonel Dufau and his wife demonstrate a clear disregard for human rights—not only do they appropriate Luz but they also arrange Eduardo's murder when he starts to ask too many questions.

63. The name was released as part of the court case related to the appropriation of the grandson's biological mother, but the Grandmothers' policy is to maintain privacy until such time as the individual is ready to come forward publicly. The Grandmothers' press release on August 6, 2014, indicates they "regret" that information was provided by the Federal Court, reiterating their commitment to protect the privacy of individuals who approach their organization. Abuelas de Plaza de Mayo, "Guido Montoya Carlotto ya conoció a su verdadera familia," August 6, 2014, http://www.abuelas.org.ar/comunicados/restituciones/res140807_0102-1.htm.

64. Comments come from his public press conference, August 8, 2014.

65. Mariela Arias, "Ignacio Guido Hurban viajó a Santa Cruz al cumpleaños 92 de su abuela paterna," *La Nación*, August 30, 2014. The issue of naming is obviously a

delicate one. During his press conference on August 8, 2014, Carlotto's grandson acknowledged the name "Guido" but requested to be called "Ignacio," gently correcting a member of the press corps who addressed him as "Guido."

66. Ari Gandsman, "'Do You Know Who You Are?' Radical Existential Doubt and Scientific Certainty in the Search for the Kidnapped Children of the Disappeared in Argentina," *ETHOS* 37, no. 4 (2009): 445. His claims are based on fourteen months of fieldwork between 2003 and 2005, consisting of interviews, archival work, and attendance at human rights events sponsored by the Grandmothers. Individuals interviewed included family members of the disappeared, human rights workers, and the Grandmothers' legal, genetic, and psychological teams, as well as grandchildren who had gone through the process of identity restitution themselves. Gandsman explains that these premises arise out of developments in genetics in the twentieth century as well as the adoption rights movement in North America and Europe that advocated for an adopted child's right to know their biological identities. His article explores the primacy of genetic "truth" when defining identity in Argentina.

67. Again, this is not to say that the Grandmothers' position is exclusively biological. I refer only to their use of biological imagery in their promotional campaign.

68. See, for example, Cecilia Sosa, "*Queering* Acts of Mourning in the Aftermath of Argentina's Dictatorship: The Mothers of Plaza de Mayo and *Los Rubios*," in *The Memory of State Terrorism in the Southern Cone: Argentina, Chile, and Uruguay*, ed. Francesca Lessa and Vincent Druliolle (New York: Palgrave Macmillan, 2011), 63–85; and Cecilia Sosa, "Queering Kinship: The Performance of Blood and the Attires of Memory," *Journal of Latin American Cultural Studies* 21, no. 2 (2012): 221–33.

69. Gandsman even observes that groups comprised of survivors occupy a marginalized position in the human rights community—when it comes to establishing authority, blood ties appear to trump experiences in clandestine detention centers. He notes that references to "directly affected" and "non-affected" groups almost exclusively reference family members, at the expense of ex-detainees. Ari Gandsman, "The Limits of Kinship Mobilizations," 206–7.

70. Ibid., 206.

71. For a detailed analysis of how the position of the Grandmothers considers identity as both biological and somewhat constructed, see Ari Gandsman, "'A Prick of a Needle Can Do No Harm': Compulsory Extraction of Blood in the Search for the Children of Argentina's Disappeared," *Journal of Latin American and Caribbean Anthropology* 14, no. 1 (2009): 162–84.

72. Osorio, *My Name Is Light*, 316.

73. Palazón Sáez, "Reconstrucción identitaria y mecanismos de la memoria," 479.

74. Osorio, *My Name Is Light*, 264.

75. Several other characters exhibit this type of internal "knowing." Eduardo, Dolores, and Laura all demonstrate moments of enlightenment based not on intellectual knowledge but on emotional (or physical) knowing. The use of words such as "feel" and "intuition" when talking about these characters' moments of discovery also underscore the importance of this type of physical understanding.

76. The tension between rhetoric and action can be seen in the title of the Grandmothers' press release regarding Carlotto's recovered grandson: "Guido Montoya Carlotto ya conoció a su verdadera familia" (Guido Montoya Carlotto finally met his true family). The use of the word "verdadera" (true or real) implies an identity rooted in biology, yet the content of the press release itself and the actions of the organization exhibit a more nuanced engagement with the issue.

77. Osorio, *My Name Is Light*, 69.

78. Ibid., 193–94.

79. Biology also defines the villains in these cultural works. In *A veinte años, Luz*, Mariana's hateful nature reflects that of her military father; meanwhile, in *Montecristo* the daughter of the torturer Lisandro is incapable of becoming a good person, despite multiple efforts by those around her to help her change, further proof that the apple does not fall far from the tree.

80. The *Teatro x la identidad* (Theatre for Identity) play cycles are perhaps the best-known fictional representations of appropriated children. The characters of military parents are often named "appropriators"—in other words, they are defined by their actions. These plays thereby emphasize the impossibility of any type of loving relationship in a family created out of violence and appropriation. In his analysis of three works that address the theme of appropriated children, Marco Kunz also notes the tendency to portray the repressors in purely negative terms, to fulfill the desire that "the bad guys are recognizable as bad." Kunz, "Identidad robada y anagnórisis," 185.

81. Complications do arise when Laura is reunited with her sister Victoria, but these stem from the fact that both women are in love with Santiago rather than from any tension between the family who raised Laura and the one who searched for her.

82. For updated numbers, refer to the official website of the Grandmothers of Plaza de Mayo, abuelas.org.ar, accessed December 8, 2015.

83. Estela Carlotto, *¿Quién soy yo?* (Bravo Films in association with the National University of San Martín, coproduction of the Encuentro channel, 2007). *Who Am I?* was produced in close coordination with the Grandmothers; the director Estela Carlotto is the president of the association.

84. There have been other cases of recovered children who were abused by the families that appropriated them, for example Carla Rutila Artés, who eventually testified against her appropriator in August 2010 when he was put on trial for crimes committed during the dictatorship.

85. The anthropologist Ari Gandsman explains his surprise to discover that the restitutions were not all unqualified success stories. In his words, "The Grandmothers' institutional literature and publications on restitution failed to prepare me for my encounter with 'incomplete' restitutions. As the Grandmothers describe it, ties between kidnappers (the 'parents') and their victim (their 'son' or 'daughter') invariably dissolve as the truth of the child's parentage becomes apparent. The experiences of numerous children of the disappeared, including one I interviewed, support this idea, but a number of children are far more ambivalent or resistant." Ari Gandsman, "Retributive Justice: Public Intimacies and the Micropolitics of the Restitution of Kidnapped

Children of the Disappeared in Argentina," *International Journal of Transitional Justice* 6 (2012): 427.

86. Both *A veinte años, Luz* and *Montecristo* repeatedly incorporate the "spoils of war" rhetoric into their tales. In Osorio's novel, Sergeant Pitiotti refers to the child he hopes to receive for Miriam as "a sort of war trophy." Osorio, *My Name Is Light*, 44. Meanwhile, Carlos bitterly remarks that for the military, "those babies were just things, plunder." Ibid., 55. In *Montecristo*, Victoria advocates DNA testing for Laura, Santiago, and Matías in order to prevent the boy from becoming caught as "botín de guerra" in the struggle between Laura and Marcos. The Grandmothers have long used this phrase to call attention to the way in which their missing grandchildren were appropriated, as if they were simply one more valuable "thing" that could be taken from the disappeared.

87. In his analysis of the complexities associated with restitution, Gandsman notes that restitution is "a term primarily used with property." Gandsman, "Retributive Justice," 426.

88. Carlotto, *¿Quién soy yo?*

89. Ibid.

90. Regarding cases of adult children who demonstrated resistance to the process of restitution, Gandsman explains, "The Grandmothers argue that since their relationship was based on deceit, no love could exist. The Grandmothers argue that the relationship between their grandchildren and their kidnappers is inherently 'perverse' because of the context in which the children were born and the kidnappers' knowledge and concealment of these origins." Gandsman, "'A Prick of a Needle Can Do No Harm,'" 169. Although the actions of the Grandmothers do demonstrate nuance regarding the construction of identity, they take an absolutist position regarding cases where grandchildren remain connected to individuals who are implicated in the dictatorship's violence, advocating punishment of guilty parties. For more on how this stance has caused tensions within the human rights community, see Gandsman, "Retributive Justice."

91. Analía Argento, *De vuelta a casa: Historias de hijos y nietos restituidos* (Buenos Aires: Marea, 2008). Until recently, few voices of these appropriated children have been heard. Some cases have been featured in the aforementioned documentaries, and selected testimonies of recovered grandchildren can be found on the Grandmothers' website, yet for the most part the story of the youngest victims of the dictatorship has been told by the Grandmothers or others closely aligned with this organization. Argento's work represents a notable exception, especially because it was published by a press with no connection to the Grandmothers.

92. Ibid., 162.

93. Ibid., 172. NN refers to "ningún nombre" (unnamed) and is a direct reference to the unmarked graves in which many victims were buried during the dictatorship. One should note that even those who advocate restoring a biological identity recognize the impact of such fundamental changes. Dr. Roberto Marquevich, the judge involved in the case of Mariana Zaffaroni, compares the act of changing Daniela Furci's name

to Mariana Zaffaroni to "a death," for one person no longer exists. Gonzalo Arijon and Virginia Martínez, *Por esos ojos*, documentary, 1997.

94. At the time of writing Evelin is described as having "the beginnings" of a relationship with her maternal grandmother, while still maintaining very close ties to her "adoptive" parents, who were sentenced to jail terms in 2011.

95. Argento, *De vuelta a casa*, 171.

96. Another complicated story is that of Matías Reggiardo Tolosa, one of the twins involved in a high-profile case of appropriation (this case is mentioned in *A veinte años, Luz*). The man who raised them, Samuel Miara, was a federal police chief who was involved in the disappearance of their biological parents, yet when the Miaras were sent to jail, the twins were still quite young. Matías describes the way in which he and his brother were taken from their "parents" as very traumatic, and he still maintains a very close loving bond with Beatriz Miara, the only mother he ever knew. In his words, "We had a happy childhood, in our ignorance or whatever you want to call it, but in a home in which they raised us with love." Ibid., 209.

97. Sosa, "Queering Kinship," 227.

98. Gandsman, "'A Prick of a Needle Can Do No Harm,'" 172.

99. Gandsman observes that "victim-oriented transitional justice should privilege what victims say they need," noting that in Argentina disagreement arises when the Grandmothers claim they know the needs of their kidnapped grandchildren, and some grandchildren deny they are victims at all. Gandsman, "Retributive Justice," 441.

100. This can be seen in another high-profile case of appropriation that worked its way through the court system in Argentina in 2010–11. Marcela and Felipe Noble-Herrera, the adoptive children of the media magnate Ernestina Herrera de Noble, categorically refused to submit to DNA testing, even after receiving a court order. Their refusal aligns with the idea that a "child" should not have to testify against a "parent"; the Grandmothers countered that they held evidence of a crime in their bodies and had an obligation to present it. According to statements made by Carlotto during January 2011, although it may not be deliberate, "the adoptive children of Ernestina Herrera de Noble are part of the cover-up of a crime" and therefore were required to offer the evidence they carried inside their bodies. See "Son parte del ocultamiento," *Página/12*, January 21, 2011.

101. The debate surrounding mandatory DNA testing for individuals suspected of being children of the disappeared introduces important issues regarding individual versus societal rights that lie outside the scope of this chapter. For an excellent treatment of the subject, see Gandsman's analysis of the Vázquez case (Gandsman, "'A Prick of a Needle Can Do No Harm.'") For a discussion of how debates surrounding identity restitution relate to broader issues of transitional justice in Argentina, see Gandsman, "Retributive Justice."

102. Gandsman, "Retributive Justice," 443.

103. During the high-profile Reggiardo Tolosa case, the Grandmothers bemoaned the lack of public understanding of the original crime, as the media exposure highlighted the emotional suffering of the twins. After this case, the Grandmothers began

to emphasize more the right to identity. Asociación de Abuelas de Plaza de Mayo, *La historia de Abuelas*, 103–4.

104. See Abuelas de Plaza de Mayo, "Clase sobre Derecho a la identidad," video posted at http://www.abuelas.org.ar/areas.php?area=juridica.htm&der1=der1_jur.php&der2=der2_areas.php, accessed December 8, 2015.

105. Friera, "No toda la sociedad es culpable." Since the first documented case of a grandchild approaching the Grandmothers organization occurred in 1998 (Paula Cortassa), the year Osorio's book was published, it seems plausible that she had no knowledge of grandchildren searching for their origins at the time of writing.

106. When considering the role of the "happy ending," one must acknowledge the role of genre; a telenovela by definition is a love story with a happy ending. María Victoria Bourdieu, *Pasión, heroísmo e identidades colectivas: Un recorrido por los últimos veinticinco años de la telenovela argentina* (Ciudad Autónoma de Buenos Aires: Biblioteca Nacional; Los Polvorines: Universidad Nacional de General Sarmiento, 2008), 17. The conflict arises from *when* and *how*, rather than *if*, the lovers will overcome the obstacles placed in their path. While one could argue that the structure of both *A veinte años, Luz* and *Montecristo* may respond more to the limits of the melodramatic genre than any societal taboos regarding how such stories are portrayed, it is equally possible that the taboos themselves help channel large-scale representations of this delicate issue toward the melodramatic mode (with its attendant happy ending). Furthermore, certain decisions—such as the representation of appropriators as unquestionably depraved individuals—do not just respond to the constraints of the genre. As Hugo Benavides has argued, in Latin America melodrama has been able to "give voice" to groups not traditionally represented in the cultural sphere. Hugo Benavides, *Drugs, Thugs, and Divas: Telenovelas and Narco-Dramas in Latin America* (Austin: University of Texas Press, 2008), 20. He cites the "enormous hegemonic possibilities" afforded by the medium, "through the disguise offered by the social constraints of stock characters, plots, and responses" (193). Although his work addresses issues of postcolonialism rather than the legacy of dictatorship, Benavides's ideas regarding popular culture's subversive potential also may be applied to *A veinte años, Luz* and *Montecristo*. Furthermore, popular representations that must provide happy endings, rather than simply signaling a lack of nuance, can help reveal which aspects of the crime of appropriation can be discussed and what remains silenced.

107. Argento, *De vuelta a casa*, 15, emphasis added.

108. Nance, *Can Literature Promote Justice?*, 107, 106.

Chapter 5. The Memory of Forgetting in Luisa Valenzuela's *La travesía*

An earlier version of this chapter appeared as an article in *Letras Femeninas*. I am grateful to the editors for permission to reprint portions of the earlier work. See Nancy J. Gates-Madsen, "Uncivilized Remembrance in Luisa Valenzuela's *La Travesía*," *Letras Femeninas* 31, no. 2 (2005): 99–121. All translations are mine unless otherwise noted.

1. "Frente al mandato—de olvido y silencio—dominante, pensamos impre-scindible crear un contradiscurso que aporte a la reconstrucción de la identidad social de nuestro pueblo." H.I.J.O.S., "H.I.J.O.S. de la misma historia," http://www.hijos -capital.org.ar/index.php?option=com_content&view=article&id=140&Itemid=401, accessed October 13, 2013.

2. As Elizabeth Jelin notes, "Memories are the object of disputes, conflicts, and struggles." *State Repression and the Labors of Memory*, xv.

3. Lyotard, *The Differend*, 13.

4. That Valenzuela's writing should be associated with secrets and silence comes as no surprise. Much of her work addresses issues of female expression, in particular the way in which woman's voice is marked by silence. Many scholars have noted how Valenzuela's writing challenges patriarchal discourse and female silencing. For exam-ple, Z. Nelly Martínez demonstrates in *El silencio que habla* how Valenzuela's writing uses various strategies to challenge the silences and silencing of women, such as high-lighting the pleasure of the text or demystifying paternal discourse. For a discussion of how Valenzuela exposes the dangers of monolithic meaning through approaching taboo topics and exposing the multiplicity of meaning and interpretation, see Sharon Magnarelli, *Reflections/Refractions: Reading Luisa Valenzuela* (New York: Peter Lang, 1988). Juanamaría Cordonos-Cook focuses more exclusively on the political aspects of Valenzuela's writing, in particular how her development of a "poetics of transgres-sion" resists and subverts authoritarian meaning. *Poética de transgresión en la novelística de Luisa Valenzuela* (New York: Peter Lang, 1991). Aside from these major studies that mention silence, individual articles too numerous to mention inevitably mention silence and secrets as central elements of Valenzuela's writing. See in particular Ksenija Bilbija, "The Rhetoric of the Repressed in *Black Novel (with Argentines)* by Luisa Valenzuela," *Letras Femeninas* 27, no. 1 (2001): 129–47; Janet Gold, "Feminine Space and the Discourse of Silence: Yolanda Oreamuno, Elena Poniatowska, and Luisa Valenzuela," in *In the Feminine Mode: Essays on Hispanic Women Writers*, ed. Noël Maureen Valis and Carol Maier (Lewisburg: Bucknell University Press, 1990), 195–203. While some of these approaches emphasize the connection to state terror, much of the writing concerning Valenzuela's silences is related to women's writing and a struggle against patriarchal modes of expression.

5. Felman and Laub, *Testimony*, 23.

6. Luisa Valenzuela, *La travesía* (Buenos Aires: Grupo Editorial Norma, 2001), 15.

7. Ibid., 25.

8. For a closer examination of the role of accident or chance in the novel, see Gwendolyn Díaz, "Una odisea hacia el caos: *La travesía* de Luisa Valenzuela," in *Luisa Valenzuela sin máscara*, ed. Gwendolyn Díaz (Buenos Aires: Feminaria, 2002), 70–82.

9. Stern, *Remembering Pinochet's Chile*, xxviii, 111–12.

10. Valenzuela, *La travesía*, 29.

11. Ibid., 47, 40, 199.

12. Ibid., 60.

13. Ibid., 154.

14. Idelber Avelar, *The Untimely Present: Postdictatorial Latin American Fiction and the Task of Mourning* (Durham, NC: Duke University Press, 1999). I am grateful to Rebecca Atencio for noting the allegorical nature of Valenzuela's text.

15. Caruth, *Unclaimed Experience*, 17.

16. Ibid., 8.

17. Felman and Laub, *Testimony*, 50, emphasis removed.

18. Valenzuela, *La travesía*, 292, 293, 299.

19. Ksenija Bilbija, "Poniendo las cartas boca abajo: *La travesía* de Luisa Valenzuela," in *Luisa Valenzuela sin máscara*, ed. Gwendolyn Díaz (Buenos Aires: Feminaria, 2002), 83–95.

20. Ibid., 89.

21. Valenzuela, *La travesía*, 299–300.

22. Michael T. Taussig, *Defacement*, 5, emphasis removed.

23. Valenzuela, *La travesía*, 300.

24. Ibid., 94.

25. In *A Lexicon of Terror*, Marguerite Feitlowitz describes how the military government often denied that missing persons were being held in clandestine camps, instead suggesting that perhaps they were living in another country (28).

26. Valenzuela, *La travesía*, 36.

27. Luisa Valenzuela, "Siete aproximaciones al secreto," *Casa de Las Américas* 42, no. 226 (2002): 91.

28. Lyotard has also likened the memory of trauma to an internal quake, claiming: "The impossibility of quantitatively measuring it does not prohibit, but rather inspires in the minds of the survivors the idea of a very great seismic force." Lyotard, *The Differend*, 56.

29. Valenzuela, *La travesía*, 39.

30. For more on how Valenzuela conceives of bodily memories, see Luisa Valenzuela, "Escribir con el cuerpo," in *Peligrosas Palabras* (Buenos Aires: Temas Grupo Editorial, 2001), 119–39. In this essay she refers in particular to "the memory of one's pores," which manifests itself in somatic rather than linguistic terms.

31. Elina Matoso, *El cuerpo, territorio escénico* (Buenos Aires: Paidós, 1992), 15.

32. Ibid., 18.

33. Ibid., 39.

34. Valenzuela, *La travesía*, 141, 81.

35. Ibid., 79.

36. Matoso, *El cuerpo, territorio escénico*, 104.

37. Valenzuela, *La travesía*, 113.

38. Cathy Caruth likens traumatic memory to a wound. Her claim that trauma "is always the story of a wound that cries out, that addresses us in the attempt to tell us of a reality or truth that is not otherwise available," becomes especially suggestive in the context of the "bleeding" couch. Caruth, *Unclaimed Experience*, 4.

39. Valenzuela, *La travesía*, 38.

40. Domingo Faustino Sarmiento, *Facundo: Civilization and Barbarism; The First Complete English Translation*, trans. Kathleen Ross (Berkeley: University of California Press, 2003), 31.

41. Ibid., 59.

42. Ibid., 91.

43. Dinorah Cortés, "Deseo patriarcal y metáfora de la paternidad literaria en Domingo Faustino Sarmiento," *Cuadrivium* 11–12, no. 7 (Fall 2009–Spring 2011): 118.

44. Sarmiento, *Facundo: Civilization and Barbarism*, 32. The association between woman and nature seen in *Facundo* has a lengthy history. As Susan Griffin remarks, "Woven everywhere into the tapestry of European art and literature and seemingly an inseparable part of most philosophical and scientific texts—even embedded in the structure of European languages—is the assumption that women are closer to nature than men are. The notion is not intended as a compliment." *Woman and Nature: The Roaring Inside Her*, 2nd ed. (San Francisco: Sierra Club Books, 1999), ix. In fact, as Carolyn Merchant explains, both Western and non-Western cultures traditionally imagined nature as feminine, with the two dominant images being the nurturing mother or the wild and uncontrollable forces such as storms. She explores how the scientific revolution brought about the idea of mastery over nature, which readily included the domination of women by her less animalistic counterpart, man. *The Death of Nature: Women, Ecology, and the Scientific Revolution* (San Francisco: Harper & Row, 1980). In a similar fashion, Sherry B. Ortner's "Is Female to Male as Nature Is to Culture?" examines more modern conceptions of the relationship, noting that "culture (still equated relatively unambiguously with men) recognizes that women are active participants in its special processes, but at the same time sees them as being more rooted in, or having more direct affinity with nature," a tribute to the permanence of the nature/culture dualism so prevalent in Western society. "Is Female to Male as Nature Is to Culture?," in *Women, Culture, and Society*, ed. Michelle Zimbalist Rosaldo and Louise Lamphere (Stanford, CA: Stanford University Press, 1974), 73.

45. Sandra M. Gilbert and Susan Gubar, *The Madwoman in the Attic: The Woman Writer and the Nineteenth-Century Literary Imagination* (New Haven, CT: Yale University Press, 1979), 6.

46. Cortés, "Deseo patriarcal y metáfora de la paternidad literaria en Domingo Faustino Sarmiento," 123.

47. Valenzuela, *La travesía*, 88.

48. Ibid., 67.

49. Ibid., 30.

50. Ibid., 68–69.

51. Ibid., 87.

52. Sarmiento, *Facundo*, 133.

53. Valenzuela, *La travesía*, 389.

54. Ibid., 57.

55. Ortner, "Is Female to Male as Nature Is to Culture?"

56. Griffin, *Woman and Nature*, 85.

57. Díaz, "Una odisea hacia el caos," 76.

58. Valenzuela, *La travesía*, 192.

59. Ibid., 86.

60. Scarry, *The Body in Pain*, 49.

61. Frank Graziano notes that Admiral Massera compared the actions of "subversives" to "plagues that scourged the world." *Divine Violence*, 132. Admiral César A. Guzzeti was even more explicit when he described how "the social body of the country is contaminated by a disease that corrodes its insides and forms antibodies. These antibodies must not be considered in the same way that one considers a germ. In proportion to the government's control and destruction of guerrilla warfare, the action of the antibodies is going to disappear." Ibid., quote on 132–33. In other words, the military's actions to fight the "plague" of guerrilla warfare would cease only when they eradicated the invasive virus of "subversion."

62. Valenzuela, *La travesía*, 61–62.

63. Ibid., 79.

64. Matoso, *El cuerpo, territorio escénico*, 102.

65. Valenzuela, *La travesía*, 288.

66. Matoso, *El cuerpo, territorio escénico*, 102, 104.

67. Díaz, "Una odisea hacia el caos," 77–78.

68. Valenzuela, *La travesía*, 274.

69. Valenzuela's critique of the hierarchy between body and mind is a recurring theme in her writing and dates back to her earliest works. Regarding *Hay que sonreír*, for example, Sharon Magnarelli notes that by speaking through body language, the protagonist Clara dispels the notion that "only by conquering or denying the body does one arrive at the spiritual." Magnarelli, *Reflections/Refractions*, 22.

70. For an excellent analysis of the letter as a vagina monologue that emphasizes the integral role of female desire as a source of creative power, see Z. Nelly Martínez, "Luisa Valenzuela's *La travesía*: The Vagina Monologues and the Experience of Wholeness," *Letras Femeninas* 30, no. 1 (2004): 92–105.

71. Paul van Zyl, interview by Terry Gross, Fresh Air with Terry Gross, December 3, 2001.

72. Valenzuela, *La travesía*, 340.

73. Ibid.

74. Ibid., 340–41.

75. Ibid., 353.

76. Ibid., 355, 356.

77. Ibid., 356

78. For a fuller discussion of how natural elements inform the reading of the novel, see Gates-Madsen, "Uncivilized Remembrance in Luisa Valenzuela's *La travesía*."

79. Valenzuela, *La travesía*, 382.

80. Ibid., 67, 355.

81. Ibid., 375.

Chapter 6. Fallout of the Memory "Boom"

1. "Discurso completo de Kirchner en la ONU," *Clarín*, September 25, 2003, emphasis added.

2. In his inauguration speech, Kirchner had already alluded to themes of truth, memory, and justice as well as to the need for a change of direction and his commitment to values and ideals formed through political struggle: "I am part of a generation that was decimated and castigated by painful absences; I joined the political struggles believing in values and convictions I do not plan to leave at the door of the Casa Rosada." Néstor Kirchner, "Discurso de asunción del Presidente Néstor Kirchner," Buenos Aires, May 25, 2003, http://www.cfkargentina.com/discurso-de-asuncion-del -presidente-nestor-kirchner/, accessed December 9, 2015. His quick action to overturn amnesty laws soon established him as a president who supported the work of human rights groups that had been marginalized and silenced under previous administrations.

3. The Kirchner era refers to the time in office of both Kirchner presidents, Néstor (2003–7) and Cristina (2007–15).

4. Néstor Kirchner, "Speech at the Creation of the Memory Museum," Buenos Aires, March 24, 2004, https://www.youtube.com/watch?v=h2TF9Hogz-I, accessed December 9, 2015.

5. Measures implemented during the first few months of Kirchner's tenure include the aforementioned nullification of the Amnesty Laws, the establishment of a National Archive of Memory, and forced retirement of the leadership of the armed forces. Although the Kirchner administration cannot take credit for all advances in the judicial realm, the clear support for ending impunity was instrumental in facilitating reforms.

6. Both Cristina and Néstor Kirchner received criticism for capitalizing on the past. Cristina Kirchner led a "memory exercise" on April 1, 2008, days after excusing her absence from an event commemorating the anniversary of the coup by stating her desire not to use memory for political gain. See Ksenija Bilbija and Leigh A. Payne, eds., "Introduction," in *Accounting for Violence: Marketing Memory in Latin America* (Durham, NC: Duke University Press, 2011), 32–33. At a commemorative protest event marking the thirtieth anniversary of the coup (March 24, 2006), event organizers read a document criticizing Néstor Kirchner's economic policies and the criminalization of social protest, among other issues. Kirchnerism in general has drawn criticism from more radical human rights organizations for paying lip service to human rights through memory initiatives at the expense of concrete reforms of neoliberal economic policy that are related to broader issues of inequalities and civil liberties.

7. The term "marketing memory" comes from Ksenija Bilbija and Leigh A. Payne's edited volume, *Accounting for Violence: Marketing Memory in Latin America* (Durham, NC: Duke University Press, 2011).

8. Jonathan Perel, interview by Daniel Gaguine, April 16, 2010, http://elcaleido scopiodelucy.blogspot.com/2010/04/tal-como-lo-habiamos-anticipado-el.html, accessed December 9, 2015.

9. Taylor, *Disappearing Acts*, 123–24.

10. For more information on the legal process leading to the transfer of the site from the military to the City of Buenos Aires, see http://www.espaciomemoria.ar/normativa.php, accessed November 8, 2015.

11. A group of ex-detainees, for example, proposed preserving the space in order to maintain its cultural value as a site of extermination or genocide; meanwhile, the Mothers of the Plaza de Mayo advocated converting the entire space into a cultural center for young people where they can practice the fine arts—eliminating any reference to past extermination in favor of constructing a better future. For a full discussion of the proposals, see Brodsky, *Memoria en construcción*.

12. Although guided visits are given, photography inside the building is forbidden, precisely because of the building's role as evidence in the "Megatrial" of those accused of crimes committed in the former detention center (information from July 2013).

13. For a fuller discussion of the purpose and practice of documentary film, see Bill Nichols, *Representing Reality: Issues and Concepts in Documentary* (Bloomington: Indiana University Press, 2007).

14. Michael Chanan, *The Politics of Documentary* (London: British Film Institute, 2007), 30.

15. In contexts of trauma, seeing does not automatically translate to knowing, as Cathy Caruth has compellingly demonstrated in her work. See *Trauma: Explorations in Memory* (Baltimore: Johns Hopkins University Press, 1995). Perel's documentary appears to respond to this claim, for throughout the film, his carefully constructed visual language demonstrates not only the disconnect between "seeing" and "knowing" but also the impossibility of truly "seeing" at all.

16. For more on the "informing logic" of documentary film, see Nichols, *Representing Reality*.

17. Ibid., 20–21.

18. For more about the authoritative power of the voice-over, in particular its capacity to suppress the "radical heterogeneity" of the documentary subject, see Pascal Bonitzer, "The Silences of the Voice (*A Propos* of *Mai 68* by Gudie Lawaetz)," in *Narrative, Apparatus, Ideology: A Film Theory Reader*, ed. Philip Rosen (New York: Columbia University Press, 1986), 319–34.

19. This is not to say that there is a lack of information regarding the activities that transpired in the ESMA when it operated as a clandestine detention center; rather, I refer to the debates regarding its contemporary role—a space to celebrate life or commemorate past horror? In short, what is the "story" the ex-ESMA should tell to those who visit?

20. Lazzara, *Chile in Transition*. See in particular chapter 4, "Lenses of Memory (On Narrating Villa Grimaldi)."

21. Perel, interview.

22. In an article written around the time of the transfer of the site from the military to the city, journalist and survivor of the ESMA Lila Pastoriza noted this tension

regarding who should participate in discussions regarding the fate of the site. Although she advocated the inclusion of new actors in the debate who can bring fresh perspective to questions usually discussed in closed circles, she cautioned that "this should not lead to questioning or devaluing the participation in the debates of the 'involved' persons (family members, ex-detainees, etc.), minimizing the weight of their opinions, supposedly 'biased by their suffering.'" Lila Pastoriza, "ESMA, modelo para armar," *Puentes* 4, no. 11 (2004): 15.

23. The lack of authoritative voice expressing an explicit "political" message also calls attention to the fundamental tension of human rights discourse as basing its moral legitimacy on apolitical grounds. As Ari Gandsman notes, human rights groups often find themselves caught between the assumption that their work should be "outside" politics and the political realities of their work itself. He explains: "The belief that human rights groups are not political is a normative one. . . . Although the work of activists is intrinsically political, human rights organizations are trapped in a double bind in which they need to retain the perception of being apolitical." "The Limits of Kinship Mobilizations," 204. By claiming no affiliation with any human rights group, Perel is recognizing the fundamentally political stance of such organizations, while suggesting (albeit problematically) that he occupies a space "outside" the official human rights discourse.

24. José Luis García, "'El Predio' de Jonathan Perel: Reinterpretando los horrores del pasado," *Cinestel.com*, March 24, 2011, http://www.cinestel.com/el-predio-de-jonathan-perel-reinterpretando-los-horrores-del-pasado/.

25. Alison Landsberg, *Prosthetic Memory: The Transformation of American Remembrance in the Age of Mass Culture* (New York: Columbia University Press, 2004), 22.

26. Although Landsberg's work focuses on mass media and commodified culture (rather than small, independent, documentary film), I believe her ideas about how cinema can open up a "transferential space" for memory transmission is applicable to Perel's documentary, for the strategies he uses to unsettle the viewer have the same somatic effect as the more popular films Landsberg analyzes in her work. Ibid., 113. For a different take on how the documentary "makes" memory, see María Guadalupe Arenillas, "Hacia una nueva ética y estética de la memoria en el cine documental argentino: *El predio* (2010) de Jonathan Perel," *A Contracorriente* 10, no. 3 (2013): 371–88. Arenillas makes a compelling case for reading the documentary as a "counter-monument" to the victims of violence.

27. *Nunca Más*. Statistics regarding prisoners are also available at the websites of the Space for Memory (www.espaciomemoria.ar, accessed November 8, 2015) and Memoria Abierta (www.memoriaabierta.org.ar, accessed November 8, 2015).

28. Bonitzer claims that the anonymous voice-over equates a "double suppression" of the voices of the subjects the documentary claims to depict. As he notes: "First, it suppresses their voice by not allowing them to speak, and second by substituting for them." "The Silences of the Voice," 325. Perhaps in recognition of this "double suppression," Perel silences all voices, thereby calling attention to the danger of substituting an "authoritative" voice for the silenced ones of the victims themselves.

29. This is not to say that human rights actors and activities are absent from the film. Numerous scenes depict activities or images associated with human rights work. Rather, I refer to the lack of an organizational logic grounded in a particular view.

30. Jonathan Perel, "Estupor y temblor," *Página/12*, March 20, 2011.

31. Important here is the fact that the images are not manipulated or faked.

32. Roland Barthes, *Camera Lucida: Reflections on Photography*, trans. Richard Howard (New York: Hill and Wang, 2010), 85. Barthes's observations are specifically about photography (as opposed to fictional film); nevertheless, his claim that photographs serve an unimpeachable evidentiary function applies as well to documentary film, which distinguishes itself from fiction through its link to historical reality. Barthes does not consider the documentary genre when he contrasts photographs with cinema.

33. I am grateful to Alfredo Alonso for calling my attention to this connection.

34. García, "'El Predio' de Jonathan Perel." Perel refers to the difficulty of watching the film in another interview, expressing his surprised delight that the audience stayed to the end rather than getting up and walking out. Perel, interview.

35. Perel, interview.

36. This might be considered Perel's "signature shot"; he employs this type of camera gaze—still shots of long duration—for two other short documentaries about former clandestine detention centers, *17 monumentos* and *El mural.*

37. Ken Burns's well-known documentary of the Civil War serves as a classic example of this panning and zooming technique.

38. The importance of the viewer is emphasized in María Guadalupe Arenillas's analysis as well. See Arenillas, "Hacia una nueva ética y estética de la memoria en el cine documental argentino."

39. Here I follow the division in visual theory between *seeing*, which involves observing and recognizing, and *looking*, which is an active process of making meaning. For an overview of terminology of the visual, see Marita Sturken and Lisa Cartwright, *Practices of Looking: An Introduction to Visual Culture*, 2nd ed. (New York: Oxford University Press, 2009).

40. Pamela Colombo, "A Space under Construction: The Spatio-Temporal Constellation of ESMA in *El Predio*," *Journal of Latin American Cultural Studies* 21, no. 4 (2012): 499.

41. By creating a feeling of discomfort, the documentary upholds one expectation regarding a film of the ex-ESMA: the experience should not be entertaining or pleasant. As the artist Horst Hoheisel argues, memorial spaces dedicated to the remembrance of atrocity should not elicit well-being in those who visit. Horst Hoheisel et al., "La destrucción de la Puerta de Brandeburgo: Conversación con Horst Hoheisel," *Punto de Vista* 83 (2005): 21. As the aforementioned debate regarding the uses of the ex-ESMA reveal, not all individuals committed to memory in the name of human rights share Hoheisel's position, but Perel's choice to create a disquieting viewing experience seems to align with a desire not to provide any type of soothing closure to such a highly charged space.

42. The highly constructed nature of Perel's gaze can also be interpreted as a critique of any type of homogenizing discourse. While the static gaze of the camera implies an unchanging, particular viewpoint (an attempt to shoehorn the ex-ESMA into some type of understandable package), through its unsettling effects, this creation of stylistic order paradoxically undermines any type of homogeneity and underscores the lack of dominant reading of the site—the impossibility of neatly containing the ex-ESMA inside one particular view or perspective.

43. Roland Barthes, *Image, Music, Text*, trans. Stephen Heath (New York: Hill and Wang, 1977).

44. Nichols, *Representing Reality*, 35–36.

45. Regarding the poetic mode, Nichols claims that "unexpected juxtapositions or stylistic departures from the norms of a text or the conventions of a genre make realism and referentiality themselves strange. They fold the viewer's consciousness back onto itself so that it comes into contact with the work of the cinematic apparatus rather than being allowed to move unimpeded toward engagement with a representation of the historical world." Ibid., 61.

46. Quoted in Michael Renov, "Toward a Poetics of Documentary," in *Theorizing Documentary*, ed. Michael Renov (New York: Routledge, 1993), 24–25.

47. Perel, "Estupor y temblor," emphasis added.

48. Marianne Hirsch, "Surviving Images: Holocaust Photographs and the Work of Postmemory," *Yale Journal of Criticism* 14, no. 1 (2001): 16.

49. The absence of the expected images associated with the ESMA may serve another function. Following Barthes, it is possible that the four-columned building and the Officer's Quarters represent the eternal *punctum* of the images presented in the rest of the documentary—that element of the image that "pricks" the viewer, in this case an element outside the camera's frame. Barthes, *Camera Lucida*, 27.

50. This is akin to Brecht's "alienation effect" in theatre. It is also important to note the aesthetic element of this shot; like many of the shots in the documentary, it is beautifully framed and visually striking. Yet again, the focus on aesthetics runs the risk of downplaying historical or political realities at play in the ex-ESMA.

51. The eventual establishing shot of the inside-looking-out sequence reveals a different location than that of the windows of the exhibition, but the immediate connection of outside-in to inside-out suggests a dialogue between them.

52. Again, this inaccessibility and strangeness is akin to the *punctum* Barthes refers to in certain photos, an element that "pricks" the viewer, causing a different reading of the image, as if it were completely new. Barthes, *Camera Lucida*, 27, 42.

53. Nichols emphasizes that one of the central expectations of a viewer of a documentary is that "the desire to know will find gratification during the course of the film." Nichols, *Representing Reality*, 30.

54. Pamela Colombo also notes the attachment to meaning for the images, describing several series of shots found within the film. Colombo, "A Space under Construction."

55. At other moments in the film, Perel also constructs moments of interpretative "pay-off," such as when an opening shot will have the sound of a burble of voices, followed by a shot of the people themselves. In this case, the aural expectation (there are people somewhere) is resolved by presenting an image of the crowd. Similarly, there are several sequences that show a beginning, middle, and end of an event (e.g., a DVD player ready to project, a shot of people entering an auditorium, a shot of part of the film, a shot at the end of the film with the people getting up to leave). Again, this represents a strategy of making a viewer interpret a scene and then revealing the resolution, setting up the expectation that the documentary will fulfill the viewer's need to know.

56. This lack of resolution regarding the visual representation of historical horror is in keeping with Ulrich Baer's ideas regarding photography and trauma, in particular that trauma represents a Democritean rather than Heraclitean vision of history, history as a series of unconnected explosions or bursts rather than a progressive flow of narrative events. Ulrich Baer, *Spectral Evidence: The Photography of Trauma* (Cambridge, MA: MIT Press, 2005).

57. Nichols, *Representing Reality*, 124.

58. This juxtaposition appears to respond to the debates surrounding the most appropriate uses of the site, for certain functions stand in direct contradiction to others. As was discussed in chapter 2 ("Julia"), there is an irresolvable tension between honoring a victim's life and focusing on his or her violent death. One particular construction of memory can unwittingly "injure" another.

59. Brodsky, *Memoria en construcción*, 212.

60. Perel's give-and-take supports the central paradox of control regarding his cinematic gaze: while appearing to cede interpretive control to the viewer (by not offering a particular interpretation), Perel also develops a highly constructed cinematic gaze, thereby revealing the presence of a filming subject who creates order in the work.

61. Scenes toward the end of the documentary showing monument bases without plaques or monuments, followed by a shot of the monument to human rights placed at the site by the Kirchner government, also suggest meditation on this topic of removal and replacement. Furthermore, the viewer may also reflect on what s/he brings to the site, as a viewer of the documentary, what assumptions, interpretations, or beliefs inform his or her viewing.

62. For the scene as invitation, see Arenillas, "Hacia una nueva ética y estética de la memoria en el cine documental argentino." For a discussion of ESMA and its boundaries, see Colombo, "A Space under Construction." In an interview with Juan Pablo Russo, Perel affirms his intent to provide a hopeful ending to the film: "Without a doubt I wanted the film to end on a hopeful note, the final image with the open door looks to the future and everything that can be constructed inside. I think everything in the ESMA is about to be constructed. The ESMA is a symbolic place that has a great redeeming power for society as a whole." Jonathan Perel, "La ESMA es un lugar simbólico que tiene un alto poder de reparación," interview by Juan Pablo Russo, March 24, 2011, http://www.escribiendocine.com/entrevista/0002475-jonathan-perel-la-esma

-es-un-lugar-simbolico-que-tiene-un-alto-poder-de-reparacion/, accessed November 8, 2015.

63. The film as a whole comments on the "use" of memory. By showing the multiple uses of the current space, by human rights groups and others, the viewer is encouraged to meditate on the function of memory in general: What purpose does it serve? Who can, does, or should control it?

64. Elsewhere I have advocated that sites of memory should provoke a move from passive to active seeing, from observer/spectator to witness. Through its distinct language of images without commentary, *El predio* activates this engaged viewing for the ex-ESMA. See Nancy J. Gates-Madsen, "Marketing and Sacred Space: The Parque de la Memoria in Buenos Aires," in *Accounting for Violence: Marketing Memory in Latin America*, ed. Ksenija Bilbija and Leigh A. Payne (Durham, NC: Duke University Press, 2011), 151–78.

Conclusion

1. This is not to suggest that human rights discourse is monolithic or fixed. The nature of human rights discourse itself is constantly shifting, and different organizations advance varying agendas. For example, the discourse of victims as heroes in the early years following the return to democracy has ceded to demands to reclaim and honor the militancy of the victims.

2. I distinguish here between those directly involved in the violence (repressors such as Alberto Lombardo and Lisandro Donoso in *Montecristo*) and those who collaborated with the crime of appropriation in a less direct fashion (such as Lisandro's wife Helena or Luz's "father" Eduardo). For a fuller discussion regarding the appropriators, see chapter 4.

3. The importance of this lack of resolution calls to mind Leigh Payne's claim that "healthy" political community is predicated on the recognition and permission of the "messy process" of allowing discussion and debate of contentious issues. *Unsettling Accounts*, 291–92.

4. Existing scholarship on the meaning of literary and cultural silence tends to fall into the aforementioned essentialist categories. On the one hand, silence may be viewed as highly expressive, even powerful in itself. Linguistic and philosophical theory of silence in particular demonstrates how silence has the same communicative value as speech (e.g., Dauenhauer, *Silence*; Jaworski, *The Power of Silence*). Silence is also viewed as a powerful tool to subvert oppression, most often seen in analyses of women's writing, especially the writing of women of color. In contrast to what is seen as a patriarchal model of interpretation that privileges discourse and associates silence with absence, feminist criticism has strained to discover the latent power in textual gaps or in the silent characters that populate women's writing. See, for example, Tillie Olsen, *Silences* (New York: Delacorte Press/Seymour Lawrence, 1978); Patricia Ondek Laurence, *The Reading of Silence: Virginia Woolf in the English Tradition* (Stanford, CA: Stanford University Press, 1991); Morrison, "Unspeakable Things Unspoken." On the

other hand, especially in contexts of historical trauma, silence is often viewed as unequivocally negative, either proof of total destruction or oppression, or something that needs to be broken to allow silenced stories of trauma to emerge. See, for example, George Steiner, *Language and Silence: Essays on Language, Literature, and the Inhuman* (New York: Atheneum, 1970); Theodor W. Adorno, "Meditations on Metaphysics: After Auschwitz," in *Negative Dialectics*, trans. E. B. Ashton (New York: Continuum, 1983), 361–65.

5. Brodsky, *Memoria en construcción*, 200–201.

6. Lazzara, *Chile in Transition*, 32–33, 154.

7. For a discussion of the Mothers' opposition to exhumations, see Cohen Salama, *Tumbas anónimas*, 106–7. Cohen Salama notes that other human rights organizations did not adhere to the Mothers' radical stance; in particular the Grandmothers supported efforts to discover and identify remains. The Mothers also opposed the construction of the Monument to the Victims of State Terrorism in the Memory Park, at one point even threatening to remove the names of their loved ones from the monument. See Patricia Tappatá de Valdez, "El Parque de la Memoria en Buenos Aires," in *Monumentos, memoriales y marcas territoriales*, ed. Elizabeth Jelin and Victoria Langland (Madrid: Siglo XXI Editores España, 2003), 107.

8. Boss, *Ambiguous Loss*.

9. This is not to claim that one can ever arrive at a total understanding of past violence or a complete rendering of the truth. Global human rights terms such as "truth" and "justice" are necessarily shaped by their local context, and one individual or organization's "whole" truth differs from that of another. I simply call attention to the reluctance to explore some of the more difficult or unpalatable legacies of the dictatorship in Argentina.

Bibliography

"1992 Annual Report." Equipo Argentino de Antropología Forense (EAAF), 1992.

"1996–97 Biannual Report." Equipo Argentino de Antropología Forense (EAAF), 1997.

Abdala, Verónica. "La apropiación de bebés, un nuevo tópico literario." *Página/12*, June 20, 1999.

Abuelas de Plaza de Mayo. "Clase sobre Derecho a la identidad." Video posted at http://www.abuelas.org.ar/areas.php?area=juridica.htm&der1=der1_jur.php&der2 =der2_areas.php. Accessed December 8, 2015.

———. "Guido Montoya Carlotto ya conoció a su verdadera familia." August 6, 2014. http://www.abuelas.org.ar/comunicados/restituciones/res140807_0102-1.htm.

Adorno, Theodor W. "Meditations on Metaphysics: After Auschwitz." In *Negative Dialectics*, translated by E. B. Ashton, 361–65. New York: Continuum, 1983.

Albuquerque, Severino João. *Violent Acts: A Study of Contemporary Latin American Theatre*. Detroit: Wayne State University Press, 1991.

Arditti, Rita. *Searching for Life: The Grandmothers of the Plaza de Mayo and the Disappeared Children of Argentina*. Berkeley: University of California Press, 1999.

Arenillas, María Guadalupe. "Hacia una nueva ética y estética de la memoria en el cine documental argentino: *El predio* (2010) de Jonathan Perel." *A Contracorriente* 10, no. 3 (2013): 371–88.

Argento, Analía. *De vuelta a casa: Historias de hijos y nietos restituidos*. Buenos Aires: Marea, 2008.

Arias, Mariela. "Ignacio Guido Hurban viajó a Santa Cruz al cumpleaños 92 de su abuela paterna." *La Nación*, August 30, 2014.

Arijón, Gonzalo, and Virginia Martínez. *Por esos ojos*. Documentary, 1997.

Asociación de Abuelas de Plaza de Mayo. *La historia de Abuelas: 30 años de búsqueda*. Buenos Aires: Abuelas de Plaza de Mayo, 2007.

Atencio, Rebecca J. *Memory's Turn: Reckoning with Dictatorship in Brazil*. Madison: University of Wisconsin Press, 2014.

Avelar, Idelber. "Five Theses on Torture." *Journal of Latin American Cultural Studies* 10, no. 3 (2001): 253–71.

————. *The Untimely Present: Postdictatorial Latin American Fiction and the Task of Mourning*. Durham, NC: Duke University Press, 1999.

Avellaneda, Andrés. *Censura, autoritarismo y cultura: Argentina 1960–1983*. Buenos Aires: Centro Editor de América Latina, 1986.

Baer, Ulrich. *Spectral Evidence: The Photography of Trauma*. Cambridge, MA: MIT Press, 2005.

Barthes, Roland. *Camera Lucida: Reflections on Photography*. Translated by Richard Howard. New York: Hill and Wang, 2010.

————. *Image, Music, Text*. Translated by Stephen Heath. New York: Hill and Wang, 1977.

Behar, Ruth. *Translated Woman: Crossing the Border with Esperanza's Story*. Boston: Beacon Press, 1993.

————. *The Vulnerable Observer: Anthropology That Breaks Your Heart*. Boston: Beacon Press, 1996.

Benavides, Hugo. *Drugs, Thugs, and Divas: Telenovelas and Narco-Dramas in Latin America*. Austin: University of Texas Press, 2008.

Beverley, John. "The Real Thing." In *The Real Thing: Testimonial Discourse and Latin America*, edited by Georg M. Gugelberger, 266–86. Durham, NC: Duke University Press, 1996.

————. "Testimonio, Subalternity, and Narrative Authority." In *Handbook of Qualitative Research*, edited by N. K. Denzin and Y. S. Lincoln, 555–65. Thousand Oaks: Sage, 2000.

Bilbija, Ksenija. "Poniendo las cartas boca abajo: *La travesía* de Luisa Valenzuela." In *Luisa Valenzuela sin máscara*, edited by Gwendolyn Díaz, 83–95. Buenos Aires: Feminaria, 2002.

————. "The Rhetoric of the Repressed in *Black Novel (with Argentines)* by Luisa Valenzuela." *Letras Femeninas* 27, no. 1 (2001): 129–47.

————. "Story Is History Is Story . . ." In *The Art of Truth-Telling about Authoritarian Rule*, edited by Ksenija Bilbija, Jo Ellen Fair, Cynthia E. Milton, and Leigh A. Payne, 112–17. Madison: University of Wisconsin Press, 2005.

Bilbija, Ksenija, Jo Ellen Fair, Cynthia E. Milton, and Leigh A. Payne, eds. *The Art of Truth-Telling about Authoritarian Rule*. Madison: University of Wisconsin Press, 2005.

Bilbija, Ksenija, and Leigh A. Payne, eds. *Accounting for Violence: Marketing Memory in Latin America*. Durham, NC: Duke University Press, 2011.

————, eds. "Introduction." In *Accounting for Violence: Marketing Memory in Latin America*, 1–40. Durham, NC: Duke University Press, 2011.

Blaustein, Daniel. "Estrategias narrativas en *La pesquisa* de Juan José Saer." *LLJournal* 2, no. 2 (2007).

Bonitzer, Pascal. "The Silences of the Voice (*A Propos of Mai 68* by Gudie Lawaetz)." In *Narrative, Apparatus, Ideology: A Film Theory Reader*, edited by Philip Rosen, 319–34. New York: Columbia University Press, 1986.

Bonner, Michelle D. "Defining Rights in Democratization: The Argentine Government and Human Rights Organizations, 1983–2003." *Latin American Politics and Society* 47, no. 4 (2005): 55–76.

Boss, Pauline. *Ambiguous Loss: Learning to Live with Unresolved Grief.* Cambridge, MA: Harvard University Press, 1999.

Bourdieu, María Victoria. *Pasión, heroísmo e identidades colectivas: Un recorrido por los últimos veinticinco años de la telenovela argentina.* Ciudad Autónoma de Buenos Aires: Biblioteca Nacional; Los Polvorines: Universidad Nacional de General Sarmiento, 2008.

Brodsky, Marcelo. *Memoria en construcción: El debate sobre la ESMA.* Buenos Aires: la marca editora, 2005.

Calveiro, Pilar. *Poder y desaparición: Los campos de concentración en Argentina.* Buenos Aires: Ediciones Colihue, 2006.

Carlotto, Estela. *¿Quién soy yo?* Bravo Films in association with the National University of San Martín. Co-production of the Encuentro channel, 2007.

Carlson, Eric Stener. *I Remember Julia: Voices of the Disappeared.* Philadelphia: Temple University Press, 1996.

Caruth, Cathy. *Trauma: Explorations in Memory.* Baltimore: Johns Hopkins University Press, 1995.

———. *Unclaimed Experience: Trauma, Narrative, and History.* Baltimore: Johns Hopkins University Press, 1996.

Cerruti, Gabriela. "La historia de la memoria." *Puentes* 1, no. 3 (2001): 14–25.

Chanan, Michael. *The Politics of Documentary.* London: British Film Institute, 2007.

Cohen Salama, Mauricio. *Tumbas anónimas: Informe sobre la identificación de restos de víctimas de la represión ilegal.* Buenos Aires: Catálogos Editora, 1992.

Colombo, Pamela. "A Space under Construction: The Spatio-Temporal Constellation of ESMA in *El Predio.*" *Journal of Latin American Cultural Studies* 21, no. 4 (2012): 497–515.

Cordones-Cook, Juanamaría. *Poética de transgresión en la novelística de Luisa Valenzuela.* New York: Peter Lang, 1991.

Cortés, Dinorah. "Deseo patriarcal y metáfora de la paternidad literaria en Domingo Faustino Sarmiento." *Cuadrivium* 11–12, no. 7 (Fall 2009–Spring 2011): 117–25.

Crenzel, Emilio A. *Memory of the Argentina Disappearances: The Political History of Nunca Más.* Translated by Laura Pérez Carrara. New York: Routledge, 2012.

Dauenhauer, Bernard P. *Silence: The Phenomenon and Its Ontological Significance.* Bloomington: Indiana University Press, 1980.

Dauphinée, Elizabeth. "The Politics of the Body in Pain: Reading the Ethics of Imagery." *Security Dialogue* 38, no. 2 (2007): 139–55.

Derrida, Jacques. *Demeure: Fiction and Testimony.* Translated by Elizabeth Rottenberg. Stanford, CA: Stanford University Press, 2000.

Dershowitz, Alan. "Tortured Reasoning." In *Torture: A Collection,* edited by Sanford Levinson, 257–80. Oxford: Oxford University Press, 2004.

Díaz, Gwendolyn. "Una odisea hacia el caos: *La travesía* de Luisa Valenzuela." In *Luisa Valenzuela sin máscara,* edited by Gwendolyn Díaz, 70–82. Buenos Aires: Feminaria, 2002.

"Discurso completo de Kirchner en la ONU." *Clarín,* September 25, 2003.

Di Stefano, Eugenio. "From Revolution to Human Rights in Mario Benedetti's *Pedro y el Capitán*." *Journal of Latin American Cultural Studies* 20, no. 2 (2011): 121–37.

Dube, Siphiwe Ignatius. "Transitional Justice Beyond the Normative: Towards a Literary Theory of Political Transitions." *International Journal of Transitional Justice* 5, no. 2 (2011): 177–97.

duBois, Page. *Torture and Truth*. New York: Routledge, 1991.

Fagen, Patricia Weiss. "Repression and State Security." In *Fear at the Edge: State Terror and Resistance in Latin America*, edited by Juan E. Corradi, Patricia Weiss Fagen, and Manuel Antonio Garretón, 39–71. Berkeley: University of California Press, 1992.

Feitlowitz, Marguerite. "A Dance of Death: Eduardo Pavlovsky's *Paso de dos*." *Drama Review* 35, no. 2 (1991): 60–73.

———. *A Lexicon of Terror: Argentina and the Legacies of Torture*. New York: Oxford University Press, 1998.

Feld, Claudia. *Del estrado a la pantalla: Las imágenes del juicio a los ex comandantes en Argentina*. Madrid: Siglo XXI de España Editores, 2002.

Feldman, Allen. "Memory Theaters, Virtual Witnessing, and the Trauma-Aesthetic." *Biography: An Interdisciplinary Quarterly* 27, no. 1 (2004): 163–202.

Felman, Shoshana, and Dori Laub. *Testimony: Crises of Witnessing in Literature, Psychoanalysis, and History*. New York: Routledge, 1992.

Fivush, Robyn. "Speaking Silence: The Social Construction of Silence in Autobiographical and Cultural Narratives." *Memory* 18, no. 2 (2010): 88–98.

Flores, Julio. "Siluetas." In *El Siluetazo*, edited by Ana Longoni and Gustavo Bruzzone, 83–107. Buenos Aires: Adriana Hidalgo, 2008.

Flynn, Michael, and Fabiola F. Salek, eds. *Screening Torture: Media Representations of State Terror and Political Domination*. New York: Columbia University Press, 2012.

Forcinito, Ana. "Testimonial Narratives in the Argentine Post-Dictatorship: Survivors, Witnesses, and the Reconstruction of the Past." In *Post-Authoritarian Cultures: Spain and Latin America's Southern Cone*, edited by Luis Martín-Estudillo and Roberto Ampuero, 77–98. Nashville: Vanderbilt University Press, 2008.

Fridman, Lea Wernick. *Words and Witness: Narrative and Aesthetic Strategies in the Representation of the Holocaust*. Albany: State University of New York Press, 2000.

Friedlander, Saul, ed. *Probing the Limits of Representation: Nazism and the "Final Solution."* Cambridge, MA: Harvard University Press, 1992.

Friera, Silvina. "No toda la sociedad es culpable." *Página/12*, October 24, 2006.

Gallo, Darío, and Olga Wornat. "Amores clandestinos." *Noticias* 21, no. 1107 (May 14, 1998): 24–29.

Gandsman, Ari. "'Do You Know Who You Are?' Radical Existential Doubt and Scientific Certainty in the Search for the Kidnapped Children of the Disappeared in Argentina." *ETHOS* 37, no. 4 (2009): 441–65.

———. "The Limits of Kinship Mobilizations and the (A)politics of Human Rights in Argentina." *Journal of Latin American and Caribbean Anthropology* 17, no. 2 (2012): 193–214.

———. "'A Prick of a Needle Can Do No Harm': Compulsory Extraction of Blood in the Search for the Children of Argentina's Disappeared." *Journal of Latin American and Caribbean Anthropology* 14, no. 1 (2009): 162–84.

———. "Retributive Justice: Public Intimacies and the Micropolitics of the Restitution of Kidnapped Children of the Disappeared in Argentina." *International Journal of Transitional Justice* 6 (2012): 423–43.

García, José Luis. "'El Predio' de Jonathan Perel: Reinterpretando los horrores del pasado." *Cinestel.com*, March 24, 2011. http://www.cinestel.com/el-predio-de-jonathan-perel-reinterpretando-los-horrores-del-pasado/.

Garretón, Manuel Antonio. "Fear in Military Regimes: An Overview." In *Fear at the Edge: State Terror and Resistance in Latin America*, edited by Juan E. Corradi, Patricia Weiss Fagen, and Manuel Antonio Garretón, 13–25. Berkeley: University of California Press, 1992.

Gates-Madsen, Nancy J. "Marketing and Sacred Space: The Parque de la Memoria in Buenos Aires." In *Accounting for Violence: Marketing Memory in Latin America*, edited by Ksenija Bilbija and Leigh A. Payne, 151–78. Durham, NC: Duke University Press, 2011.

———. "Tortured Silence and Silenced Torture in Mario Benedetti's *Pedro y el capitán*, Ariel Dorfman's *La muerte y la doncella* and Eduardo Pavlovsky's *Paso de dos*." *Latin American Theatre Review* 42, no. 1 (2008): 5–31.

———. "Uncivilized Remembrance in Luisa Valenzuela's *La travesía*." *Letras Femeninas* 31, no. 2 (2005): 99–121.

Geertz, Clifford. *Works and Lives: The Anthropologist as Author*. Stanford, CA: Stanford University Press, 1988.

Gilbert, Sandra M., and Susan Gubar. *The Madwoman in the Attic: The Woman Writer and the Nineteenth-Century Literary Imagination*. New Haven, CT: Yale University Press, 1979.

Gilmore, Leigh. *The Limits of Autobiography: Trauma and Testimony*. Ithaca, NY: Cornell University Press, 2001.

Ginzberg, Carlo. "Just One Witness." In *Probing the Limits of Representation: Nazism and the "Final Solution,"* edited by Saul Friedlander, 82–96. Cambridge, MA: Harvard University Press, 1992.

Gold, Janet. "Feminine Space and the Discourse of Silence: Yolanda Oreamuno, Elena Poniatowska, and Luisa Valenzuela." In *In The Feminine Mode: Essays on Hispanic Women Writers*, edited by Noël Maureen Valis and Carol Maier, 195–203. Lewisburg: Bucknell University Press, 1990.

Goldberg, Elizabeth Swanson. *Beyond Terror: Gender, Narrative, Human Rights*. Princeton, NJ: Rutgers University Press, 2007.

Goldberg, Florinda. "*La pesquisa* de Juan José Saer: Alambradas de la ficción." *Hispamérica: Revista de Literatura* 26, no. 76–77 (1997): 89–100.

Gordon, Avery F. *Ghostly Matters: Haunting and the Sociological Imagination*. Minneapolis: University of Minnesota Press, 1997.

Gramuglio, María Teresa. "El lugar de Saer." In *Juan José Saer por Juan José Saer*, 261–99. Buenos Aires: Editorial Celtia, 1986.

Graziano, Frank. *Divine Violence: Spectacle, Psychosexuality, and Radical Christianity in the Argentine "Dirty War."* Boulder: Westview Press, 1992.

Griffin, Susan. *Woman and Nature: The Roaring Inside Her.* 2nd ed. San Francisco: Sierra Club Books, 1999.

Grüner, Eduardo. "La invisibilidad estratégica, o la redención política de los vivos: Violencia política y representación estética en el siglo de las desapariciones." In *El Siluetazo*, edited by Ana Longoni and Gustavo Bruzzone, 285–308. Buenos Aires: Adriana Hidalgo, 2008.

Halfon, Mercedes. "Los nietos de 'Montecristo.'" *Perfil*, October 2, 2006.

Harding, Sandra. *Feminism and Methodology: Social Science Issues.* Readers Notes edition. Bloomington: Indiana University Press, 1987.

H.I.J.O.S. "H.I.J.O.S. de la misma historia." http://www.hijos-capital.org.ar/index .php?option=com_content&view=article&id=140&Itemid=401. Accessed October 13, 2013.

Hirsch, Marianne. "Surviving Images: Holocaust Photographs and the Work of Post-memory." *Yale Journal of Criticism* 14, no. 1 (2001): 5–37.

Hoheisel, Horst, Beatriz Sarlo, Graciela Silvestri, and Hugo Vezzetti. "La destrucción de la Puerta de Brandeburgo: Conversación con Horst Hoheisel." *Punto de Vista* 83 (2005): 18–22.

Jaworski, Adam. *The Power of Silence: Social and Pragmatic Perspectives.* Newbury Park: Sage, 1993.

Jehenson, Myriam Yvonne. "Book Review: *I Remember Julia: Voices of the Disappeared.*" *Humanity and Society* 23, no. 4 (1999): 388–90.

Jelin, Elizabeth. *State Repression and the Labors of Memory.* Translated by Judy Rein and Marcial Godoy-Anativia. Minneapolis: University of Minnesota Press, 2003.

Kirchner, Néstor. "Discurso de asunción del Presidente Néstor Kirchner." Buenos Aires, May 25, 2003. http://www.cfkargentina.com/discurso-de-asuncion-del-presi dente-nestor-kirchner/. Accessed December 9, 2015.

———. "Speech at the Creation of the Memory Museum." Buenos Aires, March 24, 2004. https://www.youtube.com/watch?v=h2TF9Hogz-I. Accessed December 9, 2015.

Kunz, Marco. "Identidad robada y anagnórisis: De *Nunca Más* a *Quinteto de Buenos Aires*." In *Violence politique et écriture de l'élucidation dans la bassin méditerranéen*, edited by Claude Ambroise and Georges Tyras, 179–93. Grenoble: Université Stendhal, 2002.

LaCapra, Dominick. *Representing the Holocaust: History, Theory, Trauma.* Ithaca, NY: Cornell University Press, 1994.

Landsberg, Alison. *Prosthetic Memory: The Transformation of American Remembrance in the Age of Mass Culture.* New York: Columbia University Press, 2004.

Lang, Berel. "The Representation of Limits." In *Probing the Limits of Representation: Nazism and the "Final Solution,"* edited by Saul Friedländer, 300–317. Cambridge, MA: Harvard University Press, 1992.

Langer, Lawrence L. *Holocaust Testimony: The Ruins of Memory*. New Haven, CT: Yale University Press, 1991.

———. *Versions of Survival: The Holocaust and the Human Spirit*. Albany: State University of New York Press, 1982.

Laqueur, Thomas W. "The Dead Body and Human Rights." In *The Body*, edited by Sean T. Sweeney and Ian Hodder, 75–93. Cambridge, U.K.: Cambridge University Press, 2002.

Lather, Patti. "Issues of Validity in Openly Ideological Research: Between a Rock and a Soft Place." *Interchange* 17, no. 4 (1986): 63–84.

Laurence, Patricia Ondek. *The Reading of Silence: Virginia Woolf in the English Tradition*. Stanford, CA: Stanford University Press, 1991.

Lazzara, Michael J. *Chile in Transition: The Poetics and Politics of Memory*. Gainesville: University Press of Florida, 2006.

Lindenberger, Herbert. *Historical Drama: The Relation of Literature and Reality*. Chicago: University of Chicago Press, 1975.

Longoni, Ana. "Photographs and Silhouettes: Visual Politics in Argentina." Translated by Yaiza Hernández. *Afterall Journal* 25 (2010). http://www.afterall.org/journal/issue.25/photographs-and-silhouettes-visual-politics-in-the-human-rights-movement-of-argentina.

———. *Traiciones: La figura del traidor en los relatos acerca de los sobrevivientes de la represión*. Buenos Aires: Grupo Editorial Norma, 2007.

Longoni, Ana, and Gustavo Bruzzone. "Introduccción." In *El Siluetazo*, edited by Ana Longoni and Gustavo Bruzzone, 7–58. Buenos Aires: Adriana Hidalgo, 2008.

Lyotard, Jean-François. *The Differend: Phrases in Dispute*. Translated by Georges van den Abeele. Minneapolis: University of Minnesota Press, 1988.

Magnarelli, Sharon. *Reflections/Refractions: Reading Luisa Valenzuela*. New York: Peter Lang, 1988.

Martínez, Z. Nelly. *El silencio que habla: Aproximación a la obra de Luisa Valenzuela*. Buenos Aires: Ediciones Corregidor, 1994.

———. "Luisa Valenzuela's *La travesía*: The Vagina Monologues and the Experience of Wholeness." *Letras Femeninas* 30, no. 1 (2004): 92–105.

Matoso, Elina. *El cuerpo, territorio escénico*. Buenos Aires: Paidós, 1992.

Mazziotti, Nora. "La venganza de Montecristo y la máquina novelesca." *Tram(p)as de la comunicación y la cultura* 47 (2006): 60–64.

Mennell, D. Jan. "(Im)penetrable Silence: The Language of the Unspeakable in Manuela Fingueret's *Hija del silencio*." *Revista Canadiense de Estudios Hispánicos* 27, no. 3 (2003): 485–507.

Merchant, Carolyn. *The Death of Nature: Women, Ecology, and the Scientific Revolution*. San Francisco: Harper & Row, 1980.

Miller, Nancy K. "Facts, Pacts, Acts." *Profession* (1992): 10–14.

Milton, Cynthia E., ed. *Art from a Fractured Past: Memory and Truth-Telling in Post–Shining Path Peru*. Durham, NC: Duke University Press, 2014.

Montecristo. Buenos Aires: Telefe, 2006.

Morrison, Toni. "Unspeakable Things Unspoken: The Afro-American Presence in American Literature." *Michigan Quarterly Review* 28, no. 1 (1989): 1–34.

Murray, Jessica. "Tremblings in the Distinction Between Fiction and Testimony." *Postcolonial Text* 4, no. 2 (2008): 1–19.

Nance, Kimberly. *Can Literature Promote Justice? Trauma Narrative and Social Action in Latin American Testimonio*. Nashville: Vanderbilt University Press, 2006.

Newbery, Charles. "Telefe Extends 'Montecristo' Sales." *Variety*, February 19, 2007.

Nichols, Bill. *Representing Reality: Issues and Concepts in Documentary*. Bloomington: Indiana University Press, 2007.

Nosiglia, Julio E. *Botín de guerra*. 3rd ed. Buenos Aires: Abuelas de Plaza de Mayo, 2007.

Nunca Más: Informe de la Comisión Nacional sobre la Desaparición de Personas (CONADEP). Buenos Aires: EUDEBA, 1984. http://www.desaparecidos.org/nuncamas/web/english/library/nevagain/nevagain_001.htm.

Olsen, Tillie. *Silences*. New York: Delacorte Press/Seymour Lawrence, 1978.

Ortner, Sherry B. "Is Female to Male as Nature Is to Culture?" In *Women, Culture, and Society*, edited by Michelle Zimbalist Rosaldo and Louise Lamphere, 67–87. Stanford, CA: Stanford University Press, 1974.

Osorio, Elsa. *A veinte años, Luz*. Buenos Aires: Grijalbo Mondadori, 1999.

———. *My Name Is Light*. Translated by Catherine Jagoe. New York: Bloomsbury, 2003.

Page, Philippa J. *Politics and Performance in Post-Dictatorship Argentine Film and Theatre*. Colección Tamesis. Serie A, Monografías 301. Woodbridge, Suffolk, UK: Tamesis, 2011.

Palazón Sáez, Gema. "Reconstrucción identitaria y mecanismos de la memoria: *A veinte años, Luz*." *Río de La Plata* 29–30 (2004): 475–85.

Partnoy, Alicia. *The Little School: Tales of Disappearance and Survival*. Pittsburgh, PA: Cleis Press, 1986.

Pastoriza, Lila. "ESMA, modelo para armar." *Puentes* 4, no. 11 (2004): 10–16.

Pavlovsky, Eduardo. *Paso de dos*. Buenos Aires: Ediciones Ayllu, 1990.

Payne, Leigh A. *Unsettling Accounts: Neither Truth nor Reconciliation in Confessions of State Violence*. Durham, NC: Duke University Press, 2008.

Perel, Jonathan, dir. *El predio*. Argentina, 2010. DVD.

———. "Estupor y temblor." *Página/12*, March 20, 2011.

———. "La ESMA es un lugar simbólico que tiene un alto poder de reparación." Interview by Juan Pablo Russo, March 24, 2011. http://www.escribiendocine.com/entrevista/0002475-jonathan-perel-la-esma-es-un-lugar-simbolico-que-tiene-un-alto-poder-de-reparacion/. Accessed December 9, 2015.

———. Interview by Daniel Gaguine, April 16, 2010. http://elcaleidoscopiodelucy.blogspot.com/2010/04/tal-como-lo-habiamos-anticipado-el.html. Accessed December 9, 2015.

Peters, Edward. *Torture*. Philadelphia: University of Pennsylvania Press, 1996.

Platía, Marta. "En peligro de muerte permanente." *Página/12*, July 30, 2013.

Premat, Julio. "El crimen de la escritura: La novela policial según Juan José Saer." *Latin American Literary Review* 24, no. 48 (1996): 19–38.

Reati, Fernando. "Historias de amores prohibidos: Prisioneras y torturadores en el imaginario argentino de la posdictadura." *Insula* 711 (2006): 27–32.

Rejali, Darius. "Movies of Modern Torture as Convenient Truths." In *Screening Torture: Media Representations of State Terror and Political Domination*, edited by Michael Flynn and Fabiola F. Salek, 219–37. New York: Columbia University Press, 2012.

———. "Whom Do You Trust? What Do You Count On?" In *On Nineteen Eighty-Four: Orwell and Our Future*, edited by Abbott Gleason, Jack Goldsmith, and Martha C. Nussbaum, 155–79. Princeton, NJ: Princeton University Press, 2005.

Renov, Michael. "Toward a Poetics of Documentary." In *Theorizing Documentary*, edited by Michael Renov, 12–36. New York: Routledge, 1993.

Respighi, Emanuel. "Una foto en 'Montecristo.'" *Página/12*, September 24, 2006.

Robben, Antonius C. G. M. "The Politics of Truth and Emotion among Victims and Perpetrators of Violence." In *Fieldwork under Fire: Contemporary Stories of Violence and Survival*, edited by Carolyn Nordstrom and Antonius C. G. M. Robben, 81–104. Berkeley: University of California Press, 1995.

Rorty, Richard. "Solidarity or Objectivity?" In *Post-Analytic Philosophy*, edited by John Rajchman and Cornel West, 3–19. New York: Columbia University Press, 1985.

Roseman, Mark. "Surviving Memory: Truth and Inaccuracy in Holocaust Testimony." *Journal of Holocaust Education* 8, no. 1 (1999): 1–20.

Saer, Juan José. *Glosa*. Barcelona: Destino, 1988.

———. *The Investigation*. Translated by Helen Lane. London: Serpent's Tail, 1999.

———. *La pesquisa*. Buenos Aires: Seix Barral, 1994.

———. *Lo imborrable*. Madrid: Alianza, 1993.

———. *Nadie nada nunca*. Mexico City: Siglo XXI, 1980.

Sáez, Ñacuñán. "Torture: A Discourse on Practice." In *Tattoo, Torture, Mutilation, and Adornment: The Denaturalization of the Body in Culture and Text*, edited by Frances E. Mascia-Lees and Patricia Sharpe, 126–44. Albany: State University of New York Press, 1992.

Sarmiento, Domingo Faustino. *Facundo: Civilization and Barbarism; The First Complete English Translation*. Translated by Kathleen Ross. Berkeley: University of California Press, 2003.

Scarry, Elaine. *The Body in Pain: The Making and Unmaking of the World*. New York: Oxford University Press, 1985.

———. "Five Errors in the Reasoning of Alan Dershowitz." In *Torture: A Collection*, edited by Sanford Levinson, 281–90. Oxford: Oxford University Press, 2004.

Schettini, Adriana. "El fenómeno Montecristo." *La Nación*, November 26, 2006.

Scipioni, Estela Patricia. *Torturadores, apropiadores y asesinos: El terrorismo de estado en la obra dramática de Eduardo Pavlovsky*. Kassel: Edition Reichenberger, 2000.

Scott, Shaunna L. "Dead Work: The Construction and Reconstruction of the Harlan Miners Memorial." *Qualitative Sociology* 19, no. 3 (1996): 365–93.

Serafini, Dom. "Argentina: Domestic Recovery Fuels International Boom for Telefe." *Video Age International* 27, no. 1 (January 2007). http://www.videoageinternational.com/articles/2007/01/telefe.html.

Sikkink, Kathryn. "From Pariah State to Global Protagonist: Argentina and the Struggle for International Human Rights." *Latin American Politics and Society* 50, no. 1 (2008): 1–29.

Sklodowska, Elzbieta. *Testimonio hispanoamericano: Historia, teoría, poética*. New York: Peter Lang, 1992.

Sommer, Doris. *Proceed with Caution, When Engaged by Minority Writing in the Americas*. Cambridge, MA: Harvard University Press, 1999.

"Son Parte Del Ocultamiento." *Página/12*, January 21, 2011.

Sosa, Cecilia. "*Queering* Acts of Mourning in the Aftermath of Argentina's Dictatorship: The Mothers of Plaza de Mayo and *Los Rubios*." In *The Memory of State Terrorism in the Southern Cone: Argentina, Chile, and Uruguay*, edited by Francesca Lessa and Vincent Druliolle, 63–85. New York: Palgrave Macmillan, 2011.

———. "Queering Kinship: The Performance of Blood and the Attires of Memory." *Journal of Latin American Cultural Studies* 21, no. 2 (2012): 221–33.

Steiner, George. *Language and Silence: Essays on Language, Literature, and the Inhuman*. New York: Atheneum, 1970.

Stern, Steve J. *Battling for Hearts and Minds: Memory Struggles in Pinochet's Chile, 1973–1988*. Durham, NC: Duke University Press, 2006.

———. *Reckoning with Pinochet: The Memory Question in Democratic Chile, 1989–2006*. Durham, NC: Duke University Press, 2010.

———. *Remembering Pinochet's Chile: On the Eve of London, 1998*. Durham, NC: Duke University Press, 2004.

Stern, Steve J., and Scott Straus, eds. *The Human Rights Paradox: Universality and Its Discontents*. Madison: University of Wisconsin Press, 2014.

Stevens, Evelyn. "Marianism: The Other Face of Machismo." In *Confronting Change, Challenging Tradition: Women in Latin American History*, edited by Gertrude M. Yeager, 3–17. Wilmington, DE: Scholarly Resources, 1994.

Sturken, Marita, and Lisa Cartwright. *Practices of Looking: An Introduction to Visual Culture*. 2nd ed. New York: Oxford University Press, 2009.

Swanson, Philip. "The Detective and the Disappeared: Memory, Forgetting, and Other Confusions in Juan José Saer's *La pesquisa*." In *Investigating Identities: Questions of Identity in Contemporary International Crime Fiction*, edited by Marieke Krajenbrink and Kate M. Quinn, 277–94. Amsterdam, Netherlands: Rodopi, 2009.

Tappatá de Valdez, Patricia. "El Parque de la Memoria en Buenos Aires." In *Monumentos, memoriales y marcas territoriales*, edited by Elizabeth Jelin and Victoria Langland, 97–112. Madrid: Siglo XXI Editores España, 2003.

Tate, Julee. "The Good and Bad Women of Telenovelas: How to Tell Them Apart Using a Simple Maternity Test." *Studies in Latin American Popular Culture* 26 (2007): 97–111.

Taussig, Michael T. *Defacement: Public Secrecy and the Labor of the Negative*. Stanford, CA: Stanford University Press, 1999.

Taylor, Diana. *The Archive and the Repertoire: Performing Cultural Memory in the Americas*. Durham, NC: Duke University Press, 2003.

———. *Disappearing Acts: Spectacles of Gender and Nationalism in Argentina's "Dirty War."* Durham, NC: Duke University Press, 1997.

———. *Theatre of Crisis: Drama and Politics in Latin America.* Lexington: University Press of Kentucky, 1991.

Timerman, Jacobo. *Prisoner without a Name, Cell without a Number.* Translated by Toby Talbot. New York: Knopf, 1981.

Vaisman, Noa. "'Memoria, Verdad y Justicia': The Terrain of Post-Dictatorship Social Reconstruction and the Struggle for Human Rights in Argentina." In *The Human Rights Paradox: Universality and Its Discontents*, edited by Steve J. Stern and Scott Straus, 125–47. Madison: University of Wisconsin Press, 2014.

Valenzuela, Luisa. "Escribir con el cuerpo." In *Peligrosas palabras*, 119–39. Buenos Aires: Temas Grupo Editorial, 2001.

———. *La travesía.* Buenos Aires: Grupo Editorial Norma, 2001.

———. "Siete aproximaciones al secreto." *Casa de Las Américas* 42, no. 226 (2002): 90–95.

Valle, Gustavo. "La incertidumbre elocuente (entrevista con Juan José Saer)." *Letras Libres*, June 2002. http://www.letraslibres.com/revista/convivio/la-incertidumbre-elo cuenteentrevista-con-juan-jose-saer.

van Zyl, Paul. Interview by Terry Gross, Fresh Air with Terry Gross. December 3, 2001.

Vinitsky-Seroussi, Vered, and Chana Teeger. "Unpacking the Unspoken: Silence and Collective Memory and Forgetting." *Social Forces* 88, no. 3 (2010): 1103–22.

Wagner-Pacifici, Robin, and Barry Schwartz. "The Vietnam Veterans Memorial: Commemorating a Difficult Past." *American Journal of Sociology* 97, no. 2 (1991): 376–420.

Werth, Brenda. *Theatre, Performance, and Memory Politics in Argentina.* New York: Palgrave Macmillan, 2010.

Whine, Michael, Anthony Richards, Peter Martin, Omar Malik, J. Bowyer Bell, and Linda A. Curcio-Nagy. "Book Reviews, Terrorism and Political Violence." *Terrorism and Political Violence* 11, no. 1 (2007): 133–44.

White, Hayden. *The Content of the Form: Narrative Discourse and Historical Representation.* Baltimore: Johns Hopkins University Press, 1987.

"World Report 2015." New York: Human Rights Watch, 2015.

Young, James. *The Texture of Memory: Holocaust Memorial and Meaning.* New Haven, CT: Yale University Press, 1993.

Zinsser, William. *Inventing the Truth: The Art and Craft of Memoir.* Boston: Houghton Mifflin Company, 1998.

Zolberg, Vera L. "Contested Remembrance: The Hiroshima Exhibit Controversy." *Theory and Society* 27, no. 4 (1998): 565–90.

Index

Aguerreberry, Rodolfo, 71
Albuquerque, Severino, 41, 178n45
Alfonsín, Raúl, 10
alienation effect, 211n50
Alonso, Alfredo, 210n33
ambiguities (regarding silence), 22–23,
    31–50, 66–70, 77–89, 99–110, 126–40,
    160–67, 196n50
Améry, Jean, 179n46
amnesty laws, 11, 30, 34–35, 89–92, 140,
    171n14, 193n4
Andrade, Jorge, 178n45
aniquilamiento, 61–62
Anos rebeldes, 194n16
appropriated children: biological
    narratives regarding, 98–116, 163–65,
    199n79; identity restitution and, 4, 19,
    25–26, 90–95, 99–103, 106–16, 199n85;
    pact of silence regarding, 7, 27–28,
    117–18; silence-breaking ethos and, 4,
    51–59, 68–70, 89–90, 140, 161–63,
    167–68; taboos regarding, 19, 90, 92,
    99–106, 116–18. *See also* Grandmothers
    of the Plaza de Mayo; human rights
    groups; Mothers of the Plaza de
    Mayo; *specific authors and works*
Arfuch, Leonor, 157
Argentina. *See* appropriated children;
    disappeared, the; memory; trauma;

*specific authors, groups, politicians, and
    works*
Argento, Analía, 113, 117
Artés, Carla Rutila, 199n84
Atencio, Rebecca, 18, 98, 172n25, 172n30,
    194n16
At the Mind's Limits (Améry), 179n46
audiences, 14–15, 47–50, 138–59, 174n46
Auel, Heriberto Justo, 61–62
Auschwitz, 147, 151, 189n12
A veinte años, Luz (Osorio), 25–26,
    90–106, 110, 116–18, 161–64, 197n62,
    199n79
Avelar, Idelber, 121, 180n65
Avellaneda, Andrés, 170n12

Barrio, Javier, 155–56
Barthes, Roland, 146, 210n32, 211n49
being silenced, 4, 14, 21–23, 27, 74, 120
Beloved (Morrison), 192n75
Benavides, Hugo, 202n106
Benedetti, Mario, 42–43, 119–20, 178n45
betrayal, 8, 31, 46–49
Beverley, John, 16
Beyond Terror (Goldberg), 32
Bilbija, Ksenija, 125
biology (as bottom of the well), 98–116,
    163–65, 199n79
Blaustein, Daniel, 111

guerrilla resistances, 42–44, 61–62
Guzzeti, César A., 206n61

Halbwachs, Maurice, 21
haunting, 16–18, 73, 84, 133, 136, 162
Heart of Darkness (Conrad), 74–75, 79–80
heroism, 41–42
Herrera de Noble, Ernestina, 201n100
hierarchies (of human rights groups), 12
H.I.J.O.S. (Hijos por la Identidad y la Justicia contra el Olvido y el Silencio), 5, 9–11, 92, 107, 119–20, 139, 160–61
Hirsch, Marianne, 151
Historical Drama (Lindenberger), 43
Hoheisel, Horst, 210n41
Holocaust, 17, 19–20, 65, 73, 132–33, 145, 147, 170n7, 184n32, 185n45
human rights groups: appropriated children and, 5, 89–90, 110–16, 167–68, 199n85; fiction's responsibilities and, 91–95, 98–99, 103–6; identity restitution and, 4, 12, 54–55, 99–103, 106–16, 162–63; individual-collective problems of, 51–59, 61–62, 68–70, 114–16; innocence tropes and, 35–44, 61–62; local-global paradox and, 12–13, 42–43, 51–53, 182n2, 214n9; memory's political uses and, 8, 25–26, 51–53; paradoxes and, 24–25, 42, 48, 60–66, 101–3, 111–12, 182n2, 209n23, 214n7; prescriptive expectations and, 66–70, 166; silence-breaking emphasis and, 4, 10–11, 51–59, 68–70, 89–90, 140, 161–63; sites of memory and, 26, 140–46, 160–61; taboos within, 12, 54–59, 99–103; torture and, 179n47; triumphalist narratives and, 4, 116–18, 202n106
Huyssen, Andreas, 42, 167

identity restitution, 4, 19, 25–26, 54–55, 90–95, 99–103, 106–16, 161–65, 182n6, 199n85

images, 6, 140–42, 146–59, 210n32
information-gathering (torture as), 44–49, 180n60
intellectualism, 121, 126–39, 198n75
International Convention on the Rights of the Child, 110
Inventing the Truth (Zinsser), 185n43
I Remember Julia (Carlson), 24, 51–72, 80, 83, 87–88, 162, 164, 183n8, 186n53
"Is Female to Male as Nature Is to Culture?" (Ortner), 133

Jara, René, 16
Jelin, Elizabeth, 20–21, 170n9
"Just One Witness" (Ginzberg), 65

Ken Burns effect, 148
Kexel, Guillermo, 71
Kirchner, Néstor and Cristina, 7, 11, 27–28, 140–41, 156, 159, 207n2, 207nn5–6, 212n61
Kozameh, Alicia, 171n22
Kunz, Marco, 103, 199n80

Lacan, Jacques, 125
Landsberg, Alison, 145, 209n26
Lang, Berel, 17–18
Langer, Lawrence, 49, 90, 185n45
language. *See* images; representation; speech; testimonies
La pesquisa (Saer), 25, 52, 71–72, 79–88, 121, 162, 164–65, 189n10, 191n46
Laqueur, Thomas, 54, 56, 162
La travesía (Valenzuela), 26, 119–39, 165–66
Laub, Dori, 17–18, 121
Lazzara, Michael, 13–14, 18, 144, 167
A Lexicon of Terror (Feitlowitz), 204n25
Lindenberger, Herbert, 43–44, 176n9
The Little School (Partnoy), 18
Longoni, Ana, 37, 43, 48, 87–88, 181n1
López, Jorge Julio, 11

Lorenzón, Adriana, 93, 102, 193n4, 195n35
Lyotard, Jean-François, 73–74, 84, 120, 204n28

The Madwoman in the Attic (Gilbert and Gubar), 131
Magnarelli, Sharon, 206n69
Marquevich, Roberto, 200n93
Martínez, Z. Nelly, 203n4
Matoso, Elina, 127–28, 135
memory: body and nature metaphors and, 126–39, 205n44; collective, 23; forgetting and, 19–20; Holocaust and, 17, 19–20, 65, 73, 132–33, 145, 147, 170n7, 184n32, 185n45; images and, 6, 149–59; politicization of, 8–13, 25–28, 72–73, 91, 140–42; representational limits and, 5–6, 21, 163–67, 189n19; repression and, 121–26, 163–65; silence and, 5–6, 8–13, 20–21, 119–21, 149–59, 163–69; sites of memory and, 26, 71–72, 89–90, 140–46, 149–61, 163, 208n11, 208n19, 212n61; trauma and, 4, 49–50, 124–25, 204n28, 204n38. *See also* human rights groups; silence; speech; testimonies; trauma
memory boom, 5, 7–8, 24, 27–28, 93, 118–21, 160–63
Memory Park, 160–61
Menchú, Rigoberta, 16, 119, 185n44
Menem, Carlos Saúl, 10–11, 27, 52, 72–73, 169n5, 175n2, 182n3
Merchant, Carolyn, 205n44
Miara, Samuel, 201n96
Mignone, Emilio, 61
Milagre na cela (Andrade), 178n45
Milton, Cynthia, 18, 173n42
Montecristo (telenovela), 25–26, 90–110, 116–18, 161–64, 193n4, 194n20, 195n35, 199n79
Montesini, Julia Andrea. See *I Remember Julia* (Carlson)

Morrison, Toni, 86–87, 192n75
Mothers of the Plaza de Mayo, 9–11, 25–26, 47, 54, 57, 107, 140–52, 167–68, 177n18, 181n1, 183n21, 188n72, 214n7
Murray, Jessica, 173n40
"Museo del gliptodonte" (Barrio), 155–56

Nadie nada nunca (Saer), 78–79, 191n51
Nance, Kimberly, 17–19, 95–97, 99, 117–18, 194n18
narratives. *See* fiction; first-person narration; human rights groups; memory; prescriptive expectations; representation; second-person narration; substitution (narrative)
narrative seduction, 64–65
Nichols, Bill, 154–55, 211n45, 211n53
Night and Fog (Resnais), 148–49
Nineteen Eighty-Four (Orwell), 179n46
Nunca Más report, 10, 18, 45, 171n13, 184n39, 190n39, 209n27

objectivity (appearance of), 146–49
Officer's Quarters (of ESMA), 151, 211n49
The Official Story (Puenzo), 3, 14, 166
organic memory, 126–39, 205n44
Ortner, Sherry, 133, 205n44
Orwell, George, 179n46
Osorio, Elsa, 25–26, 90–106, 116–18, 161, 164, 193n6
overt silences: appropriated children and, 90; covert silence's relation to, 55; expressivity of, 39–44; impunity and, 33–35; overt silence's relation to, 55; prescriptive expectations and, 66–70, 166; taboos, 161–63; taboos and, 26–27, 30–31; testimonies and, 29–30; torture and, 30–50. *See also* silence

21–23; expressive theories of, 4–5, 8–9, 13–21, 27, 34–35, 39–44, 119–25, 149–59, 163–69, 203n4; forgetting and, 33–35, 121–25, 174n55; gendering of, 31, 34, 39–41, 48–49; human rights frameworks and, 24–25, 51–55, 60–70, 161–63; images and, 140–49, 151–59, 209n28; impunity and, 33–35, 52, 92–93, 186n47; memory boom and, 5–6, 9–13, 20–21, 27, 119–21; military's "pact of," 7, 27–28, 117–18; overt, 14, 21–23, 27–28, 31–35, 48–49, 55, 74, 90, 124–25; preboom era and, 7, 55–60, 169n5; repression and, 120–21, 126–39; subalterns and, 60, 184n31; taboos and, 7–13, 24, 29–30, 54–59, 99–103, 110–18, 160–63; testimonies and, 16–21, 60–70. *See also* memory; representation; taboos; trauma; *specific authors and works*

Silhouette Campaign, 24, 51–53, 60–61, 68, 71–72, 181n1, 188n71

A Single, Numberless Death (Strejilevich), 171n22

Sklodowska, Elzbieta, 16, 64

Snow, Clyde, 182n5

Sommer, Doris, 19, 86, 120, 174n46, 192n75

Sosa, Cecilia, 107, 114

South Africa, 136

Space for Memory and the Defense and Promotion of Human Rights, 26, 89–90, 140–59, 163

speculative anthropology, 72–73

speech: context and, 21–23; excesses of, 25–26, 28, 55, 66, 76–82, 86–87, 141–46; human rights frameworks and, 24–25, 51–55, 60–70, 89–90; images and, 140–59; individual-collective issues in, 51–62, 68–70, 114–16; limits of, 14–15, 21, 60–66, 82–83; memory's relation to, 124–25; as silence's opposite, 11–13, 51–55, 63–65, 95–96, 118,

128–29; testimonies and, 16–21, 30. *See also* memory; representation; silence; taboos; trauma

Spivak, Gayatri, 184n31

Spoils of War (Blaustein), 111

State Repression and the Labors of Memory (Jelin), 20, 170n9

Stern, Steven J., 12–13, 20–21, 42, 123, 165, 182n2, 184n39

Stevens, Evelyn, 197n55

Stockholm syndrome, 112

Stoll, David, 16, 185n44

Strange Things Happen Here (Valenzuela), 122

Straus, Scott, 12–13, 42, 165, 182n2

Strejilevich, Nora, 171n22

Suárez, Marcos, 98, 195n35

subalterns, 16, 60, 184n31

substitution (narrative), 74–80, 86–87

"Surviving Images" (Hirsch), 151

taboos: appropriated children and, 19, 90, 98–106; audiences and, 14–15, 47–50, 138–59, 174n46; human rights community and, 11–13, 54–59, 110–16; local-global paradoxes and, 12–13, 42–43, 51–53, 182n2, 214n9; narrative ambiguities and, 4, 22–23, 31–50, 66–70, 77–89, 99–110, 126–40, 160–67, 196n50; prescriptive expectations and, 66–70, 166; silence's meaning and, 4–6, 8, 19, 21–24, 29–30, 66–70, 117–18, 160–63; torture and, 8, 28–31, 37, 47–49. *See also* contextual silences; representation; silence; trauma

Tango por la Identidad, 92

Tate, Julee, 104–5

Taussig, Michael, 10, 126

Taylor, Diana, 10, 31, 34, 47, 142, 176n9

Teatro por la Identidad, 92, 194n10

Teeger, Chana, 23

Telefe. See *Montecristo* (telenovela)

testimonies: audiences to, 138–39; the body as, 54–59, 66, 72, 78, 162; definitions of, 17; ethics and, 31–33, 187n63, 191n46; fictional narratives and, 4, 16–21, 50, 91–99, 116–18, 171n22, 173n40, 187n63; prescriptive expectations and, 66–70, 166; representational limits of, 16–21, 60–66, 185n41, 189n19; silence's relationship to, 4, 39–44, 60–66, 184n31; taboos and, 19, 28; torture and, 44–46; at trials, 29–30, 61–62, 141; witnessing and, 121–25. *See also* human rights groups; representation; silence; speech; victims (of human rights abuses)

textual silences, 21–23, 34–35. *See also* silence; *specific authors and works*

Theatre, Performance, and Memory Politics in Argentina (Werth), 38

Theatre of Crisis (Taylor), 47

"Theatre of World Memory" (Camillo), 131

Thoreau, Henry David, 134

Timerman, Jacobo, 18

Torquemada (Boal), 178n45

torture, 24, 30–50, 161–67, 176n9, 177n25, 178n23, 178n45, 179n47, 180n65

Torture and Truth (duBois), 45

Tractatus Logico-Philosophicus (Wittgenstein), 84

transitional justice, 18, 172n30, 201n99

trauma: audiences to, 14–15, 47–50, 165–66, 174n46, 176n9, 177n18; cover stories and, 55, 124–26, 132–33, 163–65, 193n78; ethics and, 31–33, 53–55; representations of, 4, 7–9, 16–21, 23–24, 26–28, 41–42, 44–50, 60–66, 73–74, 90–91, 117–18, 121–25, 171n22, 185n44, 189n19, 204n28; repression and, 121–26; silent expressions of,

13–15, 19, 30, 124–25, 163–69, 170n7; taboos regarding, 7–8, 19, 117–18, 161–62. *See also* appropriated children; disappeared, the; memory; representation; silence; speech; torture; *specific authors and works*

Trial of the Juntas, 10

Truth and Reconciliation Commission (South Africa), 136

United Nations, 140

Valenzuela, Luisa, 26, 119–39, 165–66, 203n4, 206n69

Van Zyl, Paul, 136

Vázquez, Evelin Karina, 113–16

victims (of human rights abuses): ambiguities in, 39–44, 103–6; heroic roles for, 35–44, 49–50; individual-collective paradoxes and, 51–59, 61–62, 68–70, 114–16, 173n39; innocence and, 42–44, 61–62, 100–103, 196n54, 197n55; overt silence and, 35–44; silence-breaking ethos and, 4, 51–59, 68–70, 89–90, 140, 161–63, 167–68; speaking for, 55–66, 162–63; torture and, 31–33, 35–44. *See also* representation; silence; speech; trauma

Villa Grimaldi, 144

Vinitzky-Seroussi, Vered, 23

Violent Acts (Severino), 41

voice-over, 27, 143–46, 209n28

voicing. *See* representation; speech; testimonies

Walsh, Rodolfo, 156

War on Terror, 180n60, 181n72

Werth, Brenda, 38

White, Hayden, 65, 80, 83

Who Am I? (Carlotto), 111–12

Wiesel, Elie, 189n12

wilderness metaphors, 130–31, 134–35, 205n44

Critical Human Rights

Memory's Turn: Reckoning with Dictatorship in Brazil
REBECCA J. ATENCIO

*Archiving the Unspeakable: Silence, Memory, and the Photographic Record in
Cambodia* MICHELLE CASWELL

Court of Remorse: Inside the International Criminal Tribunal for Rwanda
THIERRY CRUVELLIER; translated by CHARI VOSS

How Difficult It Is to Be God: Shining Path's Politics of War in Peru, 1980–1999
CARLOS IVÁN DEGREGORI; edited and with an introduction by
STEVE J. STERN

*Trauma, Taboo, and Truth-Telling: Listening to Silences in Postdictatorship
Argentina* NANCY J. GATES-MADSEN

From War to Genocide: Criminal Politics in Rwanda, 1990–1994
ANDRÉ GUICHAOUA; translated by DON E. WEBSTER

*Innocence and Victimhood: Gender, Nation, and Women's Activism in Postwar
Bosnia-Herzegovina* ELISSA HELMS

Amending the Past: Europe's Holocaust Commissions and the Right to History
ALEXANDER KARN

Torture and Impunity ALFRED W. MCCOY

Historical Justice and Memory Edited by KLAUS NEUMANN and
JANNA THOMPSON

The Human Rights Paradox: Universality and Its Discontents
Edited by STEVE J. STERN and SCOTT STRAUS

Human Rights and Transnational Solidarity in Cold War Latin America
Edited by JESSICA STITES MOR

Remaking Rwanda: State Building and Human Rights after Mass Violence
Edited by SCOTT STRAUS and LARS WALDORF

Beyond Displacement: Campesinos, Refugees, and Collective Action in the Salvadoran Civil War MOLLY TODD

The Social Origins of Human Rights: Protesting Political Violence in Colombia's Oil Capital, 1919–2010 LUIS VAN ISSCHOT

The Politics of Necessity: Community Organizing and Democracy in South Africa ELKE ZUERN

www.ingramcontent.com/pod-product-compliance
Lightning Source LLC
Chambersburg PA
CBHW071018280326
41935CB00011B/1397